AN EDUCATIONAL PSYCHOLOGY OF SCIENCE METHODS IN THE K-6 CLASSROOM

Educational PSYCHOLOGY

Critical Pedagogical Perspectives

Greg S. Goodman, *General Editor*

Vol. 23

The Educational Psychology series is part of the Peter Lang Education list.
Every volume is peer reviewed and meets
the highest quality standards for content and production.

PETER LANG
New York • Washington, D.C./Baltimore • Bern
Frankfurt • Berlin • Brussels • Vienna • Oxford

CHRISTOPHER THAO VANG

AN EDUCATIONAL PSYCHOLOGY OF SCIENCE METHODS IN THE K–6 CLASSROOM

Hands-on/Mind-Focused Strategies for all Learners

PETER LANG
New York • Washington, D.C./Baltimore • Bern
Frankfurt • Berlin • Brussels • Vienna • Oxford

Library of Congress Cataloging-in-Publication Data

Vang, Christopher Thao.
An educational psychology of science methods in the K–6 classroom:
Hands-on/mind-focused strategies for all learners / Christopher Thao Vang.
pages cm. — (Educational psychology: critical pedagogical perspectives; vol. 23)
Includes bibliographical references and index.
1. Science—Study and teaching (Elementary)
2. Science—Study and teaching (Elementary)—Activity programs.
3. Educational psychology. I. Title.
LB1585.V334   372.35'044—dc23   2012046177
ISBN 978-1-4331-2023-7 (hardcover)
ISBN 978-1-4331-2022-0 (paperback)
ISBN 978-1-4539-1027-6 (e-book)
ISSN 1943-8109

Bibliographic information published by **Die Deutsche Nationalbibliothek.**
Die Deutsche Nationalbibliothek lists this publication in the "Deutsche
Nationalbibliografie"; detailed bibliographic data is available
on the Internet at http://dnb.d-nb.de/.

The paper in this book meets the guidelines for permanence and durability
of the Committee on Production Guidelines for Book Longevity
of the Council of Library Resources.

© 2013 Peter Lang Publishing, Inc., New York
29 Broadway, 18th floor, New York, NY 10006
www.peterlang.com

Printed in the United States of America

Table of Contents

Tables and Figures

Figure

Foreword

Nowadays, in the field of teacher education, prospective educators and current classroom teachers are looking for a comprehensive framework for effective instruction in the multicultural setting. Thousands of experts have written textbooks about teaching inquiry elementary health and science to help prepare new teachers for what they will need to do when teaching science content area standards. But very few of those textbooks are on health and science methods in the K-6 classroom in the multicultural classroom. Many scholars have invested a huge amount of time, energy, research, and creative thinking in exploring elementary health and science teaching techniques that enhance teaching and learning in the classroom. Most of them would agree that inquiry science education is the single most important ingredient in public education that most schools ignore while preparing new teachers for today's schools.

This new book, *An Educational Psychology of Science Methods in the K-6 Classroom: Hands-on and Minds-Focused Strategies for All Learners,* was conceived to better prepare prospective and current teachers to teach inquiry elementary science with enthusiasm, joy, entertainment, intrigue, curiosity, and thought-provoking engagement. The hands-on and minds-on inquiry strategies herein equip teachers with enriched teaching principles, applications, tools, methodologies, and pedagogical skills needed to develop deliberate science lesson plans that engage all learners in the learning process.

Vang, as both an educator and a teacher trainer, knows how prospective educators and new classroom teachers feel about teaching inquiry elementary health and science curricula. It is an intricate matter that requires applying appropriate logical disciplines in a multicultural setting. Today's classroom is culturally and linguistically diverse, and the absence of a broad-based science foundation poses a wide range of concerns for new teachers who may not be familiar with minority students who do not possess middle-class values. Moreover, some children enter the classroom with minimal understanding of inquiry health and science concepts. Students' understandings may not be congruent with their teacher's expectations for student learning outcomes. Teachers cannot overcome their students' academic deficiencies without knowledge and skills for creating hands-on and minds-focused strategies for all learners of diverse backgrounds, strategies that will bridge the gap between teaching expectations and student learning outcomes. Teachers need this multi-faceted approach and these skills in order to develop inclusive teaching strategies that engage all children in learning inquiry health and science concepts.

Today's teaching is not entirely about *what* the teacher can do in class; it is more concerned with *how* the teacher can reach out to each and every learner in the classroom academically. In this book, the broad emphasis upon both the psychosocial and the educational psychology dimensions of learning opens prospective educators' and new classroom teachers' hearts and minds through a process of clinical training to better understand the feeling tone of teaching elementary health and science concepts and at the same time shows how teachers can implement science curricular activities by engaging all learners in science while managing diverse students' behaviors during instruction. This book offers hands-on and minds-focused inquiry strategies, comprehensive approaches, culturally responsive applications, and practical tools for meeting everyday needs in the multicultural classroom setting.

As an author, Vang brings a unique voice to the psychology of teaching inquiry elementary health and science methods and offers new, vibrant, sensible, and articulated support in the face of the educational challenges and demands of diverse prospective educators in teacher preparation programs. Most importantly, as a university professor, Vang is a renowned expert in the field of multicultural education, classroom management, best professional practices, health and science methodology, foundations of education, and critical multiculturalism pedagogy.

What is admirable in Vang's talent, writing, passion, discovery, and creativity is his firsthand experience in teaching college credential courses in the teacher preparation program; that is what makes this book academically relevant to the preparation and training of new teachers for today's multicultural classroom. Vang's insights have wide applicability for best professional practices in delivery of health and science concepts to all learners in elementary grades. Furthermore, in this book, Vang contributes his sensitive approach to the teaching of health and science methods and concepts that accepts and engages all of the diverse educators in today's pluralistic and multicultural settings.

As always, therefore, as a long-time friend of education, I am honored to recommend his well-researched book to all prospective educators and current student teachers who are teaching students of diverse backgrounds in the public school system and are looking for new directions to better understand the practical applications of teaching inquiry elementary health and science methods and concepts. To all teachers of teachers I say that the practical information in Vang's book will benefit both teachers and students in the learning circle. For that reason, *An Educational Psychology of Science Methods in the K-6 Classroom: Hands-on and Minds-Focused Strategies for All Learners* is a must-own, must-read, and must-have book because it explains to prospective educators and current classroom teachers the art and science of teaching elementary health and science methods with hands-on and minds-focused inquiry strategies that appeal to all learners.

—Dr. Gregory S. Goodman
Associate Professor
Clarion University of Pennsylvania

Preface

This book, *An Educational Psychology of Science Methods in the K-6 Classroom: Hands-on and Minds-Focused Strategies for All Learners*, was written to help prospective educators and new teachers address challenging and recurring obstacles in teaching inquiry elementary health and science concepts in the multicultural classroom setting. The content of this book was selected specifically for its usefulness in the everyday experiences new teachers encounter involving the design of science curricular activities and meaningful lesson plans to cover and uncover the inquiry science content area standards in the K-6 classroom.

This book gives comprehensive approaches to teacher preparation and discusses the nature of teaching inquiry elementary health and science concepts in a way that equips prospective educators with a broad array of practical tools to prepare them for unexpected challenges related to the conduct of science instruction, management, discipline, assessment, transition, and daily routine and structure. The information will lead prospective educators and new teachers to explore their own style or philosophy of teaching inquiry elementary health and science concepts to all learners of diverse backgrounds and find effective frameworks for developing their philosophy of discipline, philosophy of teaching, and philosophy of student engagement using hands-on and minds-focused inquiry strategies that maximize student learning outcomes.

Science curricula are challenging for many teachers, and for the most part, new teachers are not adequately prepared to teach science content area standards. This book illustrates how teaching inquiry elementary health and science concepts can be fun, intriguing, and entertaining. It provides prospective teachers and current teachers with foundations for designing meaningful science lesson plans.

Academically, teaching science can be integrated with teaching other subject matter. Today's classrooms contain students from diverse backgrounds as well as teachers who are culturally diverse. There is no such thing as a "best" science curriculum, "best" science activities, "best" classroom management techniques, or "best" logical consequences for discipline. No one-model-fits-all technique will work for any learning challenge that occurs in the classroom. In everyday teaching, there is no "one teaching model serves all." This new book does not present a model for teaching science; rather, it shows prospective educators and new teachers how to adjust their personal approach to teaching inquiry elementary health and science concepts, based on everyday real-life experiences, to provide the best possible professional practices in the multicultural classroom setting.

HOW EDUCATIONAL PSYCHOLOGY IS APPLIED IN THIS BOOK

The art and science of teaching is heavily influenced by the teacher's educational psychology. Many experts in the field of teacher education would agree wholeheartedly that psychology plays a major role in teaching, learning, engagement, classroom management, and student discipline. Theorists Erickson, Skinner, Feud, Jung, Rogers, Redl, Wattenberg, Dreikurs, and Ginott had psychology backgrounds and they are associated with specific therapeutic psychologies. This means that approaches to teaching, learning, encoding, decoding, retention of information, feeling tone, classroom climate, classroom management, and student discipline rely heavily on psychological premises of behavior enthusiasm, gratification, modification, stimulation, management, and manipulation.

In this book, educational psychology is the basis for helping classroom teachers and prospective educators understand the psycho-social environment, or feeling tone, of teaching inquiry elementary health and science concepts to all learners of diverse backgrounds. Understanding educational psychology is important if they are to deal with the complexities of teaching and learning in a multicultural setting where cultural diversity plays a pivotal role in how teachers engage students in inquiry science concepts in the learning circle during the delivery of instruction while managing student behaviors. At the same time, psychology factors in to how students respond to teachers' expectations and actions and modify their learning behaviors to adjust to teachers' demands.

Teaching can be cognitively demanding or cognitively undemanding; learning, however, is always cognitively demanding because it involves the transference of knowledge. For that reason, psychology has become an integral part of education, involved in teaching, learning, and assessing. Psychology helps explain the different behaviors of children and adults in instructional settings and is thus critical to the different aspects of classroom management, instructional practices, and student learning outcomes. Therefore, this book gives attention to educational psychology, which provides the foundation upon which new teachers and prospective educators can build hands-on and minds-focused inquiry strategies for all learners, thus maximizing professional practices for all their students.

WHAT THIS BOOK PROVIDES FOR EDUCATORS

This book was designed for everyone in the teacher education field, especially for prospective educators and new student teachers in teacher preparation programs. Newly hired teachers often battle with fear, consternation, dissatisfaction, and in some cases, personal disappointment when planning, designing, delivering, and implementing elementary science lesson plans. Moreover, many schools do not offer science curricular activities because most curricula are focused on math and language arts. The inability to teach any academic subject matter or content area standards has caused teachers more job-related stress than anything else. The purpose of this book is to give new teachers the best foundation possible for developing effective inquiry elementary health and science methods to address issues related to science content area standards and show how hands-on and minds-focused strategies can be implemented effectively in the multicultural setting.

Today's classrooms are composed of students from diverse backgrounds, and teachers are ethnically diverse as well. Each student brings his or her unique experiences, challenges, needs, and expectations to the classroom, and teachers are also unique, with specific expectations of their students. These challenges are real, and there is no question that teachers need help in meeting the many demands of today's classroom. However, even though classroom management and student discipline are at the top of teachers' must-master list, learning elementary health and science concepts is essential to students' everyday lives. Children need to understand science topics such as nutrition facts, germs, personal hygiene, pollution, climate changes, healthy food, growth, and physical fitness. Without sensible science curricular activities, today's teaching and learning are likely to be fragmented and disconnected from practical living since science is ubiquitous in real life.

This book takes prospective educators and new student teachers on a complete tour of their routine teaching so they can see how to include science instruction as part of their daily integrated curricular activities. This book is a complete guide for new teachers who need reassurance and an overview of teaching elementary health and science concepts with hands-on and minds-focused inquiry strategies.

TODAY'S CURRICULAR CHALLENGES

This book was written to address the curricular challenges most prospective educators and current teachers face in the classroom when dealing with the science content area standards related to the implementation of inquiry elementary health and science education. In some states, elementary health and science curricula are absent from the schools' teaching menus because school districts are focused almost solely on high-stakes testing; they teach only those subjects for which learning is measured by performance on standardized testing such as math and language arts. Even as schools are abandoning science curricula, some school districts are beginning to see its importance; some are now mandating the inclusion of physical education component because they understand that children need to be in good general health in order to be fit physically and mentally.

Another curricular challenge is presented by the composition of the modern classroom. Most American schools are now multilingual and multicultural. The number of limited English proficient (LEP) students is rising in districts all across the nation. Nearly 425 dialects are spoken in American schools; California schools alone have over 120 dialects. Nearly 40% of US students come from bilingual and/or minority backgrounds. Of the 54 million students in K-12 education, approximately 3.2 million are LEP students and 5.2 million are students with some kind of learning disability. Moreover, nearly 10 million students in the K-12 system speak a primary language at home other than English.

The current process of educating LEP students is obscure and capricious; it provides dismal academic services to LEP students. Most new teachers do not understand how schools identify LEP students, and once they are identified, teachers have no idea who is obligated to serve them. LEP students are tracked throughout the system to make sure the academic label remains intact, but so little is done to help these students excel academically. The ongoing practices of surface assessment, cosmetic education, and lip service continue to limit the academic achievement of LEP students.

Students with disabilities, like LEP students, need teachers who understand their struggles to learn. Most teachers are not clinically trained or otherwise prepared to deal with students with disabilities. In order for new teachers to receive their preliminary teaching credentials, they must meet teacher performance expectations (TPE) standards and demonstrate proficiency in teacher performance assessment (TPA) tasks, which requires demonstrating knowledge and skills in making instructional adaptations of academic content for English language learners (ELLs) and students with special needs. Most student teachers find TPE and TPA requirements to be tedious and they therefore do not embrace them wholeheartedly. However, if teachers are deficient in these areas, how can they address the needs of all their students?

Students' individualized educational plans (IEP) are legally binding, but more times than not, academic services are not delivered as mandated by the Individuals with Disabilities Education Act (IDEA), Public Law 94-142, and section 504 requirements of Public Law 93-112, known as the Rehabilitation

Act of 1973. The debate on full inclusion goes on while the system leaves students with disabilities in academic limbo. The problem is compounded by teacher shortages in general and among special education teachers in particular. The shortage of special education teachers is a pressing issue nationally; in some school districts, it is a crisis.

There is no perfect form of teaching, especially when considering the diversity in the classroom. Much teaching today is based on intervention strategies rather than instructional strategies. Today's teachers are commonly taught to use direct instruction modalities or scripted instruction; many are not equipped with any other teaching methodologies, strategies, or approaches. Although some school districts are now considering replacing direct instruction with the Sheltered Instruction Observation Protocol (SIOP) and/or Response to Instruction (RTI) models, nearly 75% of schools use direct instruction as the main instructional approach. This despite the fact that nearly half of all teachers believe that direct instruction is not an effective one-model-fits-all instructional methodology. Direct instruction leaves many students behind and, more importantly, teachers cannot use it to teach all subject matters creatively. A number of other strategies and instructional methodologies are available that are more effective. Although there is no perfect teaching methodology, the best tool for teaching and learning science is firsthand experience, and nothing works better in teaching inquiry elementary health and science concepts than the use of hands-on and minds-focused strategies.

THE NECESSITY OF SCIENCE EDUCATION

The National Center for Education Statistics released a shocking report on the nation's eighth graders' academic achievement in science in 2011. In its National Assessment of Education Progress (NAEP), the center tested approximately 120,000 eighth graders from more than 7,300 schools across the nation. Surprisingly, of the 47 states participating in this national examination, only 16 had eighth graders showing increases in their scores—only small increases—and most students in other states had flat scores. Overall, the report indicated that although the nation's eighth graders did better than 2 years previously, 7 out of 10 were still considered not academically proficient in science. In other words, even if 31% of students were considered somewhat proficient or better on the test, most US students in the eighth grade were not scientifically literate in 2011.

The report further illustrates that although the gap between minority students and White students narrowed for Blacks and Hispanics, both groups still lagged significantly behind their White counterparts in science. White students scored an average of 163 as compared to 137 for Hispanics and 129 for Blacks. The national average score was 152, up from 150 in 2009. Only the top 2% of all eighth graders had advanced skills in science. In California, only 22% percent of eighth graders reached the proficiency level.

To improve this dismal situation, the US Department of Education is working to bolster the number of top-notch science teachers in public schools. The plan is to prepare nearly 100,000 new science teachers over a 10-year period by offering incentive programs and academic bonuses for new teachers who pursue science teaching credentials. In some states, science teachers are paid more than those who teach other subjects. Meanwhile, experts believe that because the current scores are unacceptable and any gains minuscule, more needs to be done to improve children's education in science in the public schools.

This book was designed to help prospective educators and current teachers teach inquiry elementary health and science concepts to all students of diverse backgrounds before they reach eighth grade. According to the NAEP report, elementary students lack the kind of education in science in primary grades that would prepare them for the kind of national testing the Department of Education.conducted, and more importantly, the majority of minority students do not receive consistent inquiry science curricula prior to eighth grade. Although the US Congress mandates the national testing program for 4th, 8th, and 12th grade students in math, science, reading, and other academic subjects, many school districts have not taken bold steps to make science part of their everyday learning curricula. Perhaps the national incentive programs will capture their attention and encourage them to promote science curricula in elementary as well as secondary grades.

MY MOTIVATION FOR WRITING THIS BOOK

For 10 years I have taught the Health and Science Methodology Course in the multiple-subject-credential teacher preparation program. For all 10 years I have had a strong desire to write *An Educational Psychology of Science Methods in the K-6 Classroom: Hands-on and Minds-Focused Strategies for All Learners* for prospective educators and current teachers in credential programs and liberal studies programs. I have learned that prospective educators and student teachers need practical ideas they can apply to everyday teaching in the classroom. This book, however, will not answer all the questions and solve all the problems new teachers will have. It will serve as a guide to help new teachers find answers as they think about teaching inquiry elementary health and science concepts. Most importantly, teachers will be able to use the practical tools in this book from the beginning of their pursuit of their teaching credential and beyond.

HOW THIS BOOK IS ORGANIZED

This inquiry science book contains four main parts with rich and comprehensive content packed into 12 chapters. Each chapter presents a variety of topical issues in a single domain of educational objectives. In each chapter, headings and subheadings guide the reader to the various topical issues. Part I has four chapters on broad topics related to the understanding of science concepts. Part II has three chapters that present the applications of science concepts in the practical domain. The two chapters of Part III give an overview of the integration of academic content areas with science. Finally, Part IV has three chapters of information on the promotion of independent learning.

ACKNOWLEDGMENTS

I am honored to know Dr. Gregory S. Goodman. This book would not have been attempted or written without his expertise. I am indebted to Dr. Goodman for his scholarship, contributions, and invaluable guidance; he is the instrumental editor for this book. Also, Dr. Goodman's kindness, friendship, mentoring, and support made this book a reality.

As always, my special appreciation goes to Mr. Christopher Myers, the Managing Director of Peter Lang Publishing. His genuine encouragement and support have made this book possible and given me the momentum to complete it.

A PERSONAL NOTE

As always, I am passionate about the content of the books I write; the passion comes from my experiences teaching in the multiple subject credential program at California State University, Stanislaus. This book truly reflects my passion for teaching the elementary health and science methodology course. Over the years, my own professional development and personal growth have guided me in organizing the content of this book and in creating the conceptual framework applicable to the needs of prospective educators and new student teachers.

PART ONE

Understanding Science Concepts

CHAPTER ONE

The Nature OF Science

The greatest discoveries of science have always been those that forced us to rethink our beliefs about the universe and our place in it.

—ROBERT L. PARK THE *NEW YORK TIMES,*
7 DECEMBER 1999

INTRODUCTION

Nearly every single student in the classroom, regardless of grade level, has known, experienced, and learned something about science in real life. However, teachers often believe that science is a new concept and students have to grasp it from a textbook in order to understand its nature. For that reason, teachers wrongfully assume that students of diverse backgrounds bring no or little scientific experience to the classroom, and only students from middle-class families have the kind of knowledge and skills to understand science because they have been taught at home. Science is everywhere, and children of all cultural backgrounds have experienced it differently and similarly. What teachers need to do is apply their students' embedded experiences into their teaching practicum to enhance students' learning of science concepts, vocabulary, and meanings. This chapter introduces prospective educators and current teachers to the nature of science to prepare them for teaching elementary health and science concepts and to help them explore the meaning of everyday science in life.

APPROACH TO TEACHING SCIENCE

What is science? Science has a number of branches or fields of such study: biology, chemistry, botany, geology, archaeology, engineering, or physics, to name some of the more common ones. Believe it or not, two out of every three new teachers do not believe they can teach inquiry elementary science effectively. Everyone has different ways of learning or knowing science and each person has his or her own way of explaining what science is. Apparently, no definition covers it all. For this reason, the science curriculum is a burden for some; science encompasses a broad base of knowledge and skills.

Perhaps the most literal way of defining *science* is to say that it means the construction of meaning by systematically using inquiry processes of observing, communicating, thinking, measuring, experimenting, explaining, concluding, and validating. Another definition is the interconnectedness of ideas, knowledge, skills, and understandings about one's surroundings and the natural world.

For prospective educators and current teachers, the prospect of teaching elementary health and science concepts can be daunting, stressful, and frustrating, or it can be fun; many consider science a difficult subject to teach. However, science can be one of the most exciting, fun, intriguing, and enjoyable subjects to teach to students of diverse cultural backgrounds. When students are actively engaged in academic science exploration with hands-on and minds-on activities, learning takes place by doing, not by listening, memorizing, or emulating. Moreover, inquiry science content can be integrated with other subject matter to enhance students' learning of both.

How easily a teacher can teach science depends on how much the teacher can trust his or her ability to make science fun and relevant to the content area standards. Teachers must believe in themselves as lifelong learners, and at the same time they must trust their students' abilities to learn science. Believing in their students' abilities helps teachers think creatively and logically about science curricula, and creativity is what makes teachers the best artists. Science concepts are found everywhere, in the home and in the classroom, and most children are already equipped with basic scientific experiences, knowledge, and skills.

SCIENCE IS UBIQUITOUS

Science is everywhere because it is everyday life experience. Science surrounds life and life surrounds science. To begin teaching health and science concepts to elementary school students, prospective educators and teachers must overcome their personal and professional misperceptions or misconceptions about children's abilities, thinking patterns, and understanding of science. Science is everywhere and children are surrounded by it with firsthand experiences through real-life events, such as observing, watching movies, communicating, wondering, asking questions, playing, eating, throwing, swimming, crying, chasing, riding a bike, falling down, and walking. Frankly, science can be viewed as ongoing human activity or endeavor. For instance, most children can do these activities: *catching, galloping, skipping, tossing, crawling, hopping, rolling, tumbling, kicking, climbing, dancing, coloring, painting, running, pushing, pulling, and washing.* These ordinary experiences are essential in learning science concepts; however, ignoring such prior knowledge and skills in teaching science may result in *dissociated learning*, which means that the teaching isolates the meanings, facts, or connections, separating them from the real-life experiences that children have had.

In other words, students may perceive science to be something strange and form neutral attitudes or negative feelings about learning it academically. However, if teachers make teaching and learning inquiry science fun, intriguing, meaningful, and purposeful, then the concepts and facts can be connected to one another and to prior knowledge through hands-on and minds-focused activities. Figure 1.1 illustrates some of the types of real-life experiences that are actually science experiences and demonstrate that science is ubiquitous.

Children learn science best when they discover or experience things with excitement. Teachers must encourage students to learn about the world at their

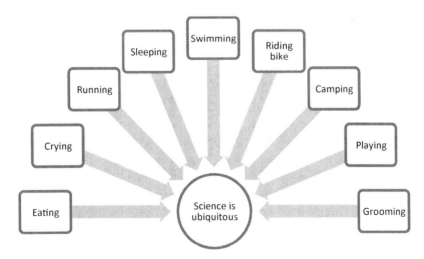

Figure 1.1 *Science is based on real-life events*

own ability levels in natural and academic ways through activities in which they are interested. Teachers can reinforce their students' personal interests and academic curiosity with meaningful teaching and learning experiences, such as investigation and experimentation.

WHAT SCIENCE MEANS

The nature of science is complex, broad, and infinite in its concepts as well as in knowledge. The very first question teachers should ask themselves before teaching science concepts is: What is science? Or what does science mean? Most of the time, teachers explain what science is based on their personal and educational experiences, or prior knowledge. In fact, there is no single definition for science; not all experts agree on what science is. For that reason, students may have a difficult time understanding what science is, what science is not, or what science means. Table 1.1 displays some of the answers college students gave to the question *What is science?*

Webster's College Dictionary defines science (2001) as "a branch of knowledge of study dealing with a body of facts or truths systematically arranged and showing the operation of general law." It further explains that the systematic knowledge of the physical or material world is gained through observation and experimentation, and knowledge, as facts or principles, is gained through systematic study. The lexical definition does not give a clear conceptual understanding of what science is. Science, in nature, is an integral part of everyday life phenomena since human activities are surrounded by it.

Children tend to believe that science is about something that is true, so their thinking about science is that it is about learning the truth of things. Academically,

Table 1.1 Selected College Students' Answers to Question *What Is Science?*

Student	Answer
1	Science is what we see around us each and every day.
2	Science is about living things and nonliving things on earth.
3	Science is how people understand the world around them.
4	Science is how we think, see, feel, understand, and know things.
5	Science is about experimentations, theories, ideas, and philosophies.
6	Science is what we do in life and how things evolve over time.
7	Science is about life, earth, rocks, ocean, weather, and physics.
8	Science is the study of complex ideas and provides answers to questions.
9	Science studies about everything on earth.
10	Science is how we understand things and how we apply ideas to things.

Table 1.2 Elementary Students' Answers to Question *What Is Science?*

Student	What is science?
A kindergartener	Science is . . . I don't know . . . about animals.
A first grader	Science is about plants and animals.
A second grader	Science tells us about animals and plants.
A third grader	Science is about life and animals.
A fourth grader	Science is the study of the world, space, and stars.
A fifth grader	Science is about how people understand things.
A sixth grader	Science is the study of matters and how people understand them.
A seventh grader	Science is the knowledge of knowing things around you.
An eighth grader	Science is the study of life, living things, nonliving things, and matter.

however, science is not the same as truth. Children's perceptions and conceptions could be exposed as false or true as they learn science. For instance, some children may not be able to describe the shape of the earth before going school; they may perceive the earth to be flat instead of round based on their personal imagination. Table 1.2 presents examples of how elementary students answered the question *What is science?*

Longman's Dictionary of American English defines science (2004) for elementary students as "knowledge about the physical world based on testing and proving facts, or work that results in knowledge." Similarly, the *Scholastic Pocket Dictionary* defines science (2005) as "the study of nature and the physical world by testing, experimenting, and measuring." Another lexical definition used by Kottmeyer, Clause, and Dockery (1973) in a student workbook explained science as "knowledge of *facts* and *laws* arranged in an orderly system, or branch of such knowledge." Again, these lexical definitions could be confusing to students. None of these definitions is very helpful to elementary students who try to look up the word *science* in the dictionary. For English language learners (ELLs), these definitions could be meaningless because they give little or no connection between everyday life experiences and the conceptual framework of science. Therefore, teachers need to fill in the gap for them; otherwise, learning science could be a daunting experience for some students.

Most children have concepts about science; however, their concepts are not concrete until they learn what science is about academically. Teachers should allow children to grow academically when teaching inquiry science concepts. Teachers may have to explain what science is and what science is not throughout the process of teaching. Figure 1.2 compares and contrasts some basic ideas of what science is and what science is not. Good teachers usually leave room for their students to grow through the experience of learning science. For instance,

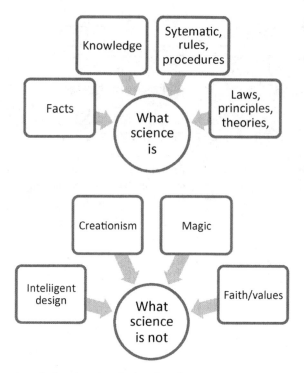

Figure 1.2 *Comparison of what science is and what science is not*

firsthand experiences change students' perceptions about things, and reinforcing learning with hands-on and minds-focused activities—such as examining rocks, fossils, and tree rings or viewing pictures of plant parts such as roots, leaves, stem, flowers, and bark—cement accurate perceptions.

Teachers can present the study of science as the search of knowledge instead of asking students to look for the answers to questions. In fact, teachers should take the time to ask students how they arrived at their answers; they should allow students to explain their findings in their own words. Teachers must affirm and reaffirm the ongoing learning of students because science cannot answer all questions.

Academically, as Howe (2002) explained, science is both knowledge, or understanding, and a way of arriving at knowledge. Science cannot answer all questions or affirm all hypotheses or theories, and science is not the only way to know things. Teachers should simply share with students that science is a way of understanding the world around them through a learning process called *inquiry*—asking and answering questions about *ideas, things, concepts, theories, facts, and principles*. Lastly, science does not mean the same as belief. For instance, people have beliefs about many things, and some of those beliefs cannot be tested. In science, hypotheses must be tested to see if they can be supported or disproven.

To help teachers understand what science means, some science basics need to be clear. *Concept* refers to the generalizations of ideas connected to each other that share common characteristics to any and all instances of a given type. *Fact* relates to the physical knowledge and is a statement or idea of inquiry observations of objects or events. *Theory* is a specific explanation of events supported by laws, principles, and scientific consequences. *Law* is basically a scientific regularity that is used to apply to all members of a broad class of phenomena, such as facts, theories, concepts, and ideas. Finally, *hypothesis* refers to an untested statement or question that involves the relationship of two or more variables.

HOW SCIENCE IS INVOLVED IN EVERYDAY LIFE

The authenticity of science is the beauty of nature. There are two basic types of science: natural science and man-made science. In ancient times, people discovered science in nature. Everyone has experienced and learned science throughout life since science surrounds all human activities and is part of everyday life. Teachers must accept the fact that science is ubiquitous in order to have trust in their students' ability to learn science. To help students think about science, teachers may ask their students this inquiry-based question: "Do you believe you are a scientist yourself?" Of course, many would say they are not scientists because they think of a scientist as someone who is a genius, an astronaut, a biologist, a teacher, a hero, or an older individual who has been recognized for doing great things in life. Children generally do not see themselves as scientists; however, they have experienced the authenticity of science already. Some female students may want to dodge the question because they think scientists are males. Girls are unsure about female scientists because throughout history there have been very few female scientists. Also, male dominance in science makes female students feel uncomfortable in answering the question.

Teachers can prompt students to understand that they are scientists with a series of questions preceded by the statement "I know you all are scientists and I believe I can prove it to you right now." In fact, teachers are scientists, too. Table 1.3 lists some questions teachers can use to check out students' prior knowledge, experiences, confidence, and ability prior to beginning a discussion of themselves as scientists. The purpose is to help students trust themselves in learning science and connect them with science concepts right away. This approach is a great start because scientific knowledge has always been part of the students' everyday life events.

Table 1.3 Questions for Inquiry-Based Approach Connecting Life Experiences with Science Concepts

Thought-Provoking Question	Yes	No	Detailed Information
Do you know how to cook?			Type of food or dish
Can you make yourself a sandwich?			Ingredients
Can you brush your teeth? Or do you know how to brush your teeth? Do you know how to comb your hair?			Two times, how often, morning or at night, etc . . .
Do you put lotion on your face, arms, legs, or body?			Rationale, reasons, etc . . .
Can you groom yourself?			Brushing, combing, clothing, cleaning, hygiene, etc . . .
Can you make your own bed?			Changing, cleaning, washing, etc . . .
Do you have five senses? Touch, taste, smell, vision, and hearing.			Like, dislike, favor, sweet, sour, bitter, soft, smooth, loud, etc . . .
Do you play videogames?			Motor skills, concentration, transmission, controlling, vision, etc . . .
Do you like rollercoaster rides?			Speed, velocity, height, wind, sensation, fear, etc . . .
What chores do you do at home? Cleaning, doing dishes, dusting, laundry, etc . . .			Cooking, mopping, waxing, vacuuming, sweeping, etc . . .
Do you take a bath or a shower every day?			How long? Water conservation, soaping, bubbles, shampoo, conditioning, etc . . .
Do you like to shop for clothes, groceries, tools, or Christmas?			List, choices, decisions, sorting, organizing, colors, sizes, etc . . .
Do you play with dolls, toys, puppets, or friends?			Shapes, sizes, made of, materials, descriptions, etc . . .
Can you ride a bike, tricycle, roller skate, roller blade, or scooter?			Balance, falling, training, learning, controlling, speed, gravity, etc . . .
Can you mix Koolaid with water?			Mixing, stirring, cool, cold, hot, chemical reaction, etc . . .
Do you like to paint or draw pictures?			Shapes, designs, colors, brush strokes, etc . . .

These questions demonstrate that students have learned or experienced science in their own lives before or during school. Regardless of their ethnic backgrounds, nearly all students answer yes to these questions. However, teachers must recognize that all students have not experienced science the same way, and each student may explain results differently based on their academic skills or cultural understanding of scientific knowledge. Furthermore, different cultures perceive the same scientific facts differently, and how people view things makes a difference in how they apply facts, principles, rules, and theories. For example, in some cultures, cooking is a very important household chore for females, but not for males;

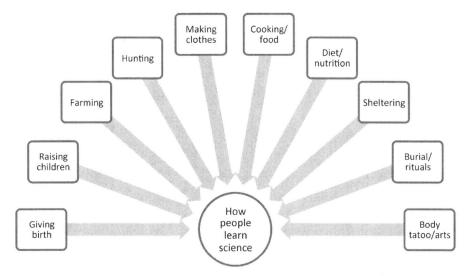

Figure 1.3 *Samples of human activities related to scientific knowledge and skills*

females must master the chore because being a good cook gives them respect and value, especially from parents or elders. In other cultures, cooking is important for males also, as evidenced by the fact that there are more male chefs than female.

Cooking is a good example of the reality that science is part of everyday life. The ingredients of various dishes; the procedures for combining them; what happens to them when they are crushed, mixed, heated, or cooled are all pieces of scientific knowledge. Figure 1.3 presents some examples of human activities that can be explained in terms of scientific knowledge. Keep in mind that science is not the answer to all questions, and most importantly, science is only one avenue for knowing, understanding, learning, and studying life phenomena and the world around us.

HOW SCIENCE IS LEARNED IN SCHOOL

In school, children are taught discovered, or natural, science along with inventive science. Discovered science is the study of natural phenomena, such as the earth, oceans, planets, wind, air, rocks, fossils, and sunlight. Inventive science has to do with man-made objects such as machines, computers, airplanes, chemical elements, cars, houses, bridges, and electricity. Students are expected to learn science by building a scaffold of different layers. Each layer helps develop their knowledge and skills acquired from their own experiences, from reading books, from seeing

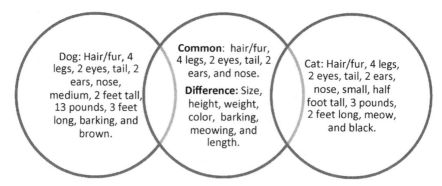

Figure 1.4 *Compare and contrast animal characteristics*

and working with peers, from doing activities or experiments, and from thinking about how things ought to be. Hands-on and minds-on activities help students learn science concepts through firsthand experience; they use meaningful activities to help students acquire knowledge, develop ideas, and understand concrete concepts. The essential element of teaching science is making sure that children are able to develop their own knowledge through scientific experiences. The goal is that students can construct their own scientific knowledge to explain their learning outcomes. Figure 1.4 illustrates an activity that shows how students can learn to classify and understand animals.

The goal of learning science is to help students construct and build their own knowledge and gain skills from their own learning experiences and thought processes; these will energize them to learn science concepts with ease and motivation. *Academic constructivism* will take place once students are able to guide themselves through the process of understanding scientific concepts with academic learned experiences; they will continue to build on their knowledge. Keep in mind that knowledge, skills, understanding, and transmission of concepts grow slowly and differently in different students. In other words, one concept may be easy for some to understand but it could be difficult for others to grasp.

Regardless of the instructional methodology used by the teacher, science must be taught as the search for knowledge rather than as knowledge itself. Students do need to have a conceptual understanding of the knowledge components of *concepts, facts, principles, theories, and hypotheses* in order to make learning science academically challenging but not difficult. Table 1.4 provides basic definitions and examples of these components. Some students have difficulty understanding science concepts because they have trouble understanding these basic ideas.

Moreover, teachers can enhance science learning with technology. Technological tools and applications help students and teachers shape the teaching and

Table 1.4 Definitions and Examples of Knowledge Components

Knowledge Component	Basic Definitions	Examples
Concept	Collection of ideas, things, evidence	Mixture, bonding, melting, evaporation
Fact	Observable object, event, idea	Sinking or floating objects in water, melting ice in palm
Principle	Generalizing idea related to relationship between concepts, objects, ideas	Atoms, molecules, particles, bonding
Theory	Guessing, predicting, imagining about ideas, concepts, principles, facts, assumption, descriptions	Surface tension, bonding of particles, estimation, prediction, Sinking, floating, buoyancy, etc . . .
Hypothesis	Untested idea, concept, principle, theory, question	Sinking or floating, compare and contrast ideas, variables

learning of science in so many ways. However, no technology can take the place of a good teacher, and the relationship between technology and science could be as complex as the science itself.

HOW SCIENTIFIC KNOWLEDGE DEVELOPS

Science knowledge and skills can develop from both natural science and inventive science. People experience science in everyday life without going to school. Some science concepts are context-embedded. Teachers as well as students have developed their understanding of science concepts from direct experiences in life such as observation, communication, collection, or restoration. The knowledge gained from these embedded experiences is referred to as *concrete concepts*. Different students have different concrete concepts because they have different real-life experiences. For instance, students who live on farms know more about cows and other farm animals than do those who live in metropolitan areas.

As mentioned earlier, children bring science experiences to the class; however, learning science concepts academically is still relatively new to some minority students of diverse backgrounds. In scientific learning, students have to think critically about their observations and experiences in order to understand their meanings. Teachers can reinforce the concrete concepts students bring with them to the classroom by connecting them with science activities through scientific investigation and experimentation. Figure 1.5 gives an example; it demonstrates prediction of whether certain objects will float or sink in water. Before conducting the experiment, teachers ask students to predict for each object whether it will float or sink, and then they allow students to test their predictions. These direct

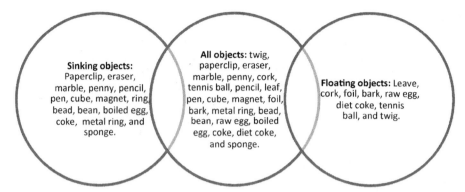

Figure 1.5 *Depiction of results of experiment on objects floating or sinking in water*

observations give students concrete concepts because the students actually conduct the experiments and experience what happens with each object.

In this experiment, some objects sink first and then float later and other objects float for a time before sinking. Teachers can explain to students why these objects belong in both categories. For instance, a paperclip floats in water if the water surface tension is not broken, and a piece of foil sinks in water if it is crumbled into a ball. Such activities should arouse students' curiosity and increase their knowledge, inspiring them to proceed to the next level of learning science concepts.

ACQUIRING ACADEMIC AND SCIENTIFIC KNOWLEDGE

If they are alert, people can find science everywhere they go and can learn it from different sources. However, in school, students have to acquire academic and scientific knowledge. Teachers should expect students to acquire specific academic and scientific knowledge that will stay with them forever. Besides *academic constructivism*, students must be guided through scientific processes to develop four types of knowledge needed for the mastery of scientific conceptual applications as shown in Table 1.5: *arbitrary knowledge, physical knowledge, logical knowledge,* and *social interactive knowledge* (Howe, 2002). Students need time to develop these types of knowledge, and different students may require different types of scientific learning to make the connections that form the knowledge. Not all knowledge can be discovered or learned from direct experiences alone. Teachers may need to fill in the gaps with books, ideas, experiments, concepts, interpretations, and observations. As mentioned previously, science does not have all the answers to every single thing, and science is constantly evolving; it is only one of the ways of knowing, understanding, examining, and learning about the world.

Table 1.5 Four Types of Knowledge

Type	Examples
Arbitrary knowledge	Names, symbols, conventions, rules, places, procedures, authentic ideas, labels, originality
Physical knowledge	Light, heavy, rough, smooth, coarse, shiny, round, oval, shapes, bright, dull, sink, float, shapes, size, mass, volume, description
Logical knowledge	Analysis, conclusion, concept, interpretation, inference, application, implication
Social interactive knowledge	Interaction with others; interpersonal relationships; cooperation; teamwork; think, pair, share; group work,; communication; sharing; discussion

PROMOTING SCIENTIFIC LITERACY IN CHILDREN

Understanding what science means requires scientific knowledge and skills developed through study. Teaching science concepts to elementary students can be challenging, but learning science can be frustrating for some students because of the use of scientific language. New vocabulary words can have different or complex meanings, and scientists use science words that have different meanings in different contexts. For instance, *archaeopteryx* is a long word with a prefix, a root, and a suffix; it means "ancient wing." *Metamorphosis* is also a long word with a prefix, a root, and a suffix and means "a process of change from one form completely to become another form." *Ecosystem* is a compound word and means "the way living and nonliving things interact in an environment." The word *interact* means different things to students, especially for non-native speakers, English language learners, and students with special needs. To help elementary students learn scientific words, teachers can explain them in different ways to make connection with concepts they already understand. For example, the word *interact* could be explained by the substitution of other words such as *survive, live together, adapt to, depend on each other, relate to, or how things understand each other*. Table 1.6 gives more examples of scientific terminology that children need to learn. Keep in mind that science literacy improves science learning.

Science is a form of language arts, and students must learn key vocabulary to help them master scientific knowledge. Teachers can create word banks with new terms or vocabulary words and ask students to define them by using the dictionary or by finding them in a book. Keep in mind that practice is the key to mastering these words. Teachers should use dictation or spelling tests as often as possible. Moreover, in science, the academic language is related to the mastery of terminology, meanings, and applications. Promoting scientific literacy is critical in learning science because the more students understand what they are studying, the more they will want to learn, and the more they enjoy learning, the more they will retain.

Table 1.6 Selected Scientific Terms

Term	Basic Meaning	Alternative Words
Adaptation	A trait that helps living things survive in a environment	Limbs, gills, scales, blubber, fur, poison, thorn
Biome	Specific location or area where living and nonliving things are found	Ocean biome, desert biome, land biome, grassland biome, mountain biome
Hypothesis	An idea, statement, concept, or explanation that can be tested, or an untested question	Experimentation, testing, guessing, predicting
Kinetic energy	Energy in the form of movement or motion, or moving energy	Moving, falling, flying, turning, dropping, running
Population	All members of a single type of living or nonliving thing in an ecosystem	Group, together, organism, collection of living or nonliving things

Today, many teachers teach science lesson plans but forget to emphasize scientific literacy. For instance, it is possible for students to perform hands-on and minds-on activities without a great deal of reading; however, if students cannot read well they will not be able to read instructions, directions, or other information independently. In other words, teachers must keep this in mind: Elementary students must be taught to read and learn content simultaneously in the early part of their education before they can be expected to read to learn for themselves in the future. So many students depend on their teachers for assistance, and in a worst-case scenario, some schools test students with open books.

The goal of promoting scientific literacy in young learners is to make sure that students are able to read, understand, and apply the key concepts, principles, rules, laws, processes, and theories in ways that are beneficial for their personal use. Literacy enhances students' ability to apply scientific knowledge in academic contexts. The benefit of literacy can last a lifetime when someone decides to become a scientist or to pursue a career in science or related fields.

TEACHING SCIENCE AS INQUIRY

Children are born with their minds largely blank slates, full of curiosity, perceptions and misperceptions, and infinite thought processes. Children wonder about the world around them. Some question everything they see and others are shy and ask very few questions, but they all are curious. Curiosity may make children inquisitive, argumentative, assertive, talkative, passive, or tenacious about learning. Scientific inquiry should be the guiding principle in the promotion, development, acquisition, and mastering of scientific knowledge.

The ongoing *process* of asking and answering questions in learning science is referred to as *guided inquiry*. Academically, *inquiry* involves students in a systematic investigation of ideas, concepts, facts, theories, or hypotheses of interest. The process of inquiry directly involves investigation and experimentation. Throughout the process, scientific progress is made by asking meaningful questions and conducting careful investigations or experimentations to answer the questions. Young children may not be able to write down their own questions for scientific investigation; however, teachers can assist students with age- and grade-level-appropriate questions for independent practice. For instance, they can use the 5Ws + H as an inquiry-based approach: asking and answering *what, when, why, where, who, and how* questions. Or they can use a *graphic organizer* chart with questions as a guide. Developing inquiry skills is a powerful tool in learning science, and all children should be encouraged to acquire as many of these skills as possible for their grade level. Examples of basic inquiry skills are shown in Table 1.7.

Inquiry skills are essential in the development and acquisition of scientific knowledge, and at the same time students are developing these skills, teachers can assess students' progress in learning science concepts based on skill levels. In science, teachers should be more concerned about the *cognitive process objective* (knowing how to do something) than the *cognitive content objective* (knowing what is being studied).

Young children may lack linguistic skills or academic language needed for communicating, interpreting, analyzing, explaining, or inferring scientific data or results; however, they may be good at other processes such as observing, classifying, drawing, coloring, organizing, or predicting possible results. Using hands-on and minds-on strategies will enhance student learning of science concepts. For that reason, teachers need to design appropriate science learning objectives based on science content standards for each grade level in order to meet the cognitive demands of the learners. Also, designing appropriate lesson plans helps teachers assess student learning outcome more quickly and accurately.

ADHERING TO SCIENCE CONTENT STANDARDS

As a practical matter, teachers know that teaching and learning have to be well structured and well organized in order for students to learn in a formalized process; little can be accomplished in a disorderly environment. There are good reasons for teachers to adhere to the science content standards because standards require specific academic instruction to be deliberately delivered in a logical sequence at each level of schooling. There are two sets of compatible national and state science standards with which all teachers should be familiar; teachers can use either

Table 1.7 Words Associated with Inquiry and Examples of Inquiry Skills

Words	Examples of Inquiry Skills
Observe	Use, apply, or allow five senses to examine, feel, determine, or learn about an object or event
Classify	Sort, put, collect, organize, separate, or place things that are the same, different, or similar in a group, or organize things that share properties together in a group
Measure	Use or apply numbers or rulers to find, label, name, or identify the size, length, distance, time, volume, area, mass, weight, height, or temperature of an object or an event
Infer	Decide, form, conclude, interpret, or finalize an idea from facts, concepts, principles, theories, results, or observation
Communicate	Discuss, interact, exchange, talk, share, elaborate, or explain information, data, or results
Interpret	Explain, tell, discuss, share, elaborate, or exchange information, data, or results of investigation or experiment
Hypothesize	Form, make, ask, or write a statement or question that can be tested to answer a question
Experiment	Use variables to perform a test to support, confirm, or disprove a hypothesis or a question of interest
Use variables	Use, identify, or label things to be changed, controlled, manipulated, or monitored in an experiment
Predict	Guess, estimate, state, or tell the possible results, number, or outcome of an event, investigation, or experimentation
Make a model	Design, craft, make, produce, or create something to represent or replicate an object, event, or experiment
Use numbers	Name, label, identify, order, count, add, subtract, multiply, or divide to explain data or results of an experiment
Record data	Note, write, log, keep, arrange, store, collect, or organize information, data, or results of science investigation or experiment
Analyze data	Decide, infer, observe, measure, communicate, apply, or use the information, data, or results collected or gathered to answer questions or to solve problems or test hypotheses

a content-compatible (not standard-based) curriculum) or a content-obligatory (standard-based curriculum) approach. Both national and state science content standards are academic guidelines that provide teachers with comprehensive lists of science concepts, procedures, and processes in order to guide instructional practices. Most importantly, these guidelines emphasize guided inquiry as the foundation for science teaching and learning for each grade level. However, science content standards are broad based; they use generalized ideas, concepts, and theories. For that reason, teachers need to think creatively as well as logically when applying science content standards to everyday teaching. Tables 1.8 and 1.9 give

Table 1.8 National Science Educational Standards

Grade level	Unifying Concepts and Processes	Science as Inquiry	Physical Science	Life Science	Earth and Space Science	Science and Technology	Science I Personal and Social Perspective	History and Nature of Science
K–4	System, order, and organization; evidence, models, and explanation; change, constancy, and measurement; evolution and equilibrium; and form and function	Ability to perform, understand, or learn scientific inquiry	Properties, objects, position, motion, light, heat, electricity, magnetism	Characteristics of plants and animals; life cycles; and ecosystems	Properties, earth's layers, objects in sky, climate changes, and materials	Use technology, differences between natural objects and made objects	Health, relationships, people, society, resources, life challenges, and changes	Science as human endeavor, discovery, and invention
5–8	System, order, and organization; evidence, models, and explanation; change, constancy, and measurement; evolution and equilibrium; and form and function	Ability to perform, understand, or learn scientific inquiry	Properties, changes, matter, motions forces, and transfer of energy	Structure, function, ecosystem, food chain/web, reproduction, heredity, behavior, people, society, adaptations, survival, and differences	Earth layers/ structure, earth history, planets, solar system, and changes	Abilities, design, understand technology, and applications	Health, resources, people, society, hazards, risks, benefits, diseases, and environments	Science as human endeavor, nature of science, and history of science

Note. Information from *A Sample of National Science Education Standards*, by Joseph M. Peters, 2006, Upper Saddle River, New Jersey: Pearson Education, and *National Science Education Standards*, 1996, Center for Science, Mathematics, and Engineering Education, Washington, DC: National Academies Press, http://books.nap.edu/html/nses/html/overview.html#content

Table 1.9 California Science Content Standards for Grades K-12

Grade level	Physical science	Life science	Earth science	Investigation/experimentation
Kindergarten	Properties of materials (clay, cloth, paper, house, car, toys, objects), observe, measure, predict, color, size, shape, weight, texture, flexibility, attraction to magnets, floating, sinking	Types of plants and animals, differences, similarities, comparing, classifying, seed-bearing plants, birds, fish, insects, stems, leaves, roots, arms, wings, legs	Earth structures, air, wind, land, water, mountains, rivers, oceans, valleys, deserts, landforms	Observe, compare, classify, describe, communicate
First	Forms and states of matter, gases, liquids, solids, properties of substances, mixed, cooled, or heated	Plants and animals, needs, survival, adaptations, food, sharp teeth: eats meat; flat teeth: eats plants, shelter, nesting, physical needs	Weather patterns, wind vane, weather conditions, temperature, thermometer, observe, measure, light, rain, fog, snow, climate changes	Observe, predict, measure, describe, communicate
Second	Motions of objects, force, strength, push, pull, sound, vibration, pitch, noise, beat	Life cycles of plants and animals, germination, pollination, reproduction, growth, development, parents, offspring, characteristics	Earth is made of materials, soil, water, fossils, rocks, minerals, resources, energy	Predict, observe, measure, describe, communicate, experiment, test, record
Third	Forms of energy and matter, light, heat, water, wind, gas, fuel, food, solid, liquid, gas, evaporation, melting, substances, atoms, particles	Adaptations, behavior, survival, reproduction, growth, extinction, biomes, life forms, ecosystems	Objects in the sky, patterns, constellations, stars, planets, day, night, dark, light, seasons, lunar cycles	Predict, observe, measure, describe, communicate, experiment, test, record

	Physical Science	Life Science	Earth Science	Skills
Fourth	Electricity, magnetism, energy, light, motions, forces, charges, poles, compass, effects, circuits, design, motors, devices, generators, magnetic field	All organisms need energy and matter to live and grow, food chain, food web, herbivores, omnivores, carnivores, consumers, decomposers, producers, recycle of plants and animals	Properties of rocks and minerals, process of formation; igneous, sedimentary, metamorphic rock; earthquakes; landslides; erosion; volcanic eruption; landforms; weathering; transportation; deposition; wind; waves	Read, predict, observe, measure, describe, communicate, infer, formulate, experiment, test, record
Fifth	Types of matter, periodic table, chemical reactions, elements, metal, nonmetal, gas, solid, liquid, chemical properties, atoms, molecules, physical properties	Plant and animal structures, respiration, transpiration, waste disposal, digestion, functions of internal organs, metabolism, chemical breakdowns	Weather cycles, patterns, conditions, seasons, evaporation, condensation, precipitation, rain, hail, snow, fog, sleet, ice, lakes, oceans, rivers, underground water, convection currents, temperature	Conduct study, read, predict, observe, measure, describe, communicate, infer, formulate, experiment, test, record
Sixth	Heat and thermal energy, climate changes, heat waves, light, radiation, flow of energy, temperature, convection currents, transfer of energy, humidity, pressure	All organisms in ecosystem, exchange energy and nutrients, sunlight, photosynthesis, produce food, food web, antibiotic factors, light, water, natural energy, material resources, air, soil, rocks, minerals, petroleum, fresh water, wildlife, forests, renewable and, nonrenewable energy	Plate tectonics and earth's structures, geological events, earthquakes, tsunamis, shakes, motions, eruptions, layers, fossils, epicenter, faults, landforms, weather patterns, climate, shapes, topography	Conduct study, read, use technology, predict, observe, measure, describe, communicate, infer, formulate, experiment, test, record, science project

(Continued)

Grade level	Physical science	Life science	Earth science	Investigation/experimentation
Seventh	Physical principles in living systems, light spectrum, light waves, reflection, refraction, electromagnetic light, wavelengths, lenses, eyes, magnify glass, telescope, microscope, camera, light colors, light travel	Cell biology, genetics, structure and function in living systems, cells, tissues, organs, muscles, joints, skeletal, genes, traits, heredity, recessive, dominant, mitosis, reproductive organs, sexual activity, pollens, seeds, fruit, fertilization, pregnancy, chromosomes, plant and animal cellular structures, species, natural selection, anatomy, fossils	Earth and life history, age of the earth, rock cycles, evolution of life on earth, geological processes, geological time scale, extinction, fossils, fire, flood, catastrophic events, eruptions, impacts of asteroids	Conduct study, read, use technology, predict, observe, measure, describe, communicate, infer, formulate, experiment, test, record, science project
Eighth	Motions, forces, structure of matter properties, density, buoyancy, forms of matter, velocity, speed, balanced, unbalanced, inertia, action, reaction, static, gravity, elastic, tension, compression, friction, atomic structure, proton, neutron, electron, properties, molecular motions, elements on periodic table, acidic, basic, neutral	Chemistry of living systems, carbon, carbohydrates, fats, proteins, DNA, principles of chemistry in living organisms	Earth in the solar system, structure and composition of the universe, milky way, stars, planets, galaxies, black hole, distance between planets, eclipse, shine, waxing, waning	Conduct study, read, use technology, predict, observe, measure, describe, communicate, infer, formulate, experiment, test, record, science project

Note. Information from *Science Content Standards for California Public Schools: Kindergarten through Grade 12,* 2003, California Department of Education, http://www.cde.ca.gov/be/st/ss/documents/sciencestnd.pdf

the National Science Educational Standards (NSES) and California Science Content Standards for the K-12 grades.

Keep in mind that these standards are guidelines and should be used accordingly in order to teach science concepts appropriately. Without guidelines, lesson plan objectives may be too difficult or too easy for students to understand. Science content standards for Grades K-2 are concerned with general concepts, but standards for Grades 4-6 deal with concrete science concepts and scientific knowledge. In other words, teachers following the standards teach science from general concepts to concrete, specific ideas. Another way to explain this is that concepts are introduced in lower grades and in-depth science is taught in higher grades.

MAKING SCIENCE FOR EVERYONE

Despite students' academic differences, teachers should help all learners believe in themselves as scientists because a strong belief that each child will learn science in accordance with his or her ability improves the teacher's attitude in teaching inquiry science to all students. This approach is not different from the current norm in school. Many schools use slogans, mottos, or names like Scholars, Mustangs, Titans, Cowboys, Tigers, Bears, Bulldogs, or Grizzlies to boost academic excellence and self-esteem. So, calling students scientists is not a nonacademic idea.

Today, nearly 80% of teachers in elementary schools use direct instruction or scripted instruction to teach science. This model of instruction benefits only the top students but neglects those in the middle and at the bottom. Because students have diverse academic abilities, teachers need to select teaching methodologies and strategies that benefit all students, maximizing student learning outcomes. There is no one-model-fits all, but there are task strategies and activity strategies that are better than others at motivating and encouraging students to actively engage in instruction and activities. For instance, cooperative learning, think-pair-share, group activity, center instruction, differentiating instruction, and hands-on/minds-on activities have been demonstrated to be more conducive to learning than direct instruction. The point here is that teachers must consider their attitudes and values regarding people to find different ways to engage all learners in learning science.

The teacher's personality is the most single important factor in teaching; it is the screen that students watch each and every day in the classroom. Also, personality affects teachers' attitudes toward the subject matter, lesson planning, instruction, activities, and most importantly, students. To engage students in the learning circle, teachers must have positive attitudes that foster both teaching and learning. Here are some examples of positive attitudes:

1. Be passionate.
2. Be patient.
3. Be enthusiastic.
4. Be excited.
5. Be creative and flexible.
6. Be inclusive and accommodating.
7. Understand the challenges facing students.
8. Balance difficult tasks and challenging tasks.
9. Make teaching and learning interesting and fun.
10. Help students be curious and eager to learn.
11. Use props, prompts, and perks to engage students.
12. Get involved in activities with students.

Teachers' attitudes and teaching methods are instructional ingredients; they must be good if the teacher is to provide effective lessons for all learners in the classroom. With good attitudes and appropriate teaching methods, teachers can make learning science an exhilarating experience for all students; that should be the goal: making science fun for everyone.

UNDERSTAND THE GOALS FOR SCIENCE EDUCATION

Like teaching any other academic subject, teaching science has learning objectives. Teachers should set learning expectations and goals early to guide the teaching of science concepts every step of the way. The final outcomes must align with the NSES and state standards for science content. As the drivers of the class, teachers can develop the knowledge and skills needed to help students reach the ultimate goals. Here are some ideas teachers should consider adding to their science teaching skills repertoire:

1. Use the guided inquiry approach.
2. Keep students curious about the world around them.
3. Incorporate investigation and experimentation with hands-on and minds-on activities.
4. Connect science activities to real-life experiences.
5. Keep students enjoying learning.
6. Promote independent thinking.
7. Model good behaviors in class.
8. Use technology to enhance learning.

9. Use creativity to engage students.
10. Assess student needs and build upon their ideas.
11. Allow academic engaged time for science activities.
12. Use integrated content to connect science with other subjects.
13. Promote scientific literacy.
14. Select appropriate teaching methods.
15. Maintain a positive attitude at all time.

These ideas are not new, and they should enable teachers to develop the technical and intellectual skills needed to prepare and organize science lesson plans and materials. Keep in mind that teaching has to be flexible and challenging, but not difficult. Moreover, teachers must present themselves as professional models, adhere to the academic principles they teach in order to learn, grow, and glow with their students and guide them to reach the following goals:

- Develop an understanding of and ability to engage in scientific inquiry
- Develop a base of factual, conceptual, and theoretical knowledge of their surroundings and the natural world
- Develop scientific attitudes and mental habits
- Understand the connections between science and technology, recognizing how science and technology affect people, life, and society as a whole, and understanding that science and technology can be helpful for improving human life
- Have knowledge and skills to apply facts, concepts, principles, theories, and laws of science to real-life experiences and events.

SUMMING UP

This chapter provides a comprehensive overview of various concepts about teaching elementary science. Questions such as *What is science?* and *What does science mean?* provoke thought and a search for knowledge. Science should be taught as inquiry; however, finding meaningful answers to these questions is not easy for elementary students. There is no single definition that fits all aspects of science. For that reason, teachers may have to suggest logical explanations when students ask them about the nature of science. This chapter also describes science as the discovery of nature and as the study of human inventions.

In earlier times, man discovered the beauty of nature in land, mountains, lakes, oceans, seas, planets, forests, animals, insects, and natural resources. Education has given man the knowledge and skills not only to discover the principles of science, but also to invent new things such as cars, machines, computers, airplanes, tanks, guns, and boats. Science surrounds life, and life surrounds science.

All children and teachers are scientists. Each brings his or her own knowledge, skills, and real-life experiences to the classroom. Teachers are responsible to help students make connections between the academic study of science and real-life experiences. Science content standards are guidelines that teachers follow to teach science in an inquiry-based approach. Science does not have all the answers to every question, and there is not only one possible way of understanding the world. Teachers have the exciting task of helping students understand what science is and what science is not by promoting scientific literacy as well as the development of scientific knowledge and skills.

CHAPTER TWO

How Children Think
AND Learn

Equipped with his five senses, man explores the universe around him and calls the adventure Science.

—EDWIN POWELL HUBBLE
THE NATURE OF SCIENCE, 1954

INTRODUCTION

Teaching science concepts to learners in Grades K-6 requires an understanding of how children think, learn, and understand the subject matter. Elementary students are children, who do not think like their teachers or other adults. The way they see things, like things, learn things, and understand things may seem odd to people who are not like them culturally or linguistically. Teachers know that not all children think the same way or do things the same way because of multiple intelligences and because of individual differences in cognitive development, motor skills, affective factors, emotional sensitivities, and behavioral issues. For instance, some children are active in learning and others are passive in learning. Children's ways of thinking and learning should shape the way teachers teach science and what teachers expect them to learn in class. This chapter presents a comprehensive overview of children's thinking and learning processes to give teachers insight into how to make teaching science concepts sensible, meaningful, appropriate, and effective in the multicultural setting.

UNDERSTANDING CHILDREN'S MISPERCEPTIONS

As mentioned in Chapter One, children are born with their minds clean slates full of wonder, curiosity, intriguing thoughts, and inquiry about all the physical, biological, and social phenomena in life. Their cognitive processing is interesting and may seem strange because they try to create logical explanations to help them make sense of the world in which they are living and of the life they are learning to navigate each and every day. For instance, children's ideas about the earth, sky, Walt Disney movies, toys, ownership, animals, plants, and food are amazing; they have great imaginations. For this reason, their naïve ideas and imaginary perceptions of the physical world and life events are generally misconceptions. Children have a premature conceptual framework for everyday life. For instance, most preschoolers learn by copying, following examples, following simple directions, playing make believe, moving, and observing.

Keep in mind that teachers were once children themselves, and as adults, they may need to talk, think, and learn like children do in order to help demystify children's misconceptions. Children's ideas are generated by inside and outside forces or influences. For instance, some children like to copy their friends' answers or ideas and believe exactly the same way; others are very imaginative, have great artistic skills, and can form their own ideas about the things they see, hear, or like. The child's mind can be manipulated by parents, peers, and teachers. Manipulations can be easy or difficult, depending on the age, gender, and temperament of the child. Because children come to the classroom with misconceptions, it is crucial for teachers to engage their students in meaningful science activities, particularly hands-on and minds-focused activities, to help them overcome simple misconceptions by doing investigation and experimentation before dealing with more difficult and complex issues. In other words, teaching for conceptual change is important for correcting or improving children's understanding of the phenomena of everyday life. Teachers have to teach conceptual change at basic and advanced levels depending on the grade level of their students. Table 2.1 lists some misconceptions that can be overcome easily; however, teachers must be careful to pay attention to the children's belief system and some religious values because science is not the same as truth.

LEARNING FROM THE THEORISTS

Teachers can figure out how children think, behave, and learn on their own, or they can learn from the many theorists, experts, researchers, and educators who have studied children's behaviors, child development, and child psychology

Table 2.1 Some Typical Childhood Misconceptions

Conceptual idea	Conceptual determination	Possible explanations
Mass, volume, matter, or physical properties	A crumbled paper is heavier than a flat sheet of the same paper, or round object s are heavier than flat objects	Children may believe that something flat paper is lighter than something round because it appears thinner.
Moon, sun, or stars	Come out at night and go home during the day, or come out during the day and go home at night	Children may believe the sun, moon, and stars are alive because they appear at night or during the day.
Nonliving things	Not moving, stand still, just sit there, not talking, quiet	Children may believe anything that is not moving, such as a plant or a rock, is dead or nonliving.
Living things	Moving, alive, talking, rolling, falling, flying, crawling, creeping	Children may believe that anything that moves, such as cars, wind, train, cartoons, shadows, is alive.
Earth shape	Round, flat, like a ball, like a pancake, like a marble, like a ring, like a disc	Children may describe things based on their imagination, copying of information, or guessing.
Walt Disney movies, animated characters, cartoons, or action heroes	Real people, real animals, real plants, alive, true, friendly	Children may believe that animated characters, cartoons, or action heroes are real people because they appear to move. Children may believe all animals can live and play together as seen in movies.
Dolls, toys, puppets, electrical or mechanical devices	Alive, moving, talking, speaking, gesturing, responding	Children may believe toys or mechanical devices are alive because they appear to talk, respond, move hands and legs.
Tooth fairy and Santa Clause	Real people, real friends, give money, bring gifts	Children may believe stories told by adults are true.

over the last two and a half centuries. From the mid 1800s to the present day, many thinkers and experts have engaged in research to learn how children behave, think, and learn throughout their life span. Their research data should be used as bases for preparing better ways to design and deliver instruction, engage students, and facilitate the learning process for all learners in science education. Table 2.2 presents the principles of several theorists and scholars who developed learning theories with direct implications for science education. They still exert influences in academia and provide educators with practical ingredients for the development of pedagogical applications to help children learn the content of all academic subjects taught in school, and their theoretical principles still help teachers understand the ways children behave, think, and learn.

Table 2.2 Theorists Who Have Influenced Education

Theorist	Year of Impact	Theory	Theoretical Principles
Arnold Gesell	1925	Maturational theory	Personal development has biological basis; bad and good experiences; body types of endomorph, ectomorph, and mesomorph.
Sigmund Freud	1935	Psychoanalytical theory	Behavior disorders, behavioral problems, and psychodynamic models designed for children with special needs.
Eric Erickson	1950	Stages of personality development	(a) oral-sensory, birth to 18 months; (b) muscular-anal, 18 months to 3 years; (c) locomotor, 3 to 6 years; (d) latency, 6 to 12 years; (e) adolescence, 12 to 18 years; (f) young adulthood, 19 to 40 years; (g) middle adulthood, 40 to 65 years; and (h) late adulthood, 65 years to death.
Jean Piaget	1952	Constructivist theory	Based on logico-mathematical knowledge, individualism, autonomy in learning.
John Dewey	1956	Learner's experience or prior knowledge approach	Learner's experience is the starting point of instruction instead of rigid and programmed curricula.
Jerome Bruner	1966	Knowledge theory	Enactive, iconic, and symbolic modes; also, the spiral curriculum approach.
Lawrence Kohlberg	1969	Constructivist theory	Preconventional stage, conventional stage, and postconventional or principled stage.
B.F. Skinner	1974	Behaviorist theory	Environment has role in individual development or behavior modification and programmed learning.
Lev Vygotsky	1978	Sociohistorical theory	Emphasis on sociohistorical context, language and literacy learning, and child's zone of proximal development.
U. Bronfenbrenner	1979	Ecological system theory	Emphasis on the influence of microsystem, mesosystem, exosystem, and macrosystem.
Howard Gardner	1983	Multiple intelligence	Eight types of intelligence: linguistic, logical/mathematical, visual/spatial, musical, bodily kinesthetic, interpersonal, intrapersonal, and naturalist.

Note. Information from *An Educational Psychology of Methods in Multilingual Education*, by C.T. Vang, 2010, New York: Peter Lang Publishing.

According to recent research, experts in the field recognize that children of diverse backgrounds have diverse learning abilities and bring different ideas, concepts, and thought processes to the classroom. Some of these challenges involved in having a wide variety of abilities and ideas interfere with daily teaching and learning, making today's learning more domain-specific and less easily transferred from one area to another than was once thought. Furthermore, teachers must take into consideration that social interaction and the context in which a cognitive skill is learned and used are important factors in the construction of meaning in learning new ideas, such as science concepts and vocabulary words.

Teachers should discard any biased beliefs they hold in regards to the *Bell Curve* controversy initiated about two decades ago, and they must believe that science is for everyone regardless of their cultural backgrounds. Teachers should also be aware of the difference in right- and left-brain learners, as presented in Table 2.3, because teacher's beliefs about children matter in the classroom, and those beliefs can affect teaching and learning positively or negatively. The national science standards require that all children should have equal opportunity to learn

Table 2.3 Contrast Between Right- and Left-Brain Learners

Right-Brain Learners	Left-Brain Learners
• Visually oriented	Analytical
• Spatially oriented	Logical
• Demonstration	Concrete
• Experience	Sequential
• Open-ended questions	Lecture
• Nonverbal approach	Discussion
• Manipulation	Verbal cues
• Divergent thinking activities	Rules
• Flash cards	Short questions and short answers
• Maps	Yes or no approach
• Idea web	Texts
• Films	Word list or word bank
• Audiotapes	Workbook exercises
• Crafts	Readings
• Drawing activities	Drills
• Wholistic approach	Linear mode approach
• Broad thinking process	Meaning and retention
• Intuitive thinking	Question-and-answer exercises
• Guess-timating	Vocabulary and definitions
• Testing ideas and principles	Note taking
• Visual and spatial mode approach	Recitation
• Use non-sequential mode	Repetition
• Total physical response	Memorization
• Integrate performance arts	Review

science concepts in an unrestrictive environment. In other words, teachers must use the information about the different ways children learn to enhance student learning instead of using it to denigrate certain student learning styles.

HOW CHILDREN LEARN BEFORE COMING TO SCHOOL

Life begins at home, and parents are children's first teachers. There is little that teachers can do, if anything, about children's lives before they are enrolled in school. As Vang (2010) explained, some factors that can impede learning are poor physical health, poor family status, reaction to loss, unexpected life disruption, lack of a support system at home, and social stress related to the failure to have basic human needs met. Vang further pointed out that cultural factors as well as environmental factors can influence the course of development in children. Moreover, individual personality factors, cultural norms, socioeconomic status, environment, and language barriers may also influence the pace of a child's development. The attempt to fill unsatisfied needs may motivate children to behave, think, and learn in certain ways (Maslow, 1954). Figure 2.1 illustrates the hierarchy of basic human needs that influence the course of development in children.

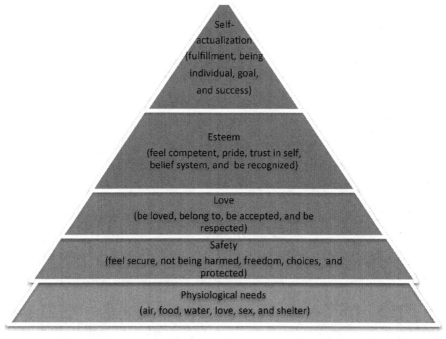

Figure 2.1 *The hierarchy of basic human needs.*

Table 2.4 Typical Progression of Early Language Development

Stage	Time of development	Examples
Hearing	Birth and beyond (unless born deaf)	Sensing, feeling, comfort, holding, recognizing, identifying, knowing
Crying	Birth to 2 months	Discomfort, hungry, thirsty, sick, ill, scare, frightening
Cooing	2 to 4 months	Comfort, satisfaction, pleasure, enjoyment
Babbling	4 to 9 months	Hear sounds, emulate sounds, learn to speak or talk, echo (echolalic babbling), smile, laugh, facial expression
One-word utterance	9 to 18 months	Make sounds, smile, laugh, recognize noises, learn to talk or speak, emulate, gesture
Two-word utterance	18 months to 2½ years	Speak; talk; smile; laugh; recognize words; understand sounds, noise, or words; use syntax; ask; answer
Oral language skills	2½ to 4 years	Talking, speaking, asking, answering, use syntax, understand words, basic communication skills

Before coming to school, children learn survival skills along with the critical stages of language development. Language at this early stage is known as child-directed speech or "motherese." Lessow-Hurley (2000) described the typical progress of early language development (Table 2.4). Not all children go through these steps in this orderly a fashion because biological and social factors may inhibit children from making the same progression in learning a language from their biological parents.

Keep in mind that the stages of progression of early language development should go hand in hand with the stages of personality development unless the process is altered by internal and/or external factors. For instance, a dysfunctional family life, conflicts, crises, and unexpected life events shape personality positively, negatively, or both. Moreover, abused children develop personality differently from non-abused children (Vang, 2010). Most importantly, teachers must know that developmental milestones cannot be rigidly assigned ages or specific places in a child's development.

HOW CHILDREN LEARN IN SCHOOL

Children enter school to gain new knowledge and skills to add to what they have been taught by their parents at home or have gained throughout their life experiences. In some cases, children have to relearn many things in class because of the mismatch between home and school. For instance, children who come to school speaking a language other than English, such as Hmong, Vietnamese, Chinese,

French, Greek, Spanish, Urdu, or Punjabi, have to learn new linguistic skills needed for academic tasks in the classroom. In states such as California, teachers have to make instructional adaptations for ELL and special-needs students.

Despite the fact that their students come from diverse ethnic backgrounds, teachers expect all students in their class to be at similar stages of moral development, but some students may require more time to develop a sense of moral responsibility. Teachers must bear in mind that children's development of a sense of right and wrong depends on the age and gender of the child. Developing the ability to make moral choices and to act righteously on these decisions is a long and slow process, and most children take many years to develop morally. Remember, teachers can modify a child's behaviors but cannot modify the child's pride, dignity, and values.

To recognize the characteristics of the stages of moral development in children, it is helpful to look at the model developed by Kohlberg (1969). First, in the *preconventional stage*, most children accept the right of authority figures, such as parents, teachers, principals, and other adults, to exercise power, and they try to obey the rules, limitations, and boundaries the authority figures set to avoid logical consequences. With children in this stage, teachers have to be fair, logical, flexible, firm, and consistent in applying rules; otherwise, children may feel they are being treated unfairly.

Second, in the *conventional stage*, most children want to do what is right to please the authority figures, and they try to live up to the expectations, limitations, and rules set by the authority figures. Normally at this stage, children are honest, loyal, respectful, truthful, altruistic, and benevolent; however, they may change these values over time if they experience conflicts or personal favoritism.

Third, in the *postconventional stage*, student behaviors are based on the awareness and recognition of other people's values and opinions. Students try to believe that these values and opinions are relative to the needs of a group. In this stage, students can develop cultural and social norms as part of their values.

Fourth, in the *principle stage*, similarly to the previous stage, children validate their beliefs, morals, opinions, and commitments based on their benefits to the greater good of a group of people. They try to show respect, promote equality, recognize individual differences, and embrace social norms.

Teachers play a key role in helping children develop a good sense of moral responsibility by modeling responsible moral behavior at each step as children progress through the stages sequentially. In other words, children must be guided throughout the process in order to learn what is necessary at each stage.

To understand the way children think and learn in school, teachers can examine Gardner's paradigm of multiple intelligences, as showed in Table 2.5, and the stages of complete human development modeled on Erickson's theory of eight stages of personality development (Table 2.6). Keep in mind that the *critical*

Table 2.5 Multiple Intelligences

Type of Intelligence	Basic Definition	Areas of Interest	Areas of Strength	Possible Learning Styles
Linguistic	Word-smart or understand words and language easily	Read, write, memorize, and tell stories	Memorization and reading.	Reading, saying, hearing, or seeing words: The word player.
Logical/ mathematical	Logical-smart, number-smart, or understand logical connections among different ideas, concepts, and theories	Do experiments, work with numbers, ask questions, explore patterns or relationships between objects, and infer results	Math, reasoning, logic, problem solving, analogy, and details.	Categorizing, ordering, sequencing, classifying, abstracting, and explaining patterns or relationship: The questioner.
Spatial/ visual	Picture-smart or understand the expressions of arts, visual images, or mental images	Draw, build, design, look at pictures, examine objects, and create images	Imagination, visualization, sensing, reading maze, interpret charts, and solving puzzles.	Visualizing, dreaming, mental imaging, drawing pictures, creating photographs: The visualizer
Musical/ audio	Music-smart, sound-smart, rhythm-smart, or understand the patterns of sound systems	Sing, hum tunes, listen, play to music, write songs, respond to music, or create rhythm	Memorization, picking sounds, understanding rhythms, or sensitivity to sounds	Sound, rhythm, melody, music, voices, or artful: The music lover
Bodily/ kinesthetic	Hand-smart, body-smart, sports-smart, physical fitness, agility, or understand patterns of body movement	Move, use body language, gesture, touch and talk, or act out	Perform physical activities, dance, sports, acting, crafts design, drafting, or hands-on	Touching, moving, interacting, processing, sensations of body movement, or feeling the physical appearance: The mover

(*Continued*)

Type of Intelligence	Basic Definition	Areas of Interest	Areas of Strength	Possible Learning Styles
Interpersonal	People-smart, friends-smart, social-smart, or understand grouping and social relationships	Make friends, like people, talk to people, join groups, share with people, depending on, or player of team	Sharing, understanding, socializing, leading, following, organizing, communicating, listening, mediating, showing, or manipulating	Sharing, comparing, relating, cooperating, socializing, communicating, following, or leading: The socializer
Intrapersonal	Self-centered, self-smart, self-propelled, or understand own ways	Be a loner, be isolated, pursue own interests, set up personal goals, or independent	Focusing on self, dealing with inward feelings, pursuing personal interests more, like own ways of doing things, choose own goals, or following instincts	Being a loner, working alone, being very independent, being self-centered, having own space, creating own turf, liking individualized project, or being introvert: The individual
Natural	Flexible, adaptable, accommodating, considerate, or understand diverse needs and differences	Have flexible and adaptable patterns of thinking, feeling, understanding, or communicating with people	Focusing on all forms of learning, interests, considering all things as important, adjusting to needs accordingly, or being able to manage change well.	Having the ability to adapt to different learning environment or subject matter, adjusting to needs accordingly, or controlling changes with flexibility: The flexible learner

Note. Information from *Multiple Intelligences: The Theory in Practice*, by H. Gardner, 1993, New York: Basic Books; and *Frames of mind: The theory of multiple intelligences*, by H. Gardner, 1983, New York: Basic Books.

Table 2.6 Stages of Human Development

Stage	Approx. Age	Basic Biological/ Physical Maturation	Basic Psychological Development	Basic Cognitive Development	Basic Social Development
Newborn period	0–4 months	Sensory capacity, reflexes, movement of head and limbs	Basic trust formation and bonding with mother	Using reflexes, crying for food, movement of limbs, sleeping patterns	Bond to mother and feel her presence or absence
Infancy period	4 months to 2 years	Rapid growth, mobility, coordination, pulling and pushing ability, roll over, crawling, walking, and control of basic body functions	Basic trust continues, use mouth for gratification, bond with mother, respond to activities, alert	Learn to use limbs, cause and effects process, playful, recognize objects, learn to speak or have basic speech development	Recognize siblings, playful, self-mobility, clumsy walking, pulling or pushing objects, learn environment
Preschool period	2 years to 4 years	Slow growth, motor skills development, coordination skills, change from infantile to juvenile body, control body functions	Learn to say no, autonomy, anal phase, understand basic needs and training	Learn to manipulate symbols, pick up words, imitate others, playful	Like friends, recognize peers, learn about siblings, like to do like others, go to school
Juvenile period	4 years to 6 years	Continue to improve motor skills and coordination, run around, playful, learn about speed and agility	In oedipal phase, learn about gender difference, have curious mind, bonding with parents continues	Recognize numbers, quantity, and time; understand basic questions (what, why, how, etc.); ask for details	Start school, make friends, learn school rules and routines, adjust to social norms, playful with friends

(Continued)

Stage	Approx. Age	Basic Biological/ Physical Maturation	Basic Psychological Development	Basic Cognitive Development	Basic Social Development
Latency period	7 years to 11 years	Growth slows, motor skills and coordination continue to improve, balance and mobility increase, teething slows, know personal grooming needs, increase appetite, like activities	Form strong identity for self, learn to follow rules, recognize fairness and justice, be close to friends, develop personality	Develop reasoning skills, use ideas, solve problems, understand more complex issues, apply imagination, curious about learning	Like to make friends of same age group, follow and copy others, recognize gender issues, socialize with friends
Preadolescence	11 years to 14 years	Enter another rapid growth period, reach puberty, body changes, muscular development, make transitions	Recognize self-identity, acceptance of peers, physical changes, orient toward self-actualization, develop personality and independence	Enter rapid intellectual growth, reasoning skills, recognize mental ability and brain games, ability to accept challenges, become autonomous in learning	Friends become important part of daily life, encounters with opposite sex, interests are high, hang around with peers, make independent decisions, take personal responsibility
Adolescence	14 years to 21 years	Physical growth slows, puberty continues, hormone changes, body changes, cosmetic period, voice changes, grooming and personality development continue	Continue to form personal identity for self to achieve independence, attracted to opposite sex for physiological needs, learn to be responsible, face social and emotional struggles	Have abstract reasoning skills, engage in complex ideas, have great ability to use the mind to deal with academic learning	Center values with peers, some conflict at home, dating games take place, form social class, recognize wealth and assets, learn societal values

Young adulthood	21 years to 35 years	Have stable growth, enter procreation and parenting stages, prepare for family values and life style	Find intimacy; have sense of competence; recognize self-worth, self-image, self-esteem, and self-concept	Learn through life experience, develop learning capacity, increase level of understanding, apply concrete details, choose learning style to meet peak performance	Recognize societal values, class status, employment, education, friendship, peers at work, continue to have love and intimacy for survival
Adult transition period	35 years to 40 years	Life is stable, family values continue, be parents, reach peak physical strength and prowess, women cease to conceive children	Reassess self-actualization, success, relationships, intimacy, career, financial stability	Have stable cognitive development, improve through training and experience, and continue to develop wisdom	Reach peak life expectations, make necessary changes, realign social life, midlife adjustments, continue looking for quality of life
Middle age	40 years to 60 years	Decline in physical health in general, sexual changes, encounter more health issues, engage in less physical activities	Face identity crisis, body changes and images, deal with unhappiness or happiness in life, live alone after children leave home, learn to cope with retirement	Decline in cognitive abilities, build reasoning skills and abilities, continue to improve wisdom, retain information but lack rapid processing	Center around friends, peers, and family members for comfort; employment could be issue; involved in children's lives; become grandparents; engage in civic responsibilities
The older years	60 years and older	Face sensory loss, skeletal degeneration, more health issues, brain functions slow, aging continues	Face loss of many things, such as sensory loss, family members, and friends; explore new interests; encounter confusion and depression; face changes in life; time to relax and enjoy life	Decline in cognitive functioning and development, wisdom increases based on life experience, explore new interests, create new mastery of skills	Enter retirement, health problems, tough financial needs, neglect by family members, live in isolation, lose friends, subject to medical care facility, enjoy life with family and friends

Note. Information from *A Mutual Challenge: Training and Learning with the Indochinese in Social Work*, by Training Center for Indochinese Paraprofessionals, 1982, Boston University School of Social Work.

Table 2.7 Correlation Between Mode of Learning and Retention

Mode	Retention	Possible Explanations
Reading	10%	Students retain only what is relevant to their real-life experiences or interests.
Listening or hearing	20%	Students retain only what is interesting and exciting.
Seeing	30%	Students retain only the highlights of scenes, actions, and episodes they like.
Combining listening and seeing	40%	Students retain only their favorite parts of the story that are relevant to their personal life experiences and what they can remember by encoding and decoding the messages.
Engaging in discussion or saying	70%	Discourse, conversation, or discussion allows students to retain more information by engaging in critical thinking and analysis of situations.
Experiencing, practicing, or doing hands-on activity	90%	Experiencing, doing, practicing, engaging in hands-on activity or firsthand experience enhances students' knowledge, skills, critical thinking, analysis, and logical application.

Note. Information from *Elementary Classroom Management* (3rd ed.), by C. M. Charles and G. W. Senter, 2002, Boston: Allyn and Bacon.

pedagogy of teaching and learning has to do with the way teachers teach the content of academic subjects and the way students are taught to learn and retain content through quality instruction. In other words, teachers must develop teaching styles that will benefit the students and accommodate their learning needs instead of expecting students to have learning styles that will fit into teachers' teaching styles.

Knowing how students think and learn may not completely encompass the constructivism in science teaching and learning for Grades K-6 grades. Teachers have to incorporate effective task and activity strategies, such as hands-on and minds-on activities, to keep students focused on guided practice and to keep students engaged in the learning task. Also, teachers have to provide enough academic engaged time so students can practice working with science concepts in class. As demonstrated in Table 2.7, the correlation between mode of learning and retention is critical. If students can learn the lesson plan objective in a ways that are enjoyable, they will retain the key concepts that are the content of the lesson, as illustrated in figure 2.2.

Figure 2.2 *Constituents of retention*

CHILDREN'S PRIOR KNOWLEDGE AND SKILLS

Remember, science is ubiquitous. Most science education for children is about the relearning of what is already known or experienced in life. Science concepts are not the same as real science subjects, such as biology, physics, chemistry, or botany. Teachers need to think about elementary science as conceptual teaching rather than real science teaching.

Teachers must take into consideration that all children of diverse backgrounds come to the classroom with knowledge and skills in science. When teachers disregard children's embedded knowledge and skills, they judge their students by their cultural identity and physical appearance, not by the content of their experiences. Prior knowledge and skills enable and guide the construction of new knowledge and skills developed through teaching. For instance, all K-6 students can eat, drink, bathe, run, jump, walk, throw, make sounds, draw pictures, color books, and brush their teeth. These experiences are preludes to new concepts they can learn and new skills they can develop. However, some disabled children have physical and mental limitations to performing some of these tasks. Every child needs certain skills to survive, and unless they are severely handicapped, children come to school with survival knowledge and skills already embedded. As Table 2.8 shows, much of the prior knowledge children bring to the classroom in the form of survival skills is related to science learning.

Children discover and explore their surroundings to gain more experience about real-life events. This process is known as *discovery learning* because it takes place naturally, inspired by curiosity or interest. Children also learn things from people, books, videos, movies, games, and other sources. This process is called *acquisition learning* because it entails acquiring new knowledge and skills from information that is given. Children also learn about real life through emulation or imitation. This type of learning takes time and energy; it is called *learning with understanding*. In some cultures, this process is highly valuable and involves recitation of religious rites, ceremonial scriptures, or oral traditions.

Whether they know it or not, teachers use the prior knowledge of science children bring to school to deal with behavioral issues. They apply science to classroom management and student discipline when they use *natural consequences, arbitrary consequences,* and *logical consequences* to resolve behavioral problems. The idea that actions have consequences is a scientific concept. Well-behaved students are trained and disciplined at home by their parents, and the parents, like teachers, often use psychological applications of scientific principles to train their children to behave responsibly. The key point here is that family structure and classroom structure affect children's behaviors positively, negatively, or both. Any structure that incorporates actions and consequences is based on scientific approaches.

Table 2.8 Prior Knowledge and Skills Related to Science Learning

Prior Knowledge	Social Knowledge/Skills	Survival Knowledge/Skills	Related to the development of science knowledge and skills standards
Tasting, eating, chewing, swallowing, digesting, drinking, etc . . .	✓	✓	Life and physical science standards
Running, walking, throwing, jumping, climbing, swimming, diving, sliding, somersaulting, etc . . .	✓	✓	Life and physical science standards
Animals: birds, frogs, cats, dogs, fish, goats, ducks, chickens, bears, horses, cows, sheep, deer, monkeys, etc . . . : Insects: butterflies, ants, bugs, roaches, flies, ladybugs, worms, dragonflies, beetles, etc . . .	✓		Life science standards and some earth science standards
Plants: Seeds, budding, germination, pollination, growth, leaves, flowers, stems, vines, roots, branches, fruit, etc . . .	✓		Life science standards and some earth science standards
Observations: Moon, sun, stars, day, night, morning, noon, evening, galaxy, eclipse, clouds, fog, etc . . .	✓	✓	Earth and physical science standards
Real life experience: heat, hot, cold, snow, wind, weather conditions, seasons, rain, fog, etc.	✓	✓	Earth and physical science standards
Playing with toys: Riding tricycle, bicycle, scooter, rollerblades; shooting marbles; speeding; pushing; pulling; hauling	✓	✓	Physical science standards, some earth and life science standards
Hygiene: Clothes, dressing up, grooming, body deodorant, washing, brushing, potty training, etc.	✓	✓	Life and physical science standards

In other words, teachers as well as parents use scientific concepts and skills to teach, train, foster, guide, and nurture children.

Children's prior knowledge should be part of everyday science teaching and learning. The embedded context allows students to assimilate and accommodate new information learned in class. The ability to integrate new information with existing information makes learning happen faster. For instance, teaching about animals is not new because nearly all children have seen some domesticated and wild animals via different sources, such as having family pets, playing video games, seeing pictures and movies, visiting a zoo, searching the Internet, or going to a pet shop. Children can apply the knowledge they have about animals to learning about an exotic animal they have not heard of. Similarly, in teaching about plants, nearly all children have seen flowers such as roses, daisies, sunflowers, or oleanders. However, they may not know the different parts of a flower, such as stigma, stamen, style, pistil, petal, ovule, ovary, sepal, and receptacle, but they can integrate this new information with what they already know about plants.

Teachers need to recognize the variety of prior knowledge and skills in their classes. Some children have lived on farms and others have grown up in metropolitan or suburban areas. The perspectives of the different children on life, earth, and physical science could be different because of their different life experiences. However, no child comes to class without some basic science knowledge and skills. Teachers should build upon children's embedded contexts to make science learning relevant to their everyday life experiences.

Misconceptions embedded in students' prior knowledge may support or refute the new learning to which they are exposed in class. For instance, students may have learned unhealthy social and survival skills, such as not brushing teeth properly or eating a poor diet, and these may be altered by new learning. The life experiences children bring from the home can be significant helps or hindrances in learning science. Remember, teachers are as bridge builders for their students regardless of the students learning abilities and limitations.

CHILDREN LEARN BY DOING

Teachers know that children learn more by doing than by listening. The direct instruction approach to teaching is a learning-by-listening method; it does not engage children in hands-on and minds-on activities to help them focus on specific learning outcome. Vang (2010) pointed out different forms of learning: habituation, sensitization, observation, language acquisition, and language learning. Academic learning can take place inside or outside the classroom through formal or informal processes. Formal learning usually takes place in school under the guidance of a well-trained professional, whereas informal learning takes place through emulation, observation, experience, and listening to folktales.

All children do not learn the same way although they all progress through the cognitive stages listed in Table 2.9. Some acquire new knowledge and skills quickly, whereas others take a longer time to develop specific skills. Academic learning is closely related to memory in the conscious and the subconscious mind, both short-term and long-term memory. Learning by doing improves cognitive

Table 2.9 Piaget's Stages of Cognitive Development

Cognitive Stage	Approximate Age	Characteristics of Cognitive Development
Sensory motor	Birth to 2 years	Adaptability; learning the surroundings; coordinating human actions; understanding space, time, substance, activities, causality; exploring the external world
Preoperational	2 to 7 years	Developing sensory motor skills and capabilities, understanding physical knowledge of different things, develop knowledge and skills in verbal forms, forming patterns of thinking, comprehending things based on perceptions, lacking conceptual knowledge, having limited thought-processes
Concrete operational	5 to 11 years	Continuing to develop cognitive skills, improving capabilities, increasing thought-processes, understanding of different things, having basic knowledge and skills to differentiate things, recognizing relationships among things, forming opinions about things, organizing basic data or information
Formal operational	12 to adulthood	Continuing to develop cognitive skills and knowledge, developing critical thinking associated knowledge and skills, using higher-order thought processes, having opinions, forming hypotheses, engaging in concrete learning, comprehending mathematical data or information, applying complex capabilities, learning to apply constructive knowledge and skills in solving problems

Note. Information from *The child's conception of the world*, 1965, by J. Piaget, London: Routledge and Kegan Paul.

development and increases construction of new knowledge and skills. The correlation between active participation in academic learning and retention of information increases children's ability to perform tasks based on prior knowledge or newly learned experiences (Vang, 2010). Although children progress through stages in their cognitive development, all of Piaget's characteristics of children's cognitive thinking may not be applied to all learners; teachers must recognize that academic learning in children is affected by factors such as age, gender, motivation, prior experience, intelligence, life crises, trauma, nutrition, disabilities, language proficiency, and developmental disorders.

CHILDREN WITH DIVERSE NEEDS AND ABILITIES

Today's student population is culturally and linguistically diverse. Nearly 60% of US public school children are socioeconomically disadvantaged as measured by federal poverty guidelines. Of that number, approximately 75% receive free

Table 2.10 California and National Student Demographics

Characteristic	California	Nation
White	31.9%	58.0%
Black	8.0%	16.9%
Asian/Pacific Islander	11.0%	4.4%
Hispanic	45.2%	19.5%
American Indian/Alaska Native	0.8%	1.2%
Economically disadvantaged	47.9%	36.7%
English language learners	24.9%	7.8%
Students with disabilities	10.6%	12.8%
Migrant students	2.5%	0.6%
LEP students	1.5 million	5.2 million

Note. Data from "Language Can't Be a Barrier (425 first languages)," by Mary Ellen Flannery, January 1, 2006, *NEA Today*, and California Department of Education, 2005-2006. Some numbers are rounded.

or reduced-price school lunches. Of the 55 million students in K-12 schools in 2006, the National Education Association (NEA) reported that Whites made up 62%, followed by Blacks (17%), Hispanics (16%), Asians and Pacific Islanders (4%), and American Indians and Alaska Natives (1%). Yet the number of English language learners had increased by nearly 65% in the 13 years between 1993 and 2006 (Vang, 2010).

In California, 31.9% of the 6 million students in K-12 schools in 2004 were White, 8% were Black, 11% were Asian or Pacific Islander, 45.2% were Hispanic, and 0.8% were American Indian or Alaska Native (Vang, 2010). Moreover, 47.9% of students were economically disadvantaged, 24.9% were English language learners, 10.6% were students with disabilities, and 2.5% were migrant students. California is home to approximately 1.5 million LEP students and nearly 1 million FEP students. Table 2.10 compares California and national student demographics including migrant students, students with disabilities, and LEP students.

As the figures in Table 2.10 indicate, cultural diversity and diverse abilities will continue to shape teaching and learning in the educational system. Sociologists predict that the students of color will make up nearly half of the nation's school-age youth, and of that number, nearly one third will be in poverty (Banks, 2008).

UNDERSTANDING CHILDREN WITH EXCEPTIONALITIES

As Vang (2010) explained, the term *exceptionalities* is used of students with special needs. Table 2.11 shows the numbers of exceptional students nationally with one or more disabilities (Manning & Baruth, 2009). This group of students with

Table 2.11 U.S. Students with Selected Disabilities

Types of disability	Approximate total number	Percentage
1. With specific learning disabilities	2,800,000	55.5%
2. Speech or language impairments	1,000,000	19.0%
3. Mental retardation	614,000	10.8%
4. Emotional disturbance	470,000	8.2%
5. With other health impairments	254,000	4.5%
6. Multiple disabilities	113,000	2.0%
7. Hearing impairments	72,000	1.3%
8. Orthopedics impairments	71,000	1.3%
9. Autism	65,000	1.3%
10. Visual impairments	27,000	0.6%
11. Developmental delay	19,000	0.38%
12. Traumatic brain injury	14,000	0.24%
13. Deaf-blindness	2,000	0.03%

Note. Information from *To assess the free appropriate education of all children with disabilities: Twenty-first annual report to Congress on the implementation of the Individuals with Disabilities Education Act (IDEA)*, 1999, U.S. Department of Education, Washington, DC. Some numbers are rounded.

disabilities is as diverse as the general student population and has been categorized into three major groups: students with disabilities, gifted and talented students, and students with linguistically and culturally diverse backgrounds. IDEA guidelines mandate that students with disabilities be provided a free and appropriate education in the "least restrictive environment." This requirement is known as *full inclusion*. Gifted and talented students are learners with academic abilities above typical children of their age, and they must receive special adaptations and accommodations. Students with linguistically and culturally diverse backgrounds must receive instructional services that are sensitive to their cultural and language differences.

A widely used definition for learning disabilities is the following offered by Kirk (1962, as cited in McNamara, 2007, p. 3):

> A learning disability refers to retardation, disorder, or delayed development in one or more of the processes of speech, language, reading, writing, arithmetic, or other school subjects resulting from a psychological handicap caused by a possible cerebral dysfunction and/ or emotional or behavioral disturbance. It is not the result of mental retardation, sensory deprivation, or cultural and instructional factors.

McNamara listed 10 of the most common characteristics of students classified as having a learning disability: (a) hyperactivity; (b) perception impairments; (c) emotional ability; (d) general coordination deficits; (e) disorders of attention, short attention span, distractibility preservation; (f) impulsivity; (g) disorders of memory and thinking; (h) specific learning disabilities—reading, arithmetic,

Table 2.12 Ethnic Distribution of Students in Gifted and Talented Programs

Ethnicity	Percentage
White	74
Black	8
Hispanic	10
Asian or Pacific Islander	7
American Indian or Alaska Native	1

Note. Data from the National Education Association, 2006.

writing, spelling; (i) disorders of speech and learning, and (j) equivocal neurologi-cal signs and EEG irregularities.

In addition to giving attention to students with disabilities, educators should be aware of students who are gifted and talented because they are often neglected, sometimes unidentified, unrecognized, and ignored in regular classrooms (Man-ning & Baruth, 2009). As Table 2.12 shows, the profiles of gifted and talented students are culturally diverse; however, Native American/Alaska Native chil-dren are underrepresented. According to Gollnick and Chinn (2009), gifted and talented students have very high intelligence or possess unusual gifts and talents in the arts. They need specially designed educational programs or curricula in order to reach their full potential.

Ryan and Cooper (2001) pointed out that gifted children usually have high intellectual ability, and talented children have creative or artistic abilities. Gifted and talented children give evidence of potential for high achievement or per-formance in academic, creative, artistic, or leadership areas. As with all other children, gifted and talented students have specific strengths and weaknesses. Manning and Baruth (2009) observed that these students are exceptionally diverse and sometimes appear as antisocial, creative, high-achieving, divergent thinkers, and perfectionists; they may have attention-deficit disorders, dyslexia, or other complex disorders.

Despite all these demands and needs, the system lacks adequate resources, especially special education teachers, to teach students with exceptionalities. Many of these children are placed in classes that provide them with few academic services. The shortage of special education teachers is a national crisis.

UNDERSTANDING CHILDREN'S PSYCHOSOCIAL NEEDS

Simply put, children learn as they feel. If they feel good, they will learn more; if they feel bad, they will learn less. As mentioned earlier, learning with enjoy-ment increases children's retention of information. Teaching science as inquiry

Table 2.13 Factors and Instructional Approaches Associated with Selected Domains of Psychosocial Learning

Domain	Associated Factors	Instructional Approaches
Cognitive	Comprehension, knowledge, skills, processing, and application	Knowing what and knowing how and expressing in written or verbal forms
Affective	Emotions, feelings, attitudes, personalities, behaviors, and values	Reflective responses to tasks, sharing with peers, interaction, communication, and expressing in verbal form
Psychomotor	Motor skills, coordination, comprehension, expression, and muscular control	Diagramming, mapping, manipulation, connection, idea web, and application
Social	Basic interpersonal communication skills, sharing, socialization, citizenship, and cooperation	Cooperative learning, teamwork, group activity, role and responsibility, and project
Academic	Cognitive academic language proficiency, literacy, constructivism, and context-reduced	Logical, arbitrary, social, physical, and constructive knowledge

with hands-on and minds-on activities improves students' construction of new knowledge and skills. The psychosocial learning environment determines the academic mindset inside individual students, and how they feel about the teachers or subject matter plays a significant role in cognitive, affective, psychomotor, social, and academic development, as illustrated in Table 2.13. As Vang (2010) explained, whether a child's feelings are negative or positive could be critical in determining the extent of the child's engagement in academic tasks and the learning process.

Teachers' psychosocial output also affects the processes of teaching and learning. How teachers feel about all their students or a specific student determines their genuine interest in teaching the academic subject. In other words, the overt and covert psychosocial dimensions of teachers have great influence on student learning. Therefore, teachers should use instructional approaches that elevate students' intrinsic and extrinsic motivation because the feeling tone in the classroom sets parameters for teaching and learning.

Lastly, today's classrooms are like the colors of a rainbow. Teachers must become multicultural educators in order to understand the sensitivity needed in teaching students with diverse needs and abilities. The way children learn, think, behave, and react reflects how they feel about learning in the psychosocial learning environment. To empower students to overcome psychological hurdles that so often come with minority status or cultural mismatch, teachers must do their very best to recognize their own cross-cultural incongruence, incompatibility, or insensitivity that may have negative effects on teaching and learning.

With this in mind, teachers, as educators, should view cultural diversity as a great strength rather than as a weakness in teaching science to all learners of diverse backgrounds.

SUMMING UP

This chapter gives teachers a tour of the different notions of how children think and learn; it should give insight into the teaching of science concepts to elementary students. Children are born with their minds clean, blank slates, and they have learned many things about the world around them before attending school. Teaching and learning are inseparable; they go hand-in-hand. Children learn from their surroundings through inquiry, discovery, and acquiring information. The ways they think about things and process the information depend on their unique and diverse needs, abilities, and experiences.

Children's prior knowledge and skills are varied in many ways. Each child brings a different set of values, experience, knowledge, and skills to class. Learning science concepts sometimes means relearning some of these prior knowledge and skills; however, the assimilation and acculturation process help students integrate the information as they try to construct the new knowledge and skills based on what is presented to them in class through hands-on and minds-on activities. Children learn best by doing, not by listening. Therefore, understanding how children think and learn is essential to the teaching of science.

CHAPTER THREE

Inquiry Processes OF Learning

Great scientific discoveries have been made by men seeking to verify quite erroneous theories about the nature of things.

—ALDOUS HUXLEY "WORDSWORTH IN THE TROPICS"

INTRODUCTION

Teachers know that teaching is a process rather than a product and that the means must justify the ends. To understand the teaching process, teachers need to carefully consider some basic principles of teaching and learning. A teacher's philosophical approach to teaching and learning science has to be clear and well thought through before the teacher attempts to deliver instruction. Teachers' psychological approach to academics has to be sensible, meaningful, inclusive, and appropriate for all learners in the multiple setting, and teachers' pedagogical approach has to be of high quality based on science content knowledge standards. Good science teaching is not about presenting answers to questions; rather it is about questioning the answers students get. This chapter discusses the process of instructional practices for science teaching and learning; its purpose is to guide teachers in planning to teach science process skills within the context of inquiry-based instruction. The discussion emphasizes the importance of helping students develop the mental and physical skills required for learning inquiry science concepts.

TEACHING SCIENCE PROCESSES

Today's teaching of science lacks clear, consistent, and deliberate processes that meet the needs of everyday science learning in the multicultural classroom setting. Teachers have to teach scientific processes early to lay out a learning foundation for academic and scientific development for the rest of their students' lives. Without these processes, learning inquiry science could be boring and a waste of time. Scientific processes require mental and physical skills, as well as knowledge. They entail organizing variables, collecting information, making predictions, examining objects, explaining data, elaborating on details, solving problems, answering questions, and asking questions. Most importantly, understanding the inquiry processes helps students follow step-by-step directions to find answers or follow specific guidelines. Teaching these processes alone is insufficient for students to learn science; students need to practice to become proficient in employing, applying, or developing scientific processes, which are parts of everyday learning, as shown in Figure 3.1.

Furthermore, teachers have to incorporate the teaching and learning of scientific processes in every single science lesson in order to properly train students scientifically. As Vang (2010) wrote, the teaching process is a creative art that teachers can polish; it is an ongoing process of human interaction, relationships, socialization, forming bonds, and exchange of ideas through communication. Students who can master scientific processes learn science concepts more quickly and show more interest in learning inquiry science as compared to students who lack scientific processes. Remember, *inquiry* is a process of learning science by constructing meanings.

DEFINING SCIENTIFIC PROCESSES

Process skills can generate new knowledge quickly and stimulate the thought process to ignite learning through integration of information as well as assimilation of information. In a simple lesson plan students easily follow a process. For instance, they *communicate, observe, compare and contrast, generalize, apply ideas, and conclude* their findings. In science, as indicated in Figure 3.1, a variety of terminologies is

Figure 3.1 *Selected basic scientific processes*

used to describe scientific processes. Each process can be defined for elementary school students as follows:

1. **Question**—questioning is an inquiry-based approach that asks questions, comments on possible outcomes, and prompts curiosity. Examples are the 5Ws+H, KWL, and ice breaker activities.
2. **Observation**—observing is the process of gathering and organizing information using the five senses: examining with hands, using magnifying glasses, looking in a telescope, listening to recorded messages, watching a dissection, watching video or film, or making notations of changes.
3. **Communication**—communicating is sharing, discussing, talking, interacting, and brainstorming to convey information. It may be done through pictures, visual aids, regalia, language, data, graphs, drawing, listening, verbal expression, and writing in journals.

4. *Explanation*—explaining is an important process of telling, sharing, inter-acting, elaborating, or discussing along with communicating, relating, and defining.

5. *Relation*—relating uses the relationship of space and time to describe, compare, contrast, or differentiate objects in terms of patterns, motions, locations, changes, and differences.

6. *Definition*—defining is the process of using operational definitions of scientific vocabulary words, descriptions, or limitations to set specific meanings for specific experimentations or situations.

7. *Measurement*—measuring is the process of using numerical devices or mechanical instruments such as rulers, measuring tape, or digital devices to determine the width, length, height, mass, or volume of different objects based on standard units of inches, feet, yard, miles, cubic feet, and square feet or metric measurements of millimeters, centimeters, or kilometers.

8. *Classification*—classifying is the process of sorting, separating, organizing, differentiating, or arranging objects into different groups based on specific characteristics such as shape, size, weight, height, length, big, small, color, fur, skin, scales, cold blood, warm blood, male, female, land or water, and day or night. Classifying can be categorized into two main types: *binary system* classification divides objects into major groups based on particular properties or specific characteristics; *multistage system* classification subdi-vides into many different groups or subgroups of objects.

9. *Inference*—inferring uses prior knowledge, learned experience, or concur-rent observation to interpret data or information about objects. It may be used to draw conclusions, make final predictions, or share findings.

10. *Prediction*—predicting uses the five senses to draw conclusions by guess-ing, judging, believing, or estimating something based on the individual's forecast of the final outcome.

11. *Hypothesis*—hypothesizing is the process of asking, formulating, or testing an untested statement or question, known as a hypothesis, for experimenta-tion using all the scientific processes.

12. *Experimentation*—experimenting is an important process that employs all the scientific processes using different types of variables—control, inde-pendent, dependent, responding, and manipulated variables—to test a hypothesis, statement, or question.

It is very important for teachers to integrate science content with science process; otherwise, focusing on scientific processes without carefully considering the content of science is inadequate preparation for teaching science concepts to elementary students. In other words, teachers must know how to apply science

Table 3.1 Selected Activity and Task Strategies for Teaching Scientific Processes

Scientific Process	Activity Strategies	Task Strategies
Observation	Use all five senses to observe three types of rock: igneous, sedimentary, and metamorphic	Touch, feel, smell, look at, no tasting rocks; describe the characteristics of rocks
Measurement	Use ruler or measuring tape to measure all sides of student desk	Record the width, length, and height of a desk in inches
Classification	Give a bag of animal pictures and ask students to sort them into three groups	Characteristics of animals are fur/hair, legs, feathers, beaks, teeth, mammal, reptile, land, water, farm, zoo, domesticated
Prediction	Use a bag of M&M candies and ask students to feel, touch, listen, and estimate the total number of M&Ms in the bag	Predict a total number, ask for the total of each color, which color has the most or least, and make a graph of M&M colors

processes as aids, but not as goals, while teaching inquiry science concepts. If scientific processes are used as practical tools to help teachers plan and carry out hands-on and minds-on activities and the content standards are applied as guides to support teachers as they think about science instruction, learning objectives will be well designed and students will be able to grasp specific skills with appropriate processes. Learning how to integrate science content and process is a key to successfully teaching inquiry science. Table 3.1 gives a few examples of activities that integrate content and process.

CONNECTING PROCESSES WITH SCIENCE ACTIVITIES

Teachers need to incorporate science processes in scientific investigations as much as possible because science standards are designed to stress the importance of teaching students to learn how to use science processes within a conceptual framework of teaching science as inquiry. Keep in mind that today's teaching is not as much about *what to* teach as about *how to* teach the subject matter; the same is also true for learning. Students appear to learn better and retain information for a longer period of time when they learn *how to* use the processes instead of knowing *what to* do with the processes or *what* teachers expect them to do.

Teaching science as inquiry requires good, thought-provoking questions to stimulate students' minds because curiosity makes learning science enjoyable. However, teachers need to use appropriate questions for science activities. They can design the content of questions to fit descriptive, classificatory, or experimental activities. *Descriptive* activities are scientific investigations that have students observing and/or gathering data to answer questions or test hypotheses.

Classificatory activities are scientific investigations in which students collect, organize, store, or group objects or data by sorting and comparing based on characteristics or properties of the different objects. Experimental activities are scientific investigations that require students to conduct experiments, tests, observations, or research. Table 3.2 gives examples of questions for different

Table 3.2 Examples of Questions for Scientific Investigations

Science concept	Questions for investigations	Descriptive investigation	Classificatory investigation	Experimental investigation	Basic procedural guidelines
Animals	What are farm animals? What are domesticated animals? What do cats and dogs have in common?	✓			Name animals that live on the farm, at the zoo, at home. Compare and contrast cats and dogs.
Plants	What do plants need to live? What are plants used for? Plants include what?	✓			Learn about sun, water, soil, space; talk about things made from plants; show a variety of plants.
Static electricity or magnetism	What causes static? Does a magnet attract or repel? What things are attracted to magnets and what things are repelled?	✓	✓		Collect different objects for testing, test south and north poles, and use balloons for static electricity.
State of matter	What are the four states of matter? What is density? What is the chemical property of each matter? How does heat affect matter?	✓	✓	✓	Ice cube for solid, water for liquid, and dry ice for gas; melting process, heat transfer, density, and molecular structure.
Friction, motion, reaction, and energy	What is inertia? What causes things to move? What is the cause and effect of action and reaction?	✓		✓	Use pulling or pushing to show motions; show action and reaction experiment; talk about kinetic and potential energy.

science content areas and that keep students focused on the different types of investigation while doing the tasks of those investigations. Keep in mind that all questions need to be age- and grade-level-appropriate; difficult, complex, and unclear questions should be avoided.

Teaching science requires flexibility and adaptation. Some learners may need accommodations to process questions. For instance, teachers may need to allow ELL, NNS, or LEP students to have extra time for answering questions, and some students may not fully understand the questions and may need additional input. It is always a good idea to consider students' diverse needs in lesson plan design. A science lesson can pose a question or a problem depending on the nature of the specific scientific investigation. Teachers must make instructional adjustments whenever necessary to engage all their students in science learning.

USING PROCESSES TO ENHANCE INQUIRY

What makes teaching and learning science fun? Teachers may have different or similar answers to this question, but most experienced teachers have learned from experience that science is not fun without hands-on and minds-on activities. Students want to learn science through firsthand experience, by doing and practicing. The scientific processes can be used to enhance inquiry to make learning science a dynamic, active, positive, and inclusive experience rather than a teacher-centered exercise.

If teachers control everything when teaching science, the students merely follow orders. In this case, very little inquiry would take place. However, if teachers apply a student-centered approach, students have fun doing science activities together in small groups or individually depending on the nature of the task strategies. To enhance inquiry, teachers must facilitate each of the processes with close supervision, monitoring, and assistance. Teachers have to stimulate students' thought processes to make scientific inquiry inspirational and challenging. Remember, when students engage in inquiry processes, they are curious about the learning objective, and that curiosity helps them make the best use of the inquiry processes. Practicing inquiry processes involves students in the following activities and experiences:

- Asking questions about objects
- Being somewhat scared or intimidated until they try
- Being curious and eager
- Wanting to gather information or data right away

- Wanting to discuss, share, talk, or explain
- Applying knowledge and skills from their prior and new experiences right away to answer questions
- Trying to cooperate and compete with one another to solve problems and answer questions
- Believing in their ability to solve problems or answer questions
- Wanting to challenge the question or hypothesis
- Doing the task without managing time

Regardless of how students may feel about some of these experiences, teachers have to keep students focused on completing the requirements of scientific inquiry, which are as follows:

1. Ask a simple question about the learning objective
2. Conduct a simple investigation.
3. Try to answer the question.
4. Share results with others in verbal or written form.
5. Conclude the investigation.

Not all elementary students can follow these five steps at all times; teachers need to train their students repeatedly, year after year, to make sure they understand the inquiry process. Teachers can post these processional guidelines on the board or on a wall for easy access. According to the National Research Council (1996), students must learn science concepts through these basic steps as a process; that process is illustrated in Figure 3.2. To assist students in learning this process, teachers can also write down specific instructions, clear procedures, concise guidelines, or easily readable directions.

Figure 3.2 *Basic scientific inquiry process*

INCLUDING PROCESSES IN SCIENCE LESSONS

For elementary science, teachers have to include processes in every single lesson they teach in the multicultural classroom. The inquiry skills that typically need to be included in science lessons are *observing, inferring, comparing, classifying, measuring, using numbers, communicating, predicting, recording data or information, analyzing data or information, forming a hypothesis, using variables, experimenting, and making a model.* Now, it is not true that teachers have to include all inquiry skills in each and every lesson plan; that is absolutely impossible. Teachers must decide what should be included, excluded, or limited in any given lesson. For instance, teachers may expect students to observe different objects as the main part of the lesson plan and then ask them to communicate what they have observed in small groups.

Some lessons are repeated and some are new, so teachers need to determine what processes are appropriate for each lesson in order to maximize their time because time management is key in successful teaching and learning. Teachers need enough time to introduce the concept, to use guided practices, and to answer questions, and students need to have sufficient time to practice hands-on and minds-on activities. Remember, academic engaged time is the essence of learning, and without time to practice in class, little learning will take place.

To help teachers understand the importance of including processes in teaching inquiry science, the following examples are provided of science lesson plans that incorporate basic scientific processes:

Inquiry Activity One: Plants

1. **Title:** What do plants need to live?
2. **Hypothesis**: Write a basic hypothesis or question for students to answer appropriate for the grade level. Use these questions as guide:
   a. Do plants need light?
   b. Do plants need space?
   c. Do plants need soil or dirt?
   d. Do plants need water?
   e. Do plants need sunlight?
   f. Do plants need caring?
   g. Do plants need food?
   h. Do plants need shelter?
3. **Use models**: Have at least four or five different plants to demonstrate the concepts stated in the title of the lesson plan:
   a. A plant with light and water
   b. A plant with light but no water
   c. A plant with water but no light

     d. A plant with no light and no water

     e. A plant with everything it needs except space

4. **Observation:** Ask students to observe each plant carefully and record their findings on a chart or in a journal. To keep students engaged in the task, use prompting questions:

     a. What does each plant look like?

     b. What differences do you see between plants?

     c. What plant is healthy and what plant is not? Why?

     d. How do you know the plant is growing or dying?

     e. What can you tell about the color of each plant?

5. **Hands-on and minds-on activity:** Use premade materials to save time: Students will plant a seed in a sterol cup to experiment with the concepts stated in the hypothesis: Light, water, and soil. Group labels: No light in dark, light in sunny place, and half light and half no light. Water is used for all planted seeds.

6. **Prediction:** Ask students to make predictions about the seed sprout or germination: What group will sprout first, second, and third? The plan: Students will examine their seeds or plants each day for ten days to learn about what plants need to live.

7. **Recording data or information:** Use a daily chart to help track seed sprouting or germination. For example:

Group	Day 4	Day 6	Day 8	Day 10	Day 12
No light					
Light					

8. **Analyze data gathered:** After two weeks of observation and recording data, ask students to share their results. What group grows taller? What groups look green? What group has different colors? What group looks healthiest? Why does each group grow the way it does?

9. **Conclusion:** Recap the key concept stated in the title and hypothesis: What do plants need to live?

10. **Further experiment:** What else do plants need to live? What else do plants need to have? How can people know? Ideas: Caring, pruning, fertilizers, food, space.

This activity is quite long and detailed. Teachers need to factor in the time allocation for each lesson; otherwise, time may run out. The procedural processes can be shortened after students are accustomed to the processes. For instance, teachers can use a three-step process: form a *hypothesis, test the hypothesis, and draw conclusions.* These steps or processes can be adjusted for other lesson plan formats, such as a five-step lesson or three-step lesson plan.

Inquiry Activity Two: Classifying living and nonliving things

1. **Title:** What makes living and nonliving things different?
2. **Hypothesis:** How can people tell living from nonliving?
3. **Use models:** Use analogy to compare objects:
   a. A tree and a house
   b. A tree and a desk
   c. Green grass and dry grass
   d. A green leaf and a brown leaf
   e. A fish in a tank and a fish on a dinner plate
4. **Observation:** Have a bag of mixed pictures of living and nonliving things and animals and ask students to tell what things or animals belong to the living or nonliving groups.
5. **Hands-on and minds-on activity:** Put students into small groups of 4, give them a task to do, and use a timer to time them on the task.
6. **Instruction:** Each group will sort, classify, and organize all the pictures of things and animals in the bag into two groups: living and nonliving; use a chart to record living and nonliving things and give one rationale for category placement.
7. **Record data:** Ask student groups to record their living and nonliving things and animals. For example, use a T-chart or columns.

Living characteristics	Nonliving characteristics	Living/nonliving characteristics
List all possible living things and animals on this side:	List all possible nonliving things and animals on this side:	List any things or animals that may be living or nonliving on this side:
A bear: is alive it is walking in the woods.	A brown leaf: is dead or nonliving because it looks dry.	A rock: may be dead or alive because it has moss on top.

8. **Analyze data in group:** Ask students in groups to discuss, share, and exchange ideas about living and nonliving things and animals.
9. **Conclusion:** Ask students to explain what makes living things different from nonliving things or ask students to share why they believe something is living and something is not living.
10. **Further experiment:** Ask students to name something that is living and nonliving, ask students what living things need to live and what nonliving things need to exist, or ask students about mechanical devices, such as cars, airplanes, machines, watches, clocks, or trains; do they think these things are living or nonliving, and why.

Inquiry Activity Three: Farm animals

1. **Title:** What animals are farm animals?
2. **Hypothesis:** What animals live on farms? Or what animals do farmers raise on their farms?
3. **Use models:** Using pictures of zoo, domesticated, and farm animals, ask students to identify them, or question where they would see these animals.
4. **Observation:** Show a 5–10-minute online video clip on animals.
5. **Hands-on and minds-on activity:** Pair students with partners for activity.
6. **Instructions:** Each pair will make a list of farm animals, such as horses, ducks, cows, sheep, goats, chickens, pigs, donkeys, alpaca, dogs, cats, listing as many as they can.

List of farm animals	Animal characteristics
1. Horses	Examples: Fur/hair, 4 legs, 2 legs, feather,
2. Ducks	flying, land, water
3. Chickens	
4.	
5.	
6.	
7.	
8.	
9.	
10.	

7. **Communication:** Each pair is asked to share the list of farm animals with the class.
8. **Conclusion:** All students should have learned about farm animals from the activity.
9. **Further experiment:** Ask students to learn more about farm animals: why people raise animals (perhaps for food or breeding) or how farm animals can help people.

Inquiry Activity Four: Observing Rocks

1. **Title:** Are rocks different?
2. **Use models:** Get a few rocks to observe (igneous, sedimentary, metamorphic, clay, river rock, etc.).
3. **Observation:** Ask students to observe the characteristics of the rocks. Ask if the rocks are different or the same, or ask student to use their five senses to describe, compare, or contrast the rocks.

4. **Record data:** Ask students to describe their findings about rocks on a piece paper, using a chart as a guide and using check marks to indicate their findings. For example, see chart below:

Type of rock	Smooth	Shiny	Flat	Round	Coarse or rough	Hard	Soft	Light	Heavy
River rock									
Igneous									

5. **Compare and contrast:** Use descriptive terms such as alike, different, same, similar, light, heavy, solid, or hollow.
6. **Conclusion:** Ask what students have learned about rocks today.

Inquiry Activity Five: Plant parts

1. **Action:** Select a few different plants, such as a tomato plant, bean plant, a spinach plant, and a radish plant.
2. **Engagement:** Show plants to students and talk about roots, stems, leaves, and flowers.
3. **Information:** Gather information about each plant, talk about differences and similarities, or name all parts.
4. **Activity:** To compare and contrast, draw Venn diagram or T-Chart on the board and ask students to complete the illustration.

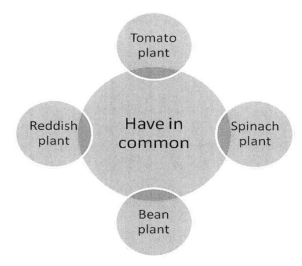

Note. This inquiry activity is a quick lab for use when time is limited.

Inquiry Activity Six: Describing different objects

1. **Title:** How do people describe objects or things?
2. **Observation:** Select any object in the classroom. Ask students to tell something about it. Ask them to describe it using adjectives. Ask about color, length, width, shape, and size. Talk about its purpose.
3. **Materials:** Use different kinds of objects for this activity, such as a pencil, pen, paper, books, crayons, ruler, plastic bags, paper bags, newspaper, magazines, eraser, strings, balls, marbles, paper weight.
4. **Hands-on and minds-on activity:** Use an idea web chart for this activity. Students describe an object selected for this activity on the idea web paper and allow their partners to guess what it is.
5. **Inference:** Partners show idea webs to each other and guess each other's object using the written descriptions.
6. **Conclusion:** Adjectives and descriptions help people know about specific objects.

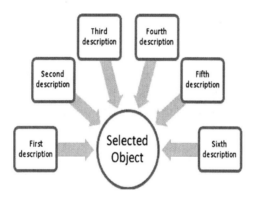

Note. Selected object must be kept secret or hidden for this activity.

Inquiry Activity Seven: What are the states of matter?

1. **Title:** How many states of matter are there?
2. **Use models:** Show students the three states of matter: solid, liquid, and gas. Place a solid ice cube, water, and a piece of dry ice in three different Ziploc bags.
3. **Observation:** Student puts a piece of ice in palm and lets it melts or in the mouth and lets it dissolves. Pour hot water into a clear container, turn off the light, and shine a flashlight at the container to allow students to observe the gas or steam coming from the water.

4. **Key words:** Use vocabulary words: liquid, solid, volume, and gas. Define each word for students: a solid has shape and volume, a liquid has volume but no shape, and a gas has no shape or volume.
5. **Communication:** Ask students why ice melts in the mouth or on the palm. What makes ice change from solid to liquid? What turns water into ice? Do people inhale or exhale gases to survive? What do people breathe to live? Does matter occupy space?
6. **Conclusion:** States of matter are solid, liquid, and gas.

Inquiry Activity Eight: How matter changes?

1. **Materials:** Take out a bag of ice cream popsicles.
2. **Engagement:** Give each student an ice cream.
3. **Observation:** Ask students to feel the temperature before opening.
4. **Hands-on and minds-on activity:** Ask students to eat the ice cream.
5. **Experiment:** Ask if it melts in their mouths.
6. **Inferences:** What causes the solid to melt in the mouth?
7. **Conclusion:** Go over key words: Energy, heat, temperature, and gas cause solids to melt or to turn into another state of matter.

Inquiry Activity Nine: What is mass?

1. **Materials:** Two sheets of paper, one green and the other white.
2. **Engagement:** Show papers to students and ask if the two papers have the same weight. Ask if the papers have the same mass. Ask if mass equals volume?
3. **Activity:** Crumble one paper with hands into a ball. Ask students if the two papers weigh the same. Ask students if they have the same mass? Ask if they have the same volume? Ask which one would take more space?
4. **Conclusion:** Two pieces of matter can have equal mass but unequal volume or equal volume but unequal mass.

Inquiry Activity Ten: How do people classify matter?

1. **Purpose:** Figure out how matter can be classified.
2. **Materials:** A bag of different objects, such as a plastic ball, pencil, pen, key, penny, comb, paperclip, rock, marble, bean, bead, nut, bolt, washer, pins, button, crayon, cap, lid, tool, utensils.

3. **Procedures:**
   a. Observe all objects.
   b. Classify objects into groups.
   c. Communicate how each group is different.
4. **Draw conclusions:**
   a. Analyze data and information: Ask how objects are grouped. Ask about objects' characteristics, purpose, properties, etc.
   b. Inference: What is classification? How can people separate things? How does grouping help people learn things quickly?
5. **Further experiment:** Can people classify animals? Can people classify insects? Can people classify cars, bikes, or boats?

Inquiry activities 1–10 are examples to show teachers ways to include processes in science lessons. Some lessons are long and others are short. The length and complexity depend on the grade level, age, time allocation, and the learning objective. Sometimes teachers can teach a concept quickly but they need to spend more time on other concepts. There is no one-model-fits-all lesson plan format. Different lessons can be designed for mastery of specific inquiry skills. Teachers should make sure the processes they include are appropriate for the particular lesson plan design. For instance, some lesson plans may only need observation and communication, but others may need hypothesis formulation, data collection, inference, and conclusions. Whatever the content of a given lesson, teachers must always include hands-on and minds-on activities because practice is vital to the construction of knowledge and skills in learning science.

Furthermore, as the inquiry activities presented here illustrate, teachers can eliminate lengthy processes in some science lesson plans because it is not necessary to go through the detail of the processes or procedural steps every time. The five-step or three-step lesson plan format may suffice. Teachers do not always have time to go through every step when the object of the lesson is not to understand the process. Once the students learn the processes, they can be part of the daily routines students go through and understanding of the processes can be maintained with occasional reminders. In order to maximize classroom time, teachers need to practice these processes with students as much as possible until students need only to be reminded by the teachers. Teaching science creatively and engaging students in hands-on and minds-on activities result in quality teaching and learning in the multicultural setting from which every learner will benefit.

Following scientific process can be taught in different ways; students can be asked to follow directions, instructions, a step-by-step process, rules, procedures, or a sequence of events. The physical education activities outlined below are designed to be implemented in a step-by-step fashion, whereas in the nutrition facts activity students are directed to follow a simple recipe.

Physical Activity One: Star Wars Game

Grade level:	3 and up
Equipment:	10–20 soft balls
Injury precaution:	Soft balls are balls that cannot hurt the players when thrown and hit

Physical Objectives:
1. Physical exercise
2. Total physical response
3. Have fun
4. Everyone can participate
5. Make team Jedi lose his or her power to revive team members
6. Hit other team's members with the soft balls

Game rules:
1. Divide the whole class into two even teams (10 and 10, 12 and 12, or 15 and 15).
2. Names for each team: The Rebels and the Imperials, The Titans and the Tigers, The Lakers and The Suns, or The Bears and the Mustangs.
3. Set a middle line that no one from either team can cross.
4. Each team chooses a "Jedi" who is the only member who can revive downed teammates.
5. When one team's members are all down, the other team wins.

How to play the game:
1. This game is played by throwing the soft balls at the other team.
2. If someone is hit by a ball, he or she is down and must sit in that spot until the Jedi of the team revives him or her by tapping to reenter the game.
3. If a ball is caught, then the thrower of that ball must sit in that spot until the Jedi revives him or her to reenter the game.
4. If a Jedi is hit by the ball or touches the ball accidentally or intentionally, he or she is down and must sit to the side for one minute and loses all his or her power permanently; the team no longer has a Jedi to revive team members.
5. When the downed Jedi reenters the game, he or she plays as a normal player and no longer has power to revive or rescue downed players.

Physical Activity Two: Ball Skills with Music

Grade level: K–3

Music: Sweet Georgia Brown

Balls: 6-inch rubber balls

All students: Each student has a ball

Physical objective:
1. Physical exercise
2. Total physical response: sitting, catching, bouncing, kneeling, bending, moving, coordinating, controlling, balancing, visual skills, physical abilities, etc.
3. Have fun
4. All can participate
5. Learn ball skills
6. Improve locomotor and psychomotor skills
7. Correlation with neurogenesis

Game rules:

Level one:
1. Set a number of bounces for practice (10 right hand and 8 left hand, or 5 right hand and 5 left hand).
2. Bounce the ball with right hand first and count the number of bounces.
3. Bounce the ball with left hand and count the number of bounces.

Level two:
1. Set a number of bounces for practice.
2. Bounce the ball with alternate hands (right and left, or left and right)
3. Count the number of bounces.

Level three:
1. Bounce the ball with both hands simultaneously.
2. Catch the ball on its return.
3. Repeat the process over and over again.

Food and Nutrition Activity: Asian Banana Split Recipe

I. Supplies:
1. Ingredients listed below
2. Spoons or forks
3. Bowls or plates
4. Knife

II. Ingredients (per child):

1 small peeled banana

½ cup low fat vanilla yogurt

1 tablespoon low fat granola

½ cup sliced strawberries

III. Directions:

1. Cut banana in half lengthwise
2. Spoon yogurt into a bowl
3. Place banana halves on both sides of yogurt
4. Top yogurt with granola and berries, then serve

ASSESSING SCIENCE PROCESSES

Teachers should plan to assess student learning of scientific processes as often as possible. Waiting to the very end of a unit to assess students' knowledge and skills can be torment for students because there may appear to be too much information or data to absorb for a test. The goal here is to help students master the science processes. Remember, teaching and learning science are processes rather than products. In the early grades, teachers should assess students' grasp of scientific processes on the basis of their performance in the three types of inquiry presented in Table 3.3: *structured inquiry, guided inquiry, and open inquiry.*

Mastery of these forms of inquiry investigation and/or experimentation enables students to become scientists. Teachers can modify the components of this model to fit the needs of their students. For structured inquiry, teachers can ask students to follow a few basic steps: form a hypothesis, test the hypothesis, make a model, use variables, try an experiment, draw conclusions, and apply inference. For guided inquiry, teachers can reduce the procedural process to three

Table 3.3 Model for Assessing Mastery of Scientific Processes

Structured Inquiry	Guided Inquiry	Open Inquiry
1. Form a hypothesis	1. Form a hypothesis	1. Ask a question
2. Procedural steps:	2. Test hypothesis	2. Form a hypothesis
a. Make a model	3. Draw conclusions	3. Test hypothesis
b. Use variables		4. Draw conclusions
c. Experiment		5. Retry
d. Retry		6. Apply inference
e. Change variables		
3. Draw conclusions		
4. Apply inference		

Table 3.4 Components in Assessing Mastery of Scientific Processes

Science Vocabulary	Concepts	Knowledge/skills
1. Create a word bank for the study of science vocabulary	1. Compare and contrast strategies	1. Compare and contrast skills
2. Use cloze strategy	2. Scientific processes or procedural steps	2. Descriptive explanations
3. Use complete sentences or definitions	3. Use hypothesis or ask question	3. Critical thinking
4. Revise or rewrite sentences or definitions to meet grade-level standards	4. Observation	4. Follow directions to read graphs or charts
5. Practice vocabulary with students	5. Conclusions	5. Read data or information given
6. Use guided practices		6. Ask questions
		7. Understand science vocabulary
		8. Observe pictures
		9. Use variables
		10. Draw conclusions

easy steps: form a hypothesis, test the hypothesis, and draw conclusions. For open inquiry, four basic steps of the scientific process are sufficient: ask a question, form a hypothesis, test the hypothesis, and draw conclusions.

With this model in mind, teachers need to identify an appropriate way to assess student learning. Keep in mind that academic assessment depends on the nature of each science lesson plan; however, progressive assessment of student learning should be conducted on an ongoing basis. A teacher-made test is one of the best tools for assessing student learning, especially for science. Table 3.4 gives a few basic guidelines for designing testing components for assessing student learning in science. Teachers need to adhere to the learning objectives, which should have *cognitive content objectives* and/or *cognitive process objectives*.

Remember, assessing students' learning outcomes is important in teaching science because scientific concepts, knowledge, and skills are difficult for many students to grasp, especially for ELLs and students with special needs. Science vocabulary words constitute academic language that all students need to have in order to master science content. Teachers can design testing instruments that measure students' knowledge and skills based on the content of each unit or lesson rather than the whole chapter. Teachers need to always remember the difference between quality and quantity.

SUMMING UP

This chapter discussed the importance of using creative processes to teach science using hands-on and minds-on activities. Creativity is what makes teachers great. Processes help teachers be creative artists. Students do not learn by listening, but by doing. For this reason, students do not benefit from teacher-centered instruction, but from student-centered methods that allow students to engage in inquiry activities. Students love to learn science if it is fun; however, science is boring if it is not based on inquiry.

Scientific processes are defined in this chapter to help teachers understand how to apply them to inquiry activities to boost student learning outcomes. Teachers have to teach science as a process rather than a product in order to achieve appropriate learning goals. Giving answers to questions will not help students construct knowledge and acquire skills. Using inquiry skills to question the answers helps students think critically. Most importantly, teachers need to make sure that the processes they teach are clear, consistent, and deliberate; otherwise, connect teaching and learning will be difficult.

Inquiry science involves process skills. Teachers engage students in inquiry process skills to conduct investigations and experimentations to answer questions. Scientific processes are tools that students need to acquire early; they will continue to use them throughout their academic careers and beyond.

CHAPTER FOUR

Linking Concepts TO Standards

Scientific principles and laws do not lie on the surface of nature. They are hidden, and must be wrested from nature by an active and elaborate technique of inquiry.

—JOHN DEWEY *RECONSTRUCTION IN PHILOSOPHY,* 1920

INTRODUCTION

The National Science Education Standards (NSES) and the California Science Content Standards for K-12 grades (CSCS) requires that school children build science knowledge, investigative skills, scientific capabilities, and facility in scientific processes through inquiry-based instruction and procedural steps that foster the development and construction of new knowledge and skills acquired through the implementation of inquiry activities. These standards emphasize the importance of teaching and learning science. They expect teachers to guide students through the process of experimentation and investigation, teaching science concepts with scientific processes to help learners develop explanations and to promote conceptual change and deeper understanding of science in all learners. This chapter describes the teaching and learning of science concepts through inquiry based on NSES and CSCS standards. It suggests ways teachers can be creative in integrating science content and processes in order for students to assume major learning responsibility for constructing positive learning outcomes and, at the same time, for teachers to deliver quality science instructions for all learners in the multicultural setting.

WHY STANDARDS REQUIRE INQUIRY

This discussion of inquiry-based instruction is necessary because teachers are used to direct instruction or scripted instruction, which is simple to implement; however, what they fail to consider is that direct instruction is a one-model-fits-all modality that leaves many learners behind. Current instructional practices are heavily based on intervention modalities rather than instructional methodologies. Direct instruction is easy to deliver, observe, and evaluate. Many teachers favor direct instruction because it can be implemented within their time constraints. Nearly 75% of everyday teaching is prescriptive and teacher-centered, not student-centered. For this reason, most teachers ignore the essential features of inquiry-based instruction, especially for science.

According to the National Research Council (2000), inquiry-based instruction is essential for teaching and learning science in Grades K-6. In science, the word *inquiry* is very meaningful; however, many teachers do not take the time to educate students on the meaning of inquiry and its importance to learning science concepts. *Inquiry* means asking or starting with a question about something in order to get the information needed to understand that thing, as shown in Figure 4.1. Without learning how to inquire, students are left with answers teachers provide to questions they did not ask, and that is not the process of teaching and learning science envisioned in the standards.

Sunal and Sunal (2003) defined inquiry as "the method by which students construct meaning and develop generalizations as they learn science."

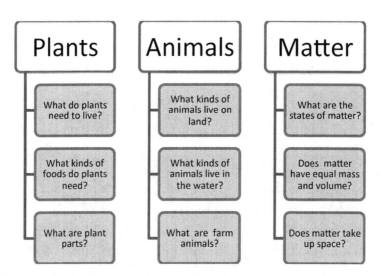

Figure 4.1 *Examples of inquiry questions*

Similarly, Howe (2002) explained that inquiry refers to different ways of experimenting, exploring, investigating, teaching, and learning science concepts. Inquiry is an approach to teaching and learning science concepts in which teachers guide students in the scientific processes of investigation and facilitate learning through different means. Inquiry-based instruction is a student-centered methodology as opposite to a teacher-centered approach. Inquiry is the process of asking and answering questions in the pursuit of learning science concepts.

INQUIRY FEATURES MATTER

Teachers should not overlook the features of inquiry because students need to learn how to develop knowledge and skills as they understand scientific processes. They need to learn how things evolve over time, how scientists discover the physical world, and how to apply academic learning to everyday, real-life experiences. Questioning generates knowledge, and answering questions is a powerful way to construct more knowledge; students can demonstrate the knowledge they have gained from the process as they report the results of their investigations. Thus the features of scientific inquiry promote cognitive development and enable students to build their capabilities, knowledge, and skills. However, teachers must always remember that the results among diverse students will be varied due to different levels of academic ability.

The national standards for science education describe how teachers are to implement inquiry-based instruction. They specify five steps that should be followed. First, teachers must use *scientific questions* to engage learners in learning science concepts. For instance, teachers may use the 5Ws+H to engage students' prior knowledge and prompt their curiosity about the subject matter. Using encouraging questions helps students think, wonder, ponder, and imagine about the subject of the lesson.

Second, the standards tell teachers to allow students the *priority to gather evidence or data* to support their experimentation or investigation. The way to do this is to have students ask a question; form a hypothesis; find evidence, data, or information needed to examine that hypothesis; make observations; engage in communication; test the hypothesis; draw conclusions; and make inferences from their conclusions. In other words, students need to engage in scientific processes to conduct their investigation to answer a question. Students could gather data or information from a variety of sources, such as textbooks, magazines articles, the Internet, databases, encyclopedias, group discussions, and science projects. One cautionary note: young children may not be able to perform these tasks without teachers' guidance, facilitation, and assistance, and teachers must be willing to provide them the help they need.

Third, the standards call for teachers to empower students to use the data or information they gather to develop *their own descriptions, explanations, understandings, and predictions.* As discussed in Chapter Three, students will use scientific processes as guides throughout the inquiry and discovery process; however, teachers need to set clear and consistent procedural guidelines for all hands-on and minds-on activities. Guidelines should include questions students can use to figure out what data or information they need. Sometimes students may find evidence that refutes rather than supports the hypothesis, and teachers need to make sure students understand that such outcomes are part of the learning process.

Fourth, after students complete the first three steps, teachers must provide guidance to help their students *build a bridge to connect scientific evidence and investigative explanations* so they can construct scientific knowledge and skills. For instance, students can examine variables used in their experimentation and develop explanations and understandings, or they can form their own theories by making inferences from the evidence to connect the dots. This process may involve abstract ideas, concrete scientific relationships between variables, observational data, and other critical thinking applications. Teachers need to bear in mind that students may not reach this level of thinking in every lesson because the nature of the inquiry activity may not require it.

Lastly, teachers must ensure that communication, interaction, or scientific discourse take place with other students so they can *share evidence, explanations, processes, data, information, and procedural results.* These discussions or communications can take place in Think Pair Share (TPS) formats, cooperative learning groups, whole-class discussions, group reports, or oral presentations. As always, teachers need to accommodate students with limitations, making whatever adaptations are necessary to include all learners; otherwise, some activities may preclude some students who may lack the communication skills required for participation.

Furthermore, teachers must pay attention to students' diverse abilities and needs in these processes because some students may not have a sufficiently high level of self-direction. Some students cannot follow several procedural steps needed to conduct an experiment; others cannot form a hypothesis to lead the investigation process. Teachers play a major role in implementing the features of inquiry. More teacher direction is needed for lower achievers than for high achievers. Teachers must take the time to provide accommodations and adaptations if necessary so learning opportunities are available to all students.

HOW INQUIRY FITS ALL STUDENTS

Teaching science concepts to children in Grades K-6 is not always fun unless teachers are creative artists because the diverse learning abilities, needs, and academic proficiencies in the classroom are challenging. On top of that, the standards set the academic goals high and the majority of students in many classrooms are either at or below grade level. Only the top 10% of students are at or above grade level. The current classroom has three groups of students: a top group, a middle group, and a bottom group. To teach science in ways that all student groups can learn, teachers have to take multicultural factors into careful consideration; these factors affect prior knowledge, language skills, academic language, equal opportunity, adaptation, equity of instruction, and instructional assistance.

In today's practice, most teachers target the middle group because it has the largest concentration of students; they neglect many of the needs of students in the top and bottom groups. Teachers believe the top students can fend for themselves and the bottom students require more time than they are either able or willing to spend. With this approach, the top and bottom students suffer academically. Teachers need to devise teaching mechanisms that benefit all students as mandated by the science standards.

To help teachers frame their inquiry instructions so they can engage all learners in science, the National Research Council (2000) gives several examples of self-direction; some are shown in Table 4.1.

Keep in mind that all children have some scientific knowledge and skills brought from home. All teachers need to do is connect what the students know to what they should learn and help them build on what they learn in class to connect to what they have experienced in a positive way that guides them to make conceptual changes.

LINKING CONCEPTS TO INQUIRY STANDARDS

Teachers need to link science concepts to inquiry standards. There is one set of national science standards; however, each state has its own set or sets of science standards that teachers are required to follow. California has both the California Science Content Standards for Grades K-12 and the California Science Framework for Grades K-12. Either is suitable for teaching science concepts in the public schools in California, but most teachers prefer to use the content standards over the framework because the standards are shorter and easier to follow. In many

Table 4.1 Self-Direction Guidelines for Different Student Groups

Inquiry Process	Bottom Group	Middle Group	Top Group
Ask a question or form hypothesis	Teachers provide questions for inquiry activity	Students select questions for inquiry activity	Students ask or form their own questions for inquiry activity
Test hypothesis, communicate, or observe	Teachers give directions for inquiry activities	Teachers guide and students carry out inquiry activities	Students carry out inquiry activities on their own
Gather data or information, communicate, observe, or analyze	Students use teachers' suggestions to draw conclusions, explanations, descriptions, and predictions	Students formulate descriptions, predictions, explanations, and conclusions based on teachers' guide	Students use their own collected data or information to formulate descriptions, explanations, predictions, and conclusions
Select variables to conduct experiment or investigation, analyze data, infer, or interpret	Teachers help connect evidence, explanations, descriptions, predictions, and conclusions to scientific processes and knowledge	Teachers guide students in connecting explanations, descriptions, predictions, and conclusions to scientific processes and knowledge	Students connect their own explanations, descriptions, predictions, and conclusions to scientific processes and knowledge
Conclusion, inference, or further study	Students follow procedural steps designed by teachers	Students use guide to perform procedural steps, such as explanations, communications, and descriptions	Students are in charge of procedural steps to communicate, explain, conclude, and infer from their results

places, there are also local or district standards, usually identical or similar to state and national standards. To see the concepts in the national and state science standards at a glance, Table 4.2 presents the NSES standards and Table 4.3 gives the California science standards. Science standards are broad based, containing general ideas, and they should be seen as guidelines for teaching science concepts. The scope of each content standard guides teachers in planning and preparing science lessons that are appropriate for each grade level or age group.

To link science concepts to standards, teachers can use idea webs or concept mapping as illustrated in Figures 4.2, 4.3, and 4.4. Teachers may need to read the science content standards often to become familiar with them; otherwise, they may teach concepts that are not aligned with the standards. For instance, a kindergarten teacher may wants to teach about volcano eruptions, but the earth science standard for kindergarten does not include this topic because it is more

Table 4.2 National Science Education Standards (NSES)

Grade Level	Unifying Concepts and Processes	Science as Inquiry	Physical Science	Life Science	Earth and Space Science	Science and Technology	Science in Personal and Social Perspective	History and Nature of Science
K-4	System, order, and organization; evidence, models, and explanation; change, constancy, and measurement; evolution and equilibrium; and form and function	Ability to perform, understand, or learn scientific inquiry	Properties, objects, position, motion, light, heat, electricity, or magnetism	Characteristic of plants and animals; life cycles; and ecosystem	Properties, earth layers, objects in the sky, climate changes, and materials	Use technology, differences between natural objects and objects made by man	Health, relationships, people, society, resources, life challenges, and changes	Science as human endeavor, discovery, and invention
5-8	System, order, and organization; evidence, models, and explanation; change, constancy, and measurement; evolution and equilibrium; and form and function	Ability to perform, understand, or learn scientific inquiry	Properties, changes, matter, motion, forces, and transfer of energy	Structure, function, ecosystem, food chain/web, reproduction, heredity, behavior, people, society, adaptations, survival, and differences	Earth layers/ structure, earth history, planets, solar system, and changes	Abilities, design, understand technology, and applications	Health, resources, people, society, hazards, risks, benefits, diseases, and environments	Science as human endeavor, nature of science, and history of science

Note. Information from *A Sampler of National Science Education Standards*, by Joseph M. Peters, 2006, Upper Saddle River, NJ: Pearson Education.

Table 4.3 California Science Content Standards

Grade Level	Physical Science	Life Science	Earth Science	Investigation/ Experimentation
Kindergarten	Properties of materials (clay, cloth, paper, house, car, toys, objects), observe, measure, predict, color, size, shape, weight, texture, flexibility, attraction to magnets, floating, sinking	Types of plants and animals, differences, similarities, comparing, classifying, seed-bearing, plants, birds, fish, insects, stems, leaves, roots, arms, wings, legs	Earth structures, air, wind, land, water, mountains, rivers, oceans, valleys, deserts, landforms	Observe, compare, classify, describe, communicate
First	Forms and states of matter, gases, liquids, solids, properties of substances, mixed, cooled, or heated	Plants and animals, needs, survival, adaptations, food, sharp teeth eats meat, flat teeth eats plants, shelter, nesting, physical needs	Weather patterns, wind vane, weather conditions, temperature, thermometer, observe, measure, light, rain, fog, snow, climate changes	Observe, predict, measure, describe, communicate
Second	Motions of objects, force, strength, push, pull, sound, vibration, pitch, noise, beat	Life cycles of plants and animals, germination, pollination, reproduction, growth, development, parents, offspring, characteristics	Earth is made of materials, soil, water, fossils, rocks, minerals, resources, energy	Predict, observe, measure, describe, communicate, experiment, test, record
Third	Forms of energy and matter, light, heat, water, wind, gas, fuel, food, solid, liquid, gas, evaporation, melting, substances, atoms, particles	Adaptations, behavior, survival, reproduction, growth, extinction, biomes, life forms, ecosystem	Objects in the sky, patterns, constellations, stars, planets, day, night, dark, light, seasons, lunar cycles	Predict, observe, measure, describe, communicate, experiment, test, record

Fourth	Electricity, magnetism, energy, light, motions, forces, charges, poles, compass, effects, circuits, design, motors, devices, generators, magnetic field	All organisms need energy and matter to live and grow, food chain, food web, herbivores, omnivores, carnivores, consumers, decomposers, producers, recycle of plants and animals	Properties of rocks and minerals, process of formation, igneous, sedimentary, metamorphic, rock cycles, earthquake, landslides, erosion, volcanic eruption, landforms, weathering, transportation, deposition, wind, waves	Read, predict, observe, measure, describe, communicate, infer, formulate, experiment, test, record
Fifth	Types of matter, periodic table, chemical reactions, elements, metal, nonmetal, gas, solid, liquid, chemical properties, atoms, molecules, physical properties	Plant and animal structures, respiration, transpiration, waste disposal, digestion, functions of internal organs, metabolism, chemical breakdowns	Weather cycles, patterns, conditions, seasons, evaporation, condensation, precipitation, rain, hail, snow, fog, sleet, ice, lakes, oceans, rivers, underground water, convection currents, temperature	Conduct study, read, predict, observe, measure, describe, communicate, infer, formulate, experiment, test, record
Sixth	Heat and thermal energy, climate changes, heat waves, light, radiation, flow of energy, temperature, convection currents, transfer of energy, humidity, pressure	All organisms in ecosystem, exchange energy and nutrients, sunlight, photosynthesis, produce food, food web, abiotic factors, light, water, natural energy, material resources, air, soil, rocks, minerals, petroleum, fresh water, wildlife, and forests, renewable energy, nonrenewable energy	Plate tectonics and earth's structures, geological events, earthquakes, tsunamis, shakes, motions, eruptions, layers, fossils, epicenter, faults, landforms, weather patterns, climate, shapes, topography	Conduct study, read, use technology, predict, observe, measure, describe, communicate, infer, formulate, experiment, test, record, science project

(Continued)

Grade Level	Physical Science	Life Science	Earth Science	Investigation/ Experimentation
Seventh	Physical principles in living systems, light spectrum, light waves, reflection, refraction, electromagnetic light, wavelengths, lenses, eyes, magnify glass, telescope, microscope, camera. light colors, light travel	Cell biology, genetics, structure and function in living systems, cells, tissues, organs, muscles, joints, skeleton, genes, traits, heredity, recessive, dominant, mitosis, reproductive organs, sexual activity, pollens, seeds, fruit, fertilization, pregnancy, chromosomes, plant and animal cellular structures, species, natural selection, anatomy, fossil	Earth and life history, age of the earth, rock cycles, evolution of life on earth, geological processes, geological time scale, extinction, fossil, fire, flood, catastrophic events, eruptions, impacts of asteroids	Conduct study, read, use technology, predict, observe, measure, describe, communicate, infer, formulate, experiment, test, record, science project
Eighth	Motions, forces, structure of matter, density, buoyancy, forms of matter, velocity, speed, balanced, unbalanced, inertia, action, reaction, static, gravity, elastic, tension, compression, friction, atomic structure, proton, neutron, electron, properties, molecular motions, elements on periodic table, acidic, basic, neutral	Chemistry of living systems, carbon, carbohydrates, fats, proteins, DNA, principles of chemistry in living organisms	Earth in the solar system, structure and composition of the universe, milky way, stars, planets, galaxies, black hole, distance between planets, eclipse, shine, waxing, waning	Conduct study, read, use technology, predict, observe, measure, describe, communicate, infer, formulate, experiment, test, record, science project

Note. Information from *Science Content Standards for California Public Schools: Kindergarten through Grade 12,* California Department of Education, 2003, http://www.cde.ca.gov/be/st/ss/documents/sciencestnd.pdf

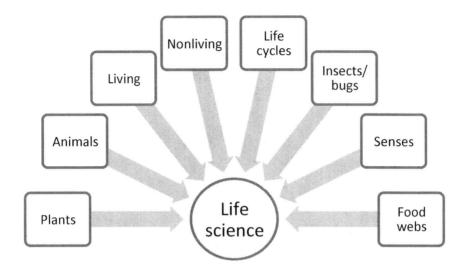

Figure 4.2 *Life science concept map*

appropriate for a higher grade level. The standards guide teachers so they do not attempt to teach science concepts that are too far below or above their students' level and for which the students are not academically prepared. Teachers must have learning objectives that align with or are derived from science content standards for their particular grade level.

Because the standards are broad, teachers need to read them carefully to see how to apply them to the science concepts. Learning objectives must be derived

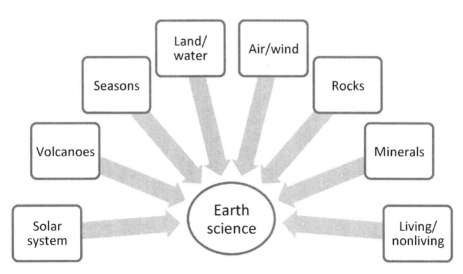

Figure 4.3 *Earth science concept map*

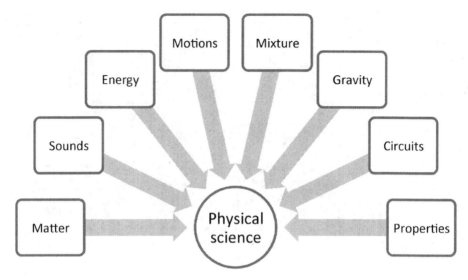

Figure 4.4 *Physical science concept map*

from the key concepts listed under each standard. Some of the science concepts are expressed as key words: biomes, plants, animals, solar system, planets, eruptions, adaptations, food chains, respiratory system, or gravity. Remember, science standards are guidelines, not learning objectives; they give teachers flexibility in planning science lessons with creative, innovative inquiry activities and hands-on and minds-on strategies that keep students focused on doing and engaged in learning.

Some teachers still believe that science, like mathematics, is not a language art; that misconception needs to be corrected. All academic subjects are language arts. For this reason, teachers can design integrated content to teach science concepts with other academic subjects. Science utilizes math skills, verbal skills, writing and reading skills, as well as social skills and can therefore be integrated with any other subject.

USING THEMATIC INQUIRY

Science should not be separated from other academic subjects, such as social studies, language arts, and mathematics. Some teachers tend to believe that science is a separate domain that should be taught with different instructional strategies or methodologies; however, science is entangled with all other subjects and should be taught with integrated content. As mentioned earlier, students need language skills, such as writing, reading, and speaking, as well as math skills and social interaction to help them learn science concepts. One way to integrate content is to use *thematic*

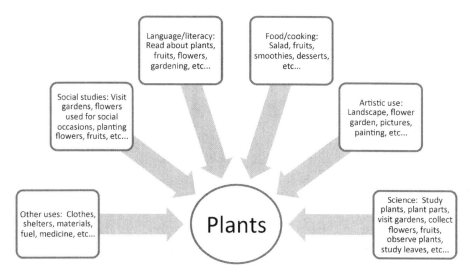

Figure 4.5 *Example of thematic teaching*

inquiry or *integrated topics* to connect concepts and ideas across the curriculum as shown in Figure 4.5. Teachers can use creative ideas to integrate math, science, language arts, and social studies. Some of the content related to the standards for these subjects, shown in Table 4.4, overlaps; teachers can use this information to explore how science can be taught with other academic disciplines.

As Table 4.4 illustrates, academic skills in one subject area are important in other subject areas also since knowledge and skills are interlocked and students learn, acquire skills, and transfer knowledge and skills as they construct new

Table 4.4 Content of Selected Subjects Related to Standards

Subject	Content According to Standards
English language arts	Reading, writing, speaking, listening, viewing, literature, grammar, conventions
Mathematics	Numbers and operations, algebra, geometry, measurement, data analysis, probability, problem solving, reasoning and proof, communication, connections, representations
Social studies	People, language, culture, time, continuity, change, places, environment, development, identity, individuals, groups, power, authority, governance, ruling, production, distribution, consumption, consumers, science, technology, society, global connections, civil ideals, practices, leaders, leadership, values, norms
Science	Life science concepts, earth science concepts, physical science concepts, earth and space science, connections, applications, hypothesis, thinking, processes, tools, technologies, communication, investigation, experimentation, properties

academic language and perform new tasks. Teachers who can integrate content across subjects enrich their students and deliver instruction that meets standards not only in science, but also in other subjects.

ALIGNING ALL CONTENT STANDARDS

The science concepts of the NSES and California standards have been reviewed and determined to be good practices in the multicultural setting. Teachers are required to align their lessons with the content standards, yet teacher preparation programs do not prepare new teachers to know and use the content standards. Most new teachers do not learn how to apply content standards until they are in the classroom, and that has been one of the frustrations that needs to be addressed. Knowing the required content of all academic subjects is one thing, but knowing how to align instructional practices to the content standards is another. It can be quite challenging for many teachers because not all schools teach science or use science curricula. Many schools focus on reading, writing, and math skills because they have to hit state targets in these subjects. Some schools implement science curricula only when they feel a need to do so. The sporadic provision of science education puts many children behind in science knowledge and skills.

The alignment of all academic content standards should be considered so that teachers can design lesson plans to teach across the curricular disciplines and include science as part of regular teaching. In other words, science does not have to be taught separately if teachers can integrate it with language arts, social studies, and math. If science is taught separately, the other subjects can be taught with it as well because the knowledge and skills in all content standards are inextricably linked. To help teachers align academic content from different subjects, Table 4.5 provides short versions of the content standards for science, math, language arts, and social studies.

APPLYING SCIENCE CONCEPTS TO STANDARDS

As Table 4.5 illustrates, the content of academic subjects overlap in a number of areas. For instance, the words *evaluate, interpret, communicate, question, analysis, information*, and *patterns* appear in science, social studies, language arts, and math content standards. These are areas in which science concepts can be integrated with the content of other academic subjects. As Tables 4.2, 4.3, 4.4, and 4.5 show, teachers have a variety of ways of applying science idea webs or concepts to specific standards, remembering that concepts must be appropriate for the grade level or

Table 4.5 Selected Standards for Science, Math, Language Arts, and Social Studies Content

Science Content Standards	Math Content Standards	Language Arts Content Standards	Social Studies Content Standards
Standard A: Science as inquiry:	*Standard A: Numbers and operations:*	*Standards:*	*Standards:*
1. Develop ability to do scientific inquiry	1. Understand numbers, ways of representing numbers, relationships among numbers and number systems	1. Read a wide range of print and non-print texts for multiple purposes	1. Have experiences that provide for the study of culture and cultural diversity
2. Understand about scientific inquiry	2. Meanings of operations and how they relate to one another	2. Read a wide range of literature from many periods and genres to build understanding of human experience	2. Provide for the study of the ways human beings view themselves in and over time
Standard B: Physical science:	3. Compute fluently and make reasonable estimate	3. Apply a wide range of strategies to comprehend, interpret, evaluate, and appreciate texts	3. Provide for the study of people, places, and environments
1. Understand properties, changes of properties in matter	*Standard B: Algebra:*	4. Adjust spoken, written, and visual language to communicate effectively for different purposes	4. Provide for the study of individual development and identity
2. Motions and forces	1. Patterns, relations, and functions	5. Employ a wide range of strategies in writing for a variety of purposes	5. Provide for the study of interactions among individuals, groups, and institutions
3. Transfer of energy	2. Represent, analyze, use algebraic symbols	6. Apply knowledge of language structure, conventions, and genre to create and discuss print and non-print texts	6. Provide for the study of how people create and change structures of power, authority, and governance
Standard C: Life science	3. Math models, quantitative relationship	7. Conduct research, generate questions, gather data, and communicate discoveries	
1. Structure and function in living system	4. Analyze changes in various contexts		
2. Reproduction and heredity	*Standard C: Geometry:*		
3. Regulation and behavior	1. Analyze characteristics, properties, shapes, arguments, and relationships		
4. Populations and ecosystems	2. Locations, spatial relationship, coordinate, and representation systems		
5. Diversity and adaptations of organisms	3. Transformation, symmetry		
Standard D: Earth and space science:			
1. Structure of the earth system			
2. Earth's history			
3. Earth in the solar system			
Standard E: Science and technology			
1. Abilities of technological design			
2. Understand about science and technologies			

(Continued)

Science Content Standards	Math Content Standards	Language Arts Content Standards	Social Studies Content Standards
Standard F: Science in personal and social perspectives:	4. Visualization, spatial reasoning, and modeling	8. Use various technologies, information sources to gather data and communicate knowledge	7. Provide for the study of how people organize for the production, distribution, and consumption of goods and services
1. Personal health	*Standard D: Measurement:*		
2. Populations, resources, and environments	1. Measurable attributes, units, systems, and processes	9. Respect for diversity in language use, patterns, and dialects	8. Provide for the study of relationships among science, technology, and society
3. Natural hazards	2. Techniques, tools, and formulas for measuring	10. Use first language to develop competency in English	
4. Risks and benefits	*Standard E: Analysis and probabilities:*	11. Participate as knowledgeable, reflective, creative, and critical members of diverse literacy communities	9. Provide for the study of global connections and interdependence
5. Science and technology in society	1. Formulate questions, collect data, analyze data, and answer questions		
Standard G: History and nature of science:	2. Statistical analysis of data	12. Use spoken, written, and visual language to accomplish own purposes	10. Provide for the study of the ideals, principles, and practices of citizenship in a democratic republic
1. Science as human endeavor	3. Evaluate, infer, and conclude based on data		
2. Nature of science	4. Concepts of probability		
3. History of science			

Note. Information from *National Science Education Standards*, Center for Science, Mathematics, and Engineering Education, 1996, Washington, DC: National Academies Press, http://books.nap.edu/html/nses/html/overview.html#content and *A Sampler of National Science Education Standards*, by Joseph M. Peters, 2006, Upper Saddle River, NJ: Pearson Education.

Table 4.6 Example of Science Concept Mapping

Grade Level	Life Science Standard	Life Science Concepts	Earth Science Standard	Earth Science Concepts	Physical Science Standards	Physical Science Concepts
Kindergarten	2, 2ab	Animals two by two, plants, and living things	3, 3c	Plants or trees	1, 1ab	Wood, fabric, paper, and texture
1–2	2, 2ab 3, 3abcde	New plants, insects, bugs, or life cycles	3, 3c; 3abcde	Pebbles, sand, and silt; air, weather, wind, or climate conditions	1, 1ab; 1, 1abcdef	Balance, motion, solids, liquids, volume, or mass
3–4	3, 3abcde; 2, 2abc; 3abcd	Structure of life, human body, or environments	4, 4ab; 5, 5abc	Water, landforms, or earth materials	1, 1abcdefghi, 2; 1, 1abcdefg	Sounds, measurements, magnetism, or electricity
5–6	1, 1abcdefghi; 1, 1abcdefg	Food, nutrition, or environments	5, 5abcde; 6, 6abc	Landforms, solar energy, or planets	3,3abcde; 6abc	Mixtures, solutions, levers, or pulleys

age of the students. Table 4.6 illustrates how teachers can do concept mapping at each grade level in order to teach with confidence, plan adequately, find necessary resources prior to teaching, and make science fun and engaging experiences for both the teachers and the students.

One cautionary note: the standards for investigation and experimentation (I/E) are not included in Table 4.6. Teachers need to apply these standards whenever they can to allow students to conduct investigations or experiments.

Table 4.7 presents science standards for inquiry activities for each grade level. Teachers should pay close attention to each of these standards in order to prescribe appropriate hands-on and minds-on activities.

Table 4.7 Science Standards for Investigation and Experimentation

Grade level	Life I/E standards	Earth I/E standards	Physical I/E standards
Kindergarten	4, 4de	4,4de	4,4de
First	4,4de	4,4de	4,4de
Second	4,4abcdefg	4,4abcdefg	4,4abcdefg
Third	5,5abcde	5,5abcde	5,fabcde
Fourth	6,6abcd	6,6abcd	6,6abcd
Fifth	6,6abcdefghi	6,6abcdefghi	6,6abcdefghi
Sixth	7,7abcdefgh	7,7abcdefgh	7,7abcdefgh

SELECTING INQUIRY APPROACHES

After learning how to link science concepts to the standards, teachers need to think about different ways to make science fun to teach and learn in the multicultural setting. Keep in mind that there is no best way or perfect way to teach all science concepts to all students, and there is no one specific way to learn all science concepts. Each content standard is different, and each lesson will be unique. Both teachers and students need to explore creative ways to teach and to learn science concepts. Teachers differ in science experience, teaching skills, and instructional strategies, and students differ in prior knowledge, experiences, cultural barriers, and academic skills. These differences make teaching and learning science challenging. They affect how teachers teach science concepts and how students learn them. The critical pedagogy involving inquiry science needs to be understood; otherwise, teachers may know what to teach but not how to develop meaningful lesson plans.

Having a repertoire of models for inquiry instruction—various instructional strategies, teaching methodologies, activity modalities, and task master techniques—should help teachers develop comprehensive approaches to teaching science. A wide repertoire enables teachers to build on different perspectives on the nature of inquiry, scientific processes, knowledge, skills, learning objectives, learning needs, and academic goals. For instance, using *guided inquiry or guided discovery* is quite popular in introducing science concepts to students. In this process, students are prompted with interesting thought-provoking questions. Teachers can use the 5Ws+H in guided inquiry to engage students right away. Teaching science is a process, not a product; therefore, models of inquiry instruction have to include scientific processes that are facilitated or guided by teachers.

Table 4.8 lists many teaching strategies that are effective in the multicultural classroom in teaching and learning science (Vang, 2010). Teachers can choose any of these strategies that fit the needs of their students as an instructional methodology, an activity strategy, or a task strategy. Some of the teaching strategies listed are more useful for intervention than for instructional purposes. For science, engaging students in observation, communication, drawing inferences, sharing, explanation, and making conclusions is key to teaching science in ways that align with standards.

TEACHING EXPECTATIONS FOR ALL

The NSES and California Science Content Standards both require teachers to teach science with an inquiry-based approach. Because the standards guide teachers in a progression through the grade levels, they should be followed

Table 4.8 Selected Teaching Strategies

Acronym	Strategy	Example of Use
TI	Thematic instruction	Organizing or framing instruction around key areas, concepts, or ideas to make connections
CALLA	Cognitive academic language approach	Involves topics, academic language skills, and language acquisition
ILA	Integrated language arts	Whole-language approach to learning new language
5W's + H	What, when, where, who, why, and how	Question-based instruction, inquiry instruction, or investigative approach
DI/EDI	Direct instruction/explicit direct instruction	Systematic approach, one-model-fits-all, use in all subject matter teaching
ELD	English language development	Transitional bilingual education programs without primary language(L1) support
ESL	English as a second language	ELD or SDAIE instruction or whole-language approach
K-W-L	What I *know*, what I *want* to learn, and what I *learned*	Student-centered approach
LEA	Language experience approach	Used mostly in language arts for writing and reading based on student's experiences and prior knowledge
PQ5Rs	Preview, question, read, recite, reflect, review, and respond	Used in all subject matter teaching and with any instructional methodologies
PR	Preview and review	Engage prior knowledge and tap into lesson plan objective
CL	Cooperative learning	Groups, centers, or stations
PW	Process writing	A process of writing or POWERS: Prewrite, organize, write, edit, rewrite, and submit
RT	Reciprocal teaching	Question-based approach used mostly in language arts for reading: 4-step process: Summary, clarification, question, and prediction
RTI	Response to intervention	Intervention strategy to identify at-risk students, SIOP components, 2-tier approaches, adaptations, modifications, accommodations, and intervention
SIOP	Sheltered instruction observation protocol	RTI components, ELD components, SDAIE components, SMART Plan, and intervention
Scaffolding	Backing out or withdrawal strategies, or building skills as layers or levels	Use in all subject matter teaching, ELD, SDAIE, TESOL, ESL, SEI, and others
SDAIE	Specially designed academic instruction in English	ELD instruction with primary language support (L1)
SEI	Sheltered English instruction	ESL, TESOL, ELD, or SDAIE instruction
TESOL	Teach English to speakers of other languages	ESL , ELD, or SDAIE instruction
TNA	The natural approach	Used mostly in language arts
TPR	Total physical response	Music, dance, physical education, or body movement
GI	Guided inquiry instruction	Student-centered, investigative instruction, question-based

every step of the way to ensure that science instruction is appropriate at each level and that knowledge builds on knowledge. However, many ELL, NNS, and SN students are excluded from instructional practices for a variety of reasons. In California, teachers have to follow another set of state standards or legal mandates to ensure that they provide inclusive instruction for all learners: the Teacher Performance Expectation Standards (TPE) and the Teacher Performance Assessment (TPA).

The TPE has a total of 13 teaching expectations, and the TPA has four major tasks teachers must accomplish to demonstrate their teaching abilities. Table 4.9 gives the TPE standards and Table 4.10 presents the TPA tasks in which new teachers must demonstrate proficiency during their student teaching practicum. The goal of the TPE and TPA standards is to make sure every child is given equal opportunity to learn in the multicultural setting.

Furthermore, TPE and TPA reinforce each other throughout the prospective teacher's clinical training in the classroom. Inequities in instructional practices caused California to mandate TPE and TPA; the goal is to make sure that teachers provide ELL and SN students with opportunity to learn academic subject matter in the classroom. These standards require that teachers develop instructional accommodations, modifications, adaptations, and interventions that include all learners, especially ELLs and SNs, in the learning processes.

Table 4.9 TPE Standards by Domain

Domain	Standards
Domain A: Making subject matter comprehensible to students	TPE 1: Specific pedagogical skills for subject matter instruction
Domain B: Assessing student learning	TPE 2: Monitoring student learning during instruction
	TPE3: Interpretation and use of assessment
Domain C: Engaging and supporting students in learning	TPE 4: Making content accessible
	TPE 5: Student engagement
	TPE 6: Developmentally appropriate teaching practices
	TPE 7: Teaching English learners
Domain D: Planning instruction and designing learning experience for all students	TPE 8: Learning about students
	TPE 9: Instructional planning
Domain E: Creating and maintaining effective environments for student learning	TPE 10: Instructional time
	TPE 11: Social environment
Doman F: Developing as a professional educator	TPE 12: Professional, legal, and ethical obligations
	TPE 13: Professional growth

Table 4.10 TPA Expectations

Task Description	Expectations
Task 1: Subject-specific pedagogy	Using subject-specific pedagogical skills (TPE 1), planning for instruction (TPE 4, 5, 6, 9), planning for assessment (TPE 3), and making adaptations (TPE 4, 6, 7)
Task 2: Designing instruction	Establishing goals and standards (TPE 8, 9), learning about student (TPE 8, 9), planning for instruction (TPE 8, 9), making adaptations (TPE 4, 6, 7), using subject-specific pedagogical skills (TPE 1), and reflection (TPE 13)
Task 3: Assessing learning	Establishing goals and standards (TPE 8, 9), planning for assessment (TPE 3), learning about students (TPE 8, 9), making adaptations (TPE 4, 6, 7), analyzing student learning evidence (TPE 3), and reflection (TPE 13)
Task 4: Culminating teaching experience	Establishing goals and standards (TPE 8, 9), learning about students (TPE 8, 9), describing classroom environment (TPE 10, 11), planning for instruction (TPE 4, 5, 6), making adaptations (TPE 1, 4, 5, 6, 7), using subject-specific pedagogical skills (TPE 1, 4, 5, 6, 7), analyzing evidence of student learning (TPE 2, 3, 13), reflection (TPE 13)

Even if teaching science as inquiry limits the involvement of some ELL and SN students, using hands-on and minds-on activities will increase the learning and the learning potential of these students because children learn by doing.

SUMMING UP

This chapter presented many ideas for helping teachers understand the nature of teaching science as inquiry based and explained how they can link science concepts to science standards. Designing inquiry instruction is essential for teaching science concepts to children in Grades K-6, and the scientific processes are the means of constructing new knowledge and skills. Inquiry starts with interesting questions and allows students to find answers to these questions using scientific processes. Throughout the inquiry activities, teachers follow standard guidelines as they guide, focus, challenge, encourage, empower, and promote student learning.

Most importantly, teachers are mentors and guides who facilitate the learning process, allowing students to discover scientific knowledge and develop skills. Of the many instructional methodologies, teachers should use instructional models that will inspire students to learn science as inquiry. In guided inquiry approaches, teachers and students can work together to form hypotheses or to generate interesting questions for investigation and experimentation.

Helping students develop inquiry abilities is key to having them learn and retain science concepts.

National standards as well as standards of some states require that teachers use inquiry-based instruction for science, but there is no one-model-fits-all instruction that teachers can adopt as a best model for teaching all science concepts to all students in the multicultural setting. Teachers need to practice their scientific arts and polish their instructional models. They must keep in mind that inquiry models of instruction can only mirror the scientific processes that are consistent with the notion that children can be motivated to learn science academically if they are encouraged to do so through constructivist approaches. Inquiry allows all children to learn with hands-on and minds-on investigation and experimentation.

PART TWO

Applications of Science Concepts in the Practical Domain

CHAPTER FIVE

Focus ON Inquiry Instruction

An experiment is a question which science poses to Nature, and a measurement is the recording of Nature's answer.

—MAX PLANCK *SCIENTIFIC AUTOBIOGRAPHY*
AND OTHER PAPERS, 1949

INTRODUCTION

Finding the right tools for teaching can be critical, but teaching itself is always a challenging task. K-6 teachers should have the basic ability to teach science skills to all learners in the multicultural classroom. There is no best way to teach science; however, there are creative ways that teachers can learn and understand in order to make teaching and learning science fun and intriguing. Students should not be grilled with facts, figures, and answers without following proper procedural guidelines. Instead, they should be taught to think critically through the use of scientific processes, finding the answers to testing questions and learning how to question the answers. Whether teachers use guided discovery or other forms of instruction, teaching science concepts requires careful planning in order to include students' prior knowledge and the content of science standards. Learning the content is essential in the development of scientific knowledge and skills. This chapter describes effective instructional practices based on inquiry approaches and discusses content-based approaches that enable teachers to develop their own principles of teaching science concepts.

SCIENCE CONTENTS APPROACH

In previous chapters, much has been said about the relevancy of science standards, teaching applications, and scientific processes, but little has been discussed about the content knowledge and skills teachers need to have to teach science concepts. Teachers need to take heed of the content knowledge required for each grade level. Some teachers do not follow standard requirements in designing lesson plans and crafting learning objectives; they teach whatever they can think of to fill gaps in time. Such piecemeal teaching is disconnected and capricious. Teachers must read and reread the content standards to learn what is expected of them in teaching science. Tables 5.1 and 5.2 list the contents of the National Science Education Standards for quick reference; however, keep in mind that standards are broad guidelines. The scope of each standard gives teachers valuable information for planning science lessons for specific concepts based on the prior knowledge, experiences, and abilities of students. Be aware of the fact that science content knowledge is the key to quality teaching of science concepts, especially, for K-6 students.

The most important element in science education is the professional teacher who can make science interesting, developmentally appropriate, and relevant to all diverse learners in the classroom. Science learning should be connected to the other curricula in the school, and science content should be embedded in a variety of curricular programs.

SCIENCE PROCESSES CONTENT

Regardless of what lesson plan format teachers select for designing the content of their lessons, they need to follow the few steps listed in the content knowledge standards as a guide helping them teach science concepts to students. In earlier chapters, scientific processes were discussed because the content standards require science concepts to be taught through processes, not as products. Therefore, teachers need to include basic procedural guidelines in their lessons that allow students to practice scientific processes on an ongoing basis. To help teachers develop their own processes, Table 5.3 gives two models for consideration. Keep in mind that different procedural guidelines may be required for each grade level or each individual group of students, depending on their level of scientific knowledge and skills. For instance, for Grades 5-6, teachers should use more complex processes for students to conduct scientific investigations and experimentations than in Grades K-3.

Table 5.1 Overview of NSES Standards for Science Education, History of Science, Science Teaching, Assessment, and Content

Science Education Program Standards	History/Nature of Science Standards	Science Teaching Standards	Assessment Standards	Content Standards
1. The program of study in science should connect to other school programs	1. Science as human endeavor	1. Plan an inquiry based-program for students	1. Assessments must be consistent with the decisions they are designed to inform	1. Ask a question about objects, organisms, and events in the environment
2. Science content must be embedded in a variety of curriculum programs that are developmentally appropriate, interesting, and relevant to students' lives	2. Nature of science	2. Guide and facilitate learning	2. Achievement and opportunity to learn science must be assessed	2. Plan and conduct a simple investigation
3. The science program should be coordinated with the mathematics program	3. History of science	3. Recognize and respond to student diversity and encourage all students to participate fully in science learning	3. The inferences made from assessment about student achievement and opportunity to learn must be sound	3. Employ simple equipment and tools to gather data and extend the senses
4. Collaborative inquiry requires adequate and safe space		4. Engage in ongoing teaching and student learning		4. Use data to construct a reasonable explanation
5. The most important source is professional teachers		5. Design and manage learning environments that provide students with the time, space, and resources needed for learning science		5. Communicate investigations and explanations
		6. Develop community of learners		

Note. Information from *National Science Education Standards*, Center for Science, Mathematics, and Engineering Education, 1996, Washington, DC: National Academies Press, http://books.nap.edu/html/nses/html/overview.html#content and *A Sampler of National Science Education Standards*, by Joseph M. Peters, 2006, Upper Saddle River, NJ: Pearson Education.

Table 5.2 Overview of NSES Standards for Life Science, Earth Science, Physical Science, Science and Technology, and Personal and Social Perspectives

Life Science Standards	Earth Science Standards	Physical Science Standards	Science and Technology Standards	Science I Personal and Social Perspectives Standards
1. Characteristics of organisms	1. Properties of earth materials	1. Properties of objects and materials	1. Abilities of technological design	1. Understand about science and technology in society
2. organisms and environments	2. Objects in the sky	2. Position and motion of objects	2. Understanding about science and technology	
	3. Changes in earth and sky	3. Forces and motion		
		4. Transfer of energy		
		5. Light, heat, electricity, and magnetism		

Note. Information from *National Science Education Standards*, Center for Science, Mathematics, and Engineering Education, 1996, Washington, DC: National Academies Press, http://books.nap.edu/html/nses/html/overview.html#content and *A Sampler of National Science Education Standards,* by Joseph M. Peters, 2006, Upper Saddle River, NJ: Pearson Education.

Inquiry investigations and experimentations should be used on a regular basis to increase students' inquiry skills in learning science. All processes require time, and students need to develop cognitive processes over time. If teachers fail to require students to use inquiry skills, their students will lack the scientific principles that are the basis for learning science concepts and acquiring skills

Table 5.3 Models of Scientific Process

Model for Grades K-3	Model for Grades 4-6
1. Ask a question	1. Make observation
2. Form a hypothesis	2. Communicate
3. Test or conduct simple investigation or experiment	3. Gather data or information
4. Draw conclusions	4. Ask a question
	5. Form a hypothesis
	6. Use variables
	7. Test or conduct investigation or experimentation
	8. Data analysis
	9. Draw conclusions
	10. Inference
	11. Results support hypothesis
	12. Results do not support hypothesis

sequentially and logically. Scientific progress is made by asking meaningful questions and conducting careful investigations and experimentations to answer such questions.

EFFECTIVE TEACHING APPROACH

Teachers need to know what is expected of them because they play many roles in the process of teaching science concepts. As the teaching standards listed in Table 5.1 indicate, teachers must know how to plan inquiry-based instruction for students and must guide the activity in the classroom to facilitate the learning process. Teachers are the prime source of instruction, the main ingredient in meaningful science education for children. Without teachers' guidance, learning science would be possible, but it would be very difficult. Therefore, finding an effective teaching approach for inquiry-based instruction is important.

Effective teaching takes a number of ingredients; effective teachers know the menu of ingredients well. Planning to guide inquiry is the very first step in effective teaching. Effective teachers gather ideas, organize thoughts, put materials together, and plan how to execute inquiry instruction based on their own knowledge, skills, and understanding of science. They pace themselves through the processes: focusing on engagement, figuring out how to provoke thoughts, deciding how to make inquiry questions challenging, and determining how to encourage their students to use their inquiry skills to answer questions.

Inquiry teaching is not about what teachers want to do with students; it is about how students are doing in the learning process with the teachers' guidance and support. Effective science teachers model ways students can develop scientific knowledge and skills from their own learning experiences. For instance, teachers can present a question and allow students to process that question individually or with a partner and express their thoughts and understandings in their own words. Teachers make decisions to initiate interactions, discussions, and clarifications whenever they need to in order to guide students. Facilitating the learning process requires consistent classroom management and student discipline. In learning science, every student should be on the same page, following the same steps as they conduct their investigations or experiments.

Effective guidance is key to effectively teaching science. Guidance is facilitating, promoting, assisting, validating, encouraging, and cooperating as students are engaged in the group process. The amount of time teachers need to spend providing each type of guidance will depend on the nature of the lesson. Teachers in Grades K-1 need to provide more assistance than teachers in Grades 3-4 because of the lower maturity level of students. Teachers must provide the opportunity for every student to participate in inquiry instruction. Some learners may not be able to discover scientific concepts, principles, and theories or acquire science skills on their own; they need teachers to help them.

Effective science teaching requires patience, passion, and time. Teachers must be flexible to accommodate students' diverse abilities and needs as they assist students in learning key concepts and acquiring content knowledge. Furthermore, teachers must incorporate different teaching styles to differentiate instruction. Including hands-on and minds-on activities always yields a high level of student engagement. Teachers can build on student activities to present new knowledge and skills by using direct or expository teaching methodologies, such as the 5Ws+H, total physical response (TPR), scaffolding, SIOP, reciprocal teaching, KWL, use of graphic organizers, ELD, and SDAIE.

Effective teaching and effective teachers go hand-in-hand. The ultimate goal in science learning is to allow students to engage in the scientific processes to discover science concepts, to explore ideas, to construct knowledge, to ask and answer questions about their surroundings, and most importantly, to develop academic understanding of the inquiry process.

THE 5-E MODEL

In 1989, the 5-E model of instruction for science was developed by the Biological Sciences Curriculum Study (BSCS) to help improve inquiry learning in children. The 5-E model consists of *engagement, exploration, explanation, elaboration, and evaluation.* In this model, students are expected to perform specific tasks for each component or phase during the inquiry instruction, as explained in Table 5.4. The five phases may not take place in the same order depending on the nature of the lesson plan and its contents. In other words, teachers may not have to walk students through all five steps in every science lesson plan. Teachers may use these steps to guide students through the scientific process.

The 5-E model of instruction can be integrated with other lesson plan formats, such as the five-step lesson plan, three-step lesson plan, direct instruction, or guided inquiry instruction. The components of 5-E are similar to components used in other lesson plan formats. However, these components alone are not sufficient to make a sound instructional model for effective teaching because a lesson plan needs more than these steps. This model is meaningful when used with the phases of the learning cycle: *exploration, concept invention, and concept application* (Jacobson & Kondo, 1968; Karplus & Thier, 1974). The effectiveness of the model depends on how teachers use the components in their science lesson plans. In the lower grades one or two components could be useful, but in the higher grades,

Table 5.4 The 5-E Model of Instruction

Component	Expectations	Examples
Engagement	Engage learners in inquiry-based instruction or ask questions about objects	What do plants need to live? How many planets in the solar system? What is the difference between insects and bugs?
Exploration	Observe, plan, or conduct simple investigation to gather data or information about objects	Water, soil, light, space; study all the planets; compare and contrast insects and bugs
Explanation	Use data and information to explain, use simple variables to label or sort out information, try to answer question	What would happen to plants if there is no light, water, soil, or space? Why planets are different in sizes? How insects and bugs are different?
Elaboration	Learn to apply new understanding to new question, or connect learned experience to real-life experience	Use results to explain different plants with details. Use information to tell how planets are different. Use characteristics of insects and bugs to explain differences and similarities
Evaluation	Engage in formal and informal learning by assessing scientific knowledge, understanding, application, and abilities	What students have learned about planets, solar system, and insects and bugs

all components might need to be used. Teachers need to decide what is best for their students' needs.

THE 8-E MODEL

Vang (2006) described the 8-E model of instruction, which contains strategies for teaching science to limited English proficient (LEP) students. The components of the 8-E model are *expectation, engagement, exploration, explanation, elaboration, experience, enjoyment, and evaluation.* Vang gave detailed information about the teacher's roles, the student's roles, and the focus of both in the learning cycle in this model. To make science lessons fun and entertaining, teachers must be able to demonstrate at least three kinds of knowledge: content knowledge, curriculum knowledge, and pedagogical knowledge.

Possessing content knowledge means that teachers have sufficient knowledge of the subject matter to plan and design a lesson based on science content standards. Curriculum knowledge is the knowledge of the way in which the subject matter is organized around the curricular content used for each grade level; it enables teachers to embed or connect science with other academic subjects. Teachers have pedagogical knowledge if they know appropriate ways to guide students into an understanding of the subject matter based on prior knowledge, learning experience, and scientific practices. These three types of knowledge and their associated skills are essential in Vang's model.

The first component, *expectation*, is the very first step in teaching. Vang asserted that setting up clear teaching and learning expectations for teachers and students is the key to making science lessons fun, intriguing, and entertaining. Teachers must facilitate and guide the scientific processes to help students achieve the learning objective stated in the lesson plan. Clear learning expectations enhance effective teaching by boosting students' motivation to excel and to develop creative thinking toward individual constructivism.

The second component, *engagement*, is the gateway into scientific learning processes. Vang explained that teachers must use an inquiry-based approach to engage students in science. Beginning with an intriguing thought, question, or statement makes students wonder about science, and science questions arouse students' curiosity. Introductory engagement is powerful for the anticipatory set. Teachers should not teach a lesson if students are not ready to go along. Time is valuable, but students' minds, attitudes, and readiness to learn are much more important than time because reteaching the same concepts will cost more time in the long run. Use engagement to prepare students and make sure they are ready for teaching and learning before tapping them into the learning objective.

Third, *exploration* is the investigative, imaginative process by which students discover new ideas that may support or may not support their prior knowledge and conceptual framework. Despite differences in linguistic abilities and skills, most students can explore science concepts through observing, classifying, communicating, measuring, predicting, and interpreting along with hands-on and minds-on activities. Exploration can be very productive if teachers provide physical examples, such as fossils, plants, lab experiments, specimens, data, or premade materials. In some cases, exploration is a real eye opener because students learn by doing, and what they learn could be shocking or surprising to them.

Fourth, *explanation* is the meat of teaching and learning science. It is based on what students did in the exploration stage. Teachers must guide this process carefully to allow students the opportunity to suggest their own explanations for what they have observed, examined, or collected. Keep in mind that some students are more articulate than others. Teachers may ask students to jot down notes or findings on paper and read them as a way of sharing with others. Or teachers may ask students to explain what they explored in brief oral and/or verbal form. Keep in mind that younger children may not be able to express details verbally.

Fifth, *elaboration* is a critical stage at which teachers need to show caring, understanding, and support for students. Not all students will be able to elaborate in detail about their exploration and explanation. Teachers' guidance is crucial in this process. For instance, teachers may need to go deeper with the concepts or provide guidance to help students differentiate, compare, contrast, explain, or combine new ideas. As Vang (2006) stated, teachers cannot assume that students comprehend unless they can demonstrate that comprehension; therefore teachers need to provide means for students to demonstrate their scientific discoveries. The means will be different at each grade level and will depend on the nature of the lesson.

Sixth, *experience* means providing students with firsthand and direct experiences, such as collecting leaves in the school yard, visiting the school garden, visiting a museum, going on a field trip, planting seeds, climbing hills, walking a trail, observing ants, measuring desks, recording data, throwing a ball, and graphing M&M colors. Experience also includes scientific investigations and experiments by which students test their hypotheses. Science concepts are best learned from experiments, not from books or teachers (Vang, 2006). Most importantly, scientific experiences must be rich, meaningful, and cognitively constructive. To achieve this, teachers may have to think outside the box to make science experiential.

Seventh, the element of *enjoyment* means that learning science is fun, and teachers should enjoy teaching science as well. To make it fun, intriguing, and entertaining, teachers have to think creatively and positively about how to make scientific practices appropriate, relevant, and conducive to learning. No doubt enjoyment can produce intrinsic and extrinsic learning motivations, and self-desire can bring great energy and enthusiasm to the critical thinking process, making learning fun, enjoyable, exciting, and refreshing (Vang, 2006). Creativity is what makes classroom teachers the greatest educators for their students. Even if inquiry activities are dirty, messy, smelly, or intimidating to some, teachers should use them to create a learning environment that is positive, inquisitive, and inclusive so all students can enjoy developing social interaction skills and academic language (Vang, 2006).

Finally, the eighth element, *evaluation*, is the closure of an inquiry activity and has a few purposes in the scientific practices. Evaluation allows teachers to check for understanding of the learning objectives, to share feedback between teachers and students, to recap key concepts in the lesson, to evaluate the effectiveness of their teaching, to affirm and reaffirm teaching and learning expectations, and to assess student learning. Keep in mind that the goal of science education is the construction of knowledge. Teachers can design teacher-made tests based on the content covered to evaluate student learning outcomes, or they can ask questions to check for comprehension, depending on the grade level. Evaluation is an essential part of reflective teaching that provides teachers with academic information so they can plan, change, grow, and glow along with students.

Furthermore, teachers can add an *independent practice* component to the 8-E model to help students stay focused and interested in learning more science concepts inside and outside the classroom. Independent practice may include short assignments, mini projects, additional reading, study guides, or reinforcement activities. These activities have to be guided discovery or inquiry based. Independent practice could be costly and some families may not have the financial resources for major projects. Teachers need to consider this limitation if independent practice is required. For younger children, independent practice must be age appropriate.

LEARNING CYCLE IN SCIENCE PROCESS

Inquiry teaching cannot be successful without scientific processes and the learning cycle. Both the 5-E and the 8-E models recognize the important roles of teachers and students in the learning cycle. However, there is no perfect role for teachers and students to play at all times, and all roles have to be flexible and accommodating. Understanding these roles generates a positive and active learning environment. Teaching and learning science can be complex and boring when teachers control everything and students are the observers or vice versa. Improper understanding of roles can lead to loss of interests, incomplete assignments, and lack of class participation (Vang, 2006). Table 5.5 explains the specific roles of teachers and students and indicates how both can work together as a team in the learning cycle. Keep in mind that teachers are the guides who will show students every step of the way, and students are learners who will ask for assistance when they are not sure about something. Sometimes these roles could be reversed depending on the grade level of students.

FOCUSING ON CONTENT INSTRUCTION

Inquiry science has to be based on content standards. Teachers need to pay close attention to the way they apply science content in planning their instructional practices. Lesson plans should be designed to cover content knowledge. Some teachers fail to recognize how important the science concepts required by content standards for each grade level really are. Teachers can navigate how to teach

Table 5.5 Roles in the Learning Cycle

Component	Teachers' Role	Students' Role	Focus of both
Expectation	Set up clear learning expectation and learning objectives for each lesson plan design. Expectation + objective = goal	Expect to understand the expectation and learning objective in the lesson and follow instructions.	Aim at same expectation, learning objective, and goal.
Engagement	Issue mentally challenging question to prompt inquiry. Enable students. Maintain good rapport with students at all times.	Ask, discuss, share the problem. Apply prior knowledge.	Read to tap into lesson and delivery of instruction.
Exploration	Use indirect approaches with support system and materials available. Give praise, encouragement, hints, or clues as necessary. Respond to questions and provide focus.	Be an active participant, engage in activity, collect data, and interpret own work and ask questions for assistance.	Facilitating, guiding, modeling, and sorting out information.
Explanation	Clarify comprehension, introduce new concepts, use appropriate teaching methodologies, and include hands-on and minds-on activities.	Learn and explain own understanding in scientific terms, apply first-hand experiences, and encode and decode new information or concepts.	Engage in discussion, clarification, questioning the answers and investigation process.
Elaboration	Provide assistance, explain procedural guidelines, guide students, and facilitate the scientific processes: Observing, communicating, classifying, measuring, relating, applying, predicting, analyzing, inferring, concluding, and taking beyond.	Expand and extend first hand experiences to gain deeper knowledge to build new concepts and develop new questions.	Reflect and review firsthand experiences and respond to unanswered or new questions.
Experience	Encourage students to conduct experiments or investigations, inspire their scientific knowledge and skills to go beyond what is learned, and supervise investigative processes.	Use learned experiences to compare and contrast, apply scientific processes to explain, elaborate, and explore the results.	Connect outside experiences with inquiry activities and textbook information.
Enjoyment	Manage, monitor, supervise, assist, guide, and facilitate students throughout the scientific processes, and allow students to work individually and cooperatively. Allow flexibility, adaptation, and accommodation.	Engage in inquiry activities, use scientific processes, conduct experiment and investigation, and work individually or cooperatively in groups.	Respect independent work or group work; engage in inquiry activities' provide support, guidance, direction; and follow guidelines. Minimize interruption.

(Continued)

Component	Teachers' Role	Students' Role	Focus of both
Evaluation	Monitor student work, evaluate progress, prescribe test, reflect on student learning outcome, give feedback, emphasize key concepts, make adaptations, and promote academic language and science literacy.	Take test, assess own learning, apply knowledge and skills, relate learned experiences to real life, use academic language and scientific process to answer questions.	What was taught is what was tested. Use teacher-made test to evaluate student progress or learning outcome.

Note. Information from "New Pedagogical Approaches for Teaching Elementary Science to Limited English Proficient Students," by C.T. Vang, 2006, *Multicultural Education*, 13(3).

science concepts by following grade-level progression as indicated in Figure 5.1 or they can demonstrate that their instruction is based on content standards by teaching from general concepts to specific concepts or from basic concepts to advanced concepts as shown in Figure 5.2. Failing to follow these requirements could make teaching and learning science concepts irrelevant to the implementation of appropriate content required for each grade level. In other words, teachers may design lesson plans that are too high or too low for a grade level. For instance, teaching gravity to K-3 students is inappropriately high because most students at that level cannot comprehend the concept without prior knowledge or adequate preparation. Most importantly, teachers must connect science concepts sequentially and orderly to guide the scientific processes. For instance, teachers must teach the concept of volcanoes before teaching the concept of eruption.

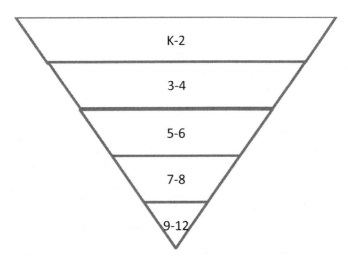

Figure 5.1 *Grade-level progression in teaching science concepts*

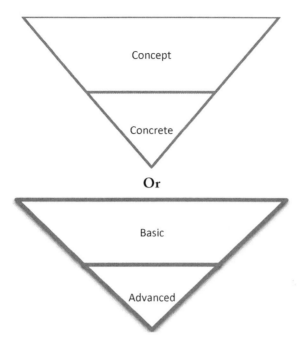

Figure 5.2 *Progression in teaching science content*

The key here is to connect scientific concepts as much as possible to make learning meaningful based on a continuous approach rather than teaching whatever the teachers can think of.

SCIENCE LESSON PLANNING

Inquiry teaching requires careful and thoughtful planning and organization. Knowing how to do science lesson planning is highly valuable in promoting effective teaching and learning. There is a difference between lesson planning and lesson plan design. Lesson plan design is the arrangement of the content of a lesson using the instructional models, such as five-step, three-step, or direct instruction. Lesson planning adds a number of components necessary for delivering the instruction. Teachers must think not only about what content needs to be covered, but also how the content of each lesson should be taught through scientific processes and how students should learn the content. Figure 5.3 illustrates some basic ideas for teachers to consider when doing science lesson planning. Remember, all of these steps are not needed in every lesson plan. Teachers need to devise their own ideas how to do lesson planning for each grade level, guided by the suggestions in Figure 5.3, recognizing that not all grade levels require the

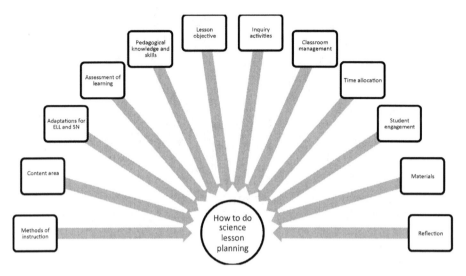

Figure 5.3 *Items included in lesson planning*

same lesson planning. Lesson planning takes time, effort, energy, and curricular knowledge. Reading the teacher's manuals may help; however, the premade lesson plans in the teacher's manual may not be aligned with or consistent with content standards; they may not cover the specific content that should be taught. Lesson planning must meet the needs of students.

Thinking through the components of lesson planning is crucial. For instance, "methods of instruction" means that teachers need to think about how the method chosen will work with students, what method best fits the students, what method contributes to good classroom management, what method fits the time allocated, what method the teachers are comfortable with, and what variations of the method can be used during instruction. All these factors contribute to the effectiveness of a lesson plan design; otherwise, poor lesson planning results in poor instructional practices.

SCIENCE LESSON FORMATS

Inquiry teaching can be done in any lesson format as long as teachers know how to include inquiry activities for investigation and experimentation. Regardless of the lesson plan format teachers use to teach science concepts, students will not gain science knowledge and skills constructively without hands-on and minds-on activities. Inquiry instruction requires activities that engage students in the inquiry processes. Today's lesson plans are scripted and teacher centered. Teachers in

Table 5.6 Basic Components of Selected Lesson Plan Formats

Direct Instruction	Guided Inquiry	Five-Step Lesson Plan	Three-Step Lesson Plan
1. Learning objectives	1. Learning objectives	1. Anticipatory set	1. Into
2. Materials	2. Materials	2. Instruction	2. Through
3. Engagement or motivation	3. Engagement or motivation	3. Guided practice	3. Beyond
4. Learning procedures: scripted presentation, guided practice, independent practice, evaluation and closure	4. Learning procedures: inquiry activities, observation, data collection, data analysis, conclusion, evaluation and closure	4. Closure/evaluation/ assessment	
5. Assessment	5. Assessment	5. Independent practice	

Grades K-3 need to be creative in teaching science concepts to students because scripted instruction does not benefit students, and for Grades 4-6, teachers need to incorporate inquiry activities that inspire students intrinsically and extrinsically.

Contemporary instructional lesson plan formats are the five-step lesson, three-step lesson, direct instruction, guided inquiry instruction, English Language Development Instruction (ELD), and Specially Designed Academic Instruction in English (SDAIE). Table 5.6 outlines some of these formats. Other instructional strategies are considered to be intervention methods, such as Response to Instruction (RTI), Sheltered Instruction Observation Protocol (SIOP), Cooperative Learning, Open Reading Court, Total Physical Response (TPR), English as a Second Language (ESL), Teach English to Speakers of Other Languages (TESOL), and KWL. Some of these are being used as instructional practices to target specific needs; however, they are more appropriate for intervention than for instructional practices for the whole class. Vang (2010) illustrated how these different teaching strategies can be beneficial in teaching as noted in Table 5.7.

Table 5.7 Intervention Strategies Used as Teaching Strategies

Acronym	Strategy	Example of Use
TI	Thematic instruction	Organizing or framing instruction around key areas, concepts, or ideas to make connections
CALLA	Cognitive academic language approach	Involve topics, academic language skills, and language acquisition
ILA	Integrated language arts	Whole-language approach to learn new language

(Continued)

Acronym	Strategy	Example of Use
5Ws + H	What, when, where, who, why, and how	Question-based instruction, inquiry instruction, or investigative approach
DI/EDI	Direct instruction/explicit direct Instruction	Systematic approach, one-model-fits-all, use in all subject matter teaching
ELD	English language development	Transitional bilingual education programs without primary language (L1) support
ESL	English as a second language	ELD or SDAIE instruction or whole-language approach
K-W-L	What I *know*, what I *want* to learn, and what I *learned*	Student-centered approach
LEA	Language experience approach	Used mostly in language arts for writing and reading based on student's experiences and prior knowledge
PQ5Rs	Preview, question, read, recite, reflect, review, and respond	Used in all subject matter teaching and with any instructional methodologies
PR	Preview and review	Engage prior knowledge and tap into lesson plan objective
CL	Cooperative learning	Groups, centers, or stations
PW	Process writing	A process of writing or POWERS: Prewrite, organize, write, edit, rewrite, and submit
RT	Reciprocal teaching	Question-based approach used mostly in language arts for reading: 4-step process: summary, clarification, question, and prediction
RTI	Response to intervention	Intervention strategy to identify at-risk students, SIOP components, 2-tier approaches, adaptations, modifications, accommodations, and intervention
SIOP	Sheltered instruction observation protocol	RTI components, ELD components, SDAIE components, SMART Plan, and intervention
Scaffolding	Backing out or withdrawal strategies, or building skills as layers or levels	Use in all subject matter teaching, ELD, SDAIE, TESOL, ESL, SEI, and others
SDAIE	Specially designed academic instruction in English	ELD instruction with primary language support (L1)
SEI	Sheltered English instruction	ESL, TESOL, ELD, or SDAIE instruction
TESOL	Teach English to speakers of other languages	ESL , ELD, or SDAIE instruction
TNA	The natural approach	Used mostly in language arts
TPR	Total physical response	Music, dance, physical education, or body movement
GI	Guided inquiry instruction	Student-centered, investigative instruction, question-based

Table 5.8 Example of English Language Development Instruction Lesson Plan

Procedural Process	Key Concepts	Examples of Activity
Title:	Volcano Eruption	What causes volcanoes to erupt?
Grade level:	4th grade	
ELD levels:		Lesson is appropriate for grade level and learning ability level of ELD students.
__ Beginning	Choose an ELD level	
__ Early intermediate		
__ Intermediate		Instruction is in English without primary support (L1).
__ Early advanced		
__ Advanced		Use thematic unit or 2–3 day lesson plan.
Date:	December 10, 2009	
Time:	15–30 minutes	
ELD standards	4th grade, ELD 1.2 or 4.1	Choose one appropriate language arts standard.
Content area standards	Link to other content area standards	Science or language arts.
Learning objective	List one specific objective or outcome.	Students will learn about volcano eruption.
Key concepts or vocabulary:	Magma, lava, eruption, explosion, temperature, fire, burning, gas	List all vocabulary on the board and recite words and definitions with students.
Materials or resources	Video, handouts, worksheet, transparencies, books, crayons, markers, and posters.	Prepare hands-on and minds-on activities for students to do in class.
Prior knowledge	Engagement, prompt, props, and intriguing questions.	Ask students to share about volcano eruption before tapping into lesson.
Reflection or reteaching	What is fun? What do students like best? Any changes?	Revise lesson plan and include new ideas for next time.

Tables 5.8 and 5.9 present samples of ELD and SDAIE lesson plan formats. ELD and SDAIE lesson plan formats are beneficial to all learners, but other lesson plan formats may not benefit ELL and SN students because they lack adaptations, modifications, accommodations, and intervention components. For science, any lesson plan format should be used with careful considerations due to the diverse needs and abilities of students.

LESSON PLAN ADAPTATIONS

For inquiry science, adapting lesson plans should not be a problem at all. In California, lesson plan adaptations are required by state mandates for all academic instruction designed for students in multicultural classrooms to target the needs

Table 5.9 Example of Specially Designed Academic Instruction in English Lesson Plan

Procedural Process	Key Concepts	Examples of Activity
Title:	Create or choose a title for the lesson	Where do animals find food to eat?
Subject area:	Science	Life science.
Grade level:	4th grade	
Date:	December 12, 2009	
Time:	15–30 minutes	
Grade-level content area standard	4th grade life science, standard 2a. Food chain or food web.	Introduce students to food chain or food web.
ELD levels: __ Beginning __ Early intermediate __ Intermediate __ Early advanced __ Advanced	Choose ELD level to focus on, even though not all students are at the same level.	For 4th grade science, the lesson should be appropriate for intermediate level; however, take the lesson from concept to concrete.
ELD standards linkage	4th grade, ELD 1.2 or 4.1.	Vocabulary building and writing sentences.
Learning objective	List one specific objective or outcome.	Students will learn about basic food chain or food web and create a food chain using plants, animals, and people.
Key concepts	Herbivores, carnivores, omnivores, decomposers, producers, and consumers.	Ask students to give examples for each group or write a sentence about each group.
Materials or resources	Video, handouts, worksheet, transparencies, books, crayons, markers, and posters.	Prepare hands-on activity for students to do in class with these materials.
Prior knowledge	Engagement, prompt, props, and intriguing questions.	Tap background knowledge into lesson and learning objective.
Procedures or steps	List specific steps for instruction: preview, review, share, and then move into lesson plan.	What is food chain? What is food web? What is the difference between the two?
Scaffolding activities: 1. Modeling 2. Bridging 3. Contextualization 4. Schema building 5. Representation of text 6. Metacognitive development 7. Summative assessment 8. Alternative assessment	Follow scaffolding techniques and procedural process.	Give and provide students with examples according to each step and follow through.
Independent practice	Use book or computer for in-class assignment and use worksheet for homework assignment.	Select a specific area for further practice: Creating a more complex food chain.
Reflection or reteaching	What is fun? What do students like best? Any changes?	Revise lesson plan and include new ideas for next time.

of ELL and SN students. It is not easy for teachers to do two or three lesson plans at once or to look at the specific needs of ELL and SN students while teaching a lesson. But teachers need to consider their challenges and obstacles as part of science lesson planning in order to include all learners. Time constraints might limit teachers' ability to reach out to all learners in the classroom; however, that should not be an excuse. Therefore, to do adaptations for ELL and SN students, teachers may have to find extra time to provide ELL and SN students with equity of instruction.

One of the ways is to adapt the whole lesson for everyone instead of adapting portions of it for one or a few students. Using hands-on and minds-on activities is such an adaptation. Firsthand experience is an adaptation from which all students benefit. It benefits everyone because it allows teachers to focus on one lesson for the whole class. If teachers choose to make separate adaptations for ELL and SN students, they need to find a way to do so academically; otherwise, adaptation is no different from giving needy students lip service without academic substance. Teachers must know the difference between accommodations, modifications, adaptations, and interventions as described in Table 5.10. These key words are important for devising lesson plans that serve all students.

Table 5.10 Examples of Lesson Plan Adaptations

Accommodations	Modifications	Adaptations	Interventions
Use list of vocabulary words, preview, review, engage prior knowledge, think-pair-share, pair-up, grouping, cooperative learning, ELD lesson, SDAIE lesson, scaffolding	Definitions, word bank, read out loud, choral reading, repetition, recitation, review, pair up, graphic organizers, graph sheet, grid, group activity, cooperative learning, video clips	Use realia, pictures, placards, word cards, model sentence, use sentence frame, cloze, cognitive learning, KWL, graphic organizer, primary language support, bilingual materials, practicing, exercise, drills, make a word dictionary	Use individualized instruction, one-on-one conference, pullout, center instruction, small-group activity, special lesson plans, formal and informal assessment
Use scaffolding, reciprocal teaching, open court reading, bridging, connecting, contextualization, schema building, thematic approaches, text representation	Use BIA, TA, translator, interpreter, bilingual materials, RTI or SIOP approaches, ELD/SDAIE approaches, TESOL, ESL, SEI approaches, slow pacing, clear enunciation, slow speech, wait time, parts to whole or whole to parts, TPR	Use hands-on and minds-on activities, practicing, drills, exercises, review, study guide, modeling, guided practices, examples, samples, demonstration, grade and age appropriate materials, illustrations, processing information, check for understanding, white boards	Use 180 program, reading clinician, pullout, ability grouping, ELD rotation, cluster grouping, paraprofessional assistance, RTI, SIOP

SCIENCE QUESTION STRATEGIES

Inquiry instruction is much more about questioning the answers than knowing the answers. For science, questioning is a powerful tool for teachers and students because great questions will lead the investigation and experimentation throughout all the scientific processes. Teachers must design key questions to help students develop inquisitive techniques to find meaningful questions to guide their scientific practices. Asking the right question triggers students' thought processes or makes students curious about the inquiry activities. In short, great questions usually produce great results.

There are different questioning strategies teachers can use to engage students in learning science as inquiry. Teachers can use *focus questions, closed questions,* and *open-ended questions* for the following reasons:

- To make students curious and eager to learn
- To motivate students to learn
- To boost students' interest
- To assess students' prior knowledge and skills
- To start an inquiry process
- To guide group discussion, explanation, communication, or conclusion
- To change the investigation and experimentation variables
- To clarify key concepts, ideas, or scientific knowledge and skills
- To reflect upon inquiry activities
- To give feedback to guide the processes

Throughout the inquiry processes, teachers should respond to student ideas, questions, concerns, or issues promptly and strategically because responsive guidance usually leads by great and inspirational questions and answers. Teachers must also learn to accept, reject, alter, or mediate questions with students; otherwise, the processes of repeating, reinforcing, clarifying, applying, summarizing, and concluding could be confusing and awkward. In other words, teachers need to find ways to develop their own questioning and responding strategies that are appropriate for the grade level or the kind of inquiry activities prescribed for students. Teachers can use the 5-E model or 8-E model to develop their questioning techniques. Table 5.11 demonstrates examples of closed and open-ended questions to help teachers create their own strategies.

Keep in mind that questions must be appropriate for the grade level and age of students. Teachers should avoid complex questions for K-2 students, perhaps using the 5Ws+H approach with simple questions for simple answers indeed of demanding detailed explanations. Moreover, some students cannot answer "why" or "why not" questions, and teachers need to model these types of questions for them.

Table 5.11 Samples of Inquiry Questions

Question	Closed strategy	Open-ended strategy	Inquiry Purposes
Do you like the taste of fortune cookies?	✓		
How do you describe the taste in your mouth?		✓	
What are the animals doing?	✓		Observing
What are the objects doing?	✓		Observing
Have you seen different animals or plants before?	✓		Observing, engaging
What do you see the animals doing in the picture?	✓		Observing, analyzing
How can you tell if animals are the same or different?		✓	Observing, comparing, contrasting, inferring,
What can you tell about the objects in the picture?		✓	Observing, inferring, concluding
What have you just observed?		✓	Explaining, inferring, concluding, elaborating,
What objects do you think will float or sink in water?		✓	Analyzing, observing, inferring, explaining, elaborating, concluding
How do you describe each animal?		✓	Observing, communicating, explaining, elaborating, analyzing, inferring, concluding
Where do these animals stay at night?		✓	Observing, predicting, hypothesizing, inferring
How can you tell the object is moving or not moving?		✓	Observing, analyzing, explaining, elaborating, experimenting, inferring, concluding

For inquiry activities, teachers can use both closed and open-ended questioning strategies; however, closed questions are generally good for short answers, like Yes or No, and open-ended questions are better for explaining, describing, elaborating, inferring, observing, or analyzing because they allow students to tell in their own words. Both strategies should be used to promote inquiry learning and either applied according to each individual student's needs. Some students like short answers and others like long answers depending on the grade level and the age of the students. Remember, scientific guidance depends on asking the right question, and that is the heart of inquiry teaching.

SUMMING UP

This chapter prepares teachers to focus on inquiry instruction based on content standards to provide effective and quality teaching for all learners in the multicultural classroom. Teaching science concepts needs to be well-organized and well-structured from the beginning all the way to the end. Students need to learn from broad concepts to concrete as required by science content standards. Teachers should avoid using improvised and impoverished inquiry instruction because it is not content based. Moreover, inquiry instruction without hands-on and minds-on activities is meaningless to students.

Scientific processes are essential in inquiry teaching. This discussion of the 5-E and 8-E models should enable teachers to recognize students' roles and teachers' roles in the learning cycle and promote inquiry teaching and use of inquiry questioning strategies. Teachers should develop their own strategies to guide their students and to respond to students' concerns during inquiry investigation and experimentation. Asking good questions serves many meaningful purposes in inquiry based-instruction. Teachers can strategize appropriate closed or open-ended questions for each grade.

Focusing on inquiry instruction allows teachers to think about science lesson planning and lesson plan formats in teaching science concepts. Different groups of students may require different lesson plan formats or lesson planning. There is no best way or one-model-fits-all format for every single science lesson plan. Creativity is what makes teachers the greatest educators. For this reason, instructional preparation and planning are essential ingredients in providing effective inquiry teaching.

CHAPTER SIX

Organize Inquiry Instruction

The important thing in science is not so much to obtain new facts as to discover new ways of thinking about them.

—William Lawrence Bragg

INTRODUCTION

Teacher preparation plays a major role in how the contents of a lesson plan are going to be taught to students. Teacher readiness makes a whole lot of difference in preparing to teach science, and teacher planning contributes to the effective teaching and learning of each lesson. In earlier chapters, teachers were introduced to the nature of science, how children think and learn, science processes of learning, linking concepts to standards, and focus on inquiry instruction. This chapter gives a comprehensive overview of how teachers can organize the learning environment to prepare students for inquiry instruction, what teachers need to do to design quality lesson plans, and how teachers can engage children in learning science. Teaching science is not about what the teachers want to do, but it is more about how the teachers get the students to become involved. That is determined by how teachers organize inquiry instruction.

PREPARE TO TEACH SCIENCE

Teachers need to carefully plan the contents of their science lessons for the grade level they are teaching. Whether the teaching plan is hourly, daily, weekly, monthly, quarterly, or yearly, science teachers need to plan inquiry-based instruction and take multicultural factors and issues into consideration. First, teachers must know the types of students in their classes. They have to know the students' reading levels, math levels, science levels, and maturity levels. Knowing these factors contribute to the effectiveness of teachers' preparation and planning, enabling them to select science content, learning objectives, lesson modalities, and inquiry activities that are appropriate, meaningful, and purposeful for these students. Second, teachers need to allow time for careful preparation because early lessons require thorough planning to set a teaching stage for the rest of the year. Even if things change and adjustments have to be made, teacher planning plays a key role in students learning science in the multicultural setting.

Third, for teaching science, teacher planning should include physical and mental readiness, planning specific science lessons, creating an inclusive learning environment, understanding classroom management and student discipline, health and safety precautions, and mastery of instructional processes such as delivery of instruction, implementation, evaluation, giving feedback, and reflective teaching. All these are necessary preparations for designing inquiry lesson plans that engage children in learning science.

Lastly, teachers must remain flexible in their preparation and planning to accommodate unanticipated situations. They need not only an excellent plan A, but also a Plan B in case plan A does not work well. Table 6.1 presents the

Table 6.1 Domains of Psychosocial Learning

Domain	Associated Factors	Instructional Approaches
Cognitive	Comprehension, knowledge, skills, processing, and application	Knowing what and knowing how and expressing in written or verbal forms
Affective	Emotions, feelings, attitudes, personalities, behaviors, and values	Reflective responses to tasks, sharing with peers, interaction, communication, and expressing in verbal form
Psychomotor	Motor skills, coordination, comprehension, expression, and muscular control	Diagramming, mapping, manipulation, connection, idea web, and application
Social	Basic interpersonal communication skills, sharing, socialization, citizenship, and cooperation	Cooperative learning, teamwork, group activity, role and responsibility, and project
Academic	Cognitive academic language proficiency, literacy, constructivism, and context-reduced	Logical, arbitrary, social, physical, and constructive knowledge

domains of psychosocial learning that can influence teacher's preparation and planning and shows the instructional approaches for each.

INCLUDE PRIOR KNOWLEDGE

Experience makes a big difference in learning science. Assessing students' prior knowledge as early as possible helps teachers prepare to teach science concepts effectively. For inquiry teaching, students' prior knowledge needs to be taken into careful consideration. Not all children possess the prior knowledge required for the content of a lesson plan; however, as mentioned earlier, all children have some kind of science prior knowledge regardless of their cultural background. Teachers need to know students' prior knowledge in order to select the most appropriate science knowledge for instruction. Teachers need to pay close attention to the concepts and principles of the content standards because some prior knowledge is needed in these areas, as shown in Figure 6.1. Knowing students' prior knowledge also enables teachers to adjust the design of a lesson plan to meet the academic challenges students may encounter as they go through the scientific processes. Most importantly, helping students build on their prior knowledge is what connects science to real-life experiences, and at the same time it allows students to construct new knowledge to deal with conceptual change.

GET READY PHYSICALLY AND MENTALLY

The physical and mental readiness of teachers is important in preparing, planning, and organizing for teaching and learning science. Physical readiness refers to environmental factors, such as the learning climate, the setup of the classroom,

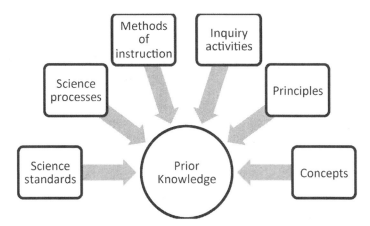

Figure 6.1 *Prior knowledge is needed for science learning*

floor diagram, materials, supplies, seating charts, stations, centers, countertops, computer lab, sinks, drinking fountains, storage, animals, plants, textbooks, and writing materials. Being physically ready and organized for science teaching does not necessarily mean that teachers are ready to implement science mentally or academically. Mental readiness depends on the teacher's confidence, beliefs, competence, and comfort.

Mental readiness refers to how strongly teachers have developed their own science background to support instruction and carrying out scientific processes, such as asking questions, launching an investigation, and conducting experiments. Teachers cannot rely heavily on textbooks for answers to questions or to respond to students' inquiries. They need to have some science background, knowledge, and skills that make teaching and learning science as natural as possible.

For instance, teachers who lack science background have difficulty answering questions or taking students beyond the learning objectives. They can give only limited information to students and they may stall learning or introduce awkwardness because the teachers they do not feel comfortable teaching science. Moreover, inadequate science background knowledge keeps teachers from using creative approaches, and that makes teaching inquiry science ineffective. Teachers should need to have physical and mental readiness to teach science; otherwise, they will use fixed-strategy instruction that is not conducive to learning. Physical readiness or lack thereof may directly impact mental readiness and vice versa. Teachers must build on their strengths in science to teach science.

CREATE A POSITIVE LEARNING ENVIRONMENT

The classroom environment has to be multidimensional for all academic learning purposes. Regardless of its size, space, age, or other limitations, teachers must use whatever classroom they have to design a positive learning environment that promotes the academic development of all students. Classroom designs vary according to several factors; however, classroom design has a direct impact on teaching and learning. Teaching science requires an environment that is accommodating, suitable, hazard free, healthy, and safe for both teachers and students. Figures 6.2 and 6.3 illustrate good classroom design. Precautions must be taken, especially in the lower grades, that students are not exposed to dangerous objects or chemicals. Cluttered, bulky, disorderly, disorganized, and messy classrooms are not good for academic purposes. The ceiling, walls, and windows can serve meaningful purposes if used properly.

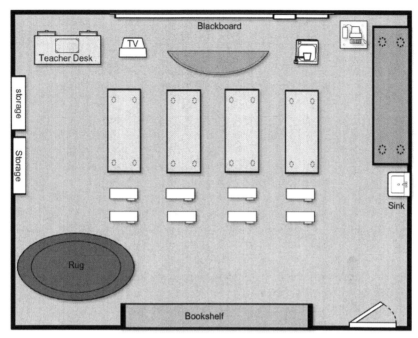

Figure 6.2 *Sample of classroom design*

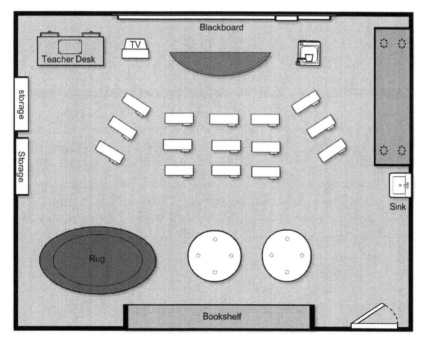

Figure 6.3 *Another sample of classroom design*

Table 6.2 Criteria for Creating a Positive Learning Environment

Criterion	Rationale
Learning centers or stations	Allocate centers or stations for learning activities, such as desks or mats
Movement or mobility	Teacher is able to move easily from group to group to monitor, supervise, or provide assistance
Smooth transitions	Make smooth transitions from one grouping to another, change from one task to another, coming in, going out, or moving from desks to mat
Accessibility	Have easy access to each other, books, materials, supplies, space
Management and discipline	Prevent disruption, correct misbehaviors, move students around, allow communication
Learning climate	Have positive psychosocial environment, consider students' and teachers' feelings, such as comfort, enjoyment, frustration, anger, boredom, security
Social interaction	Have social interaction with one another, allow opportunities for sharing, talking, discussing, processing
Class participation	Can involve, engage, participate, or support one another
Visibility	Can see all students, can visualize things on the board, have easy visibility
Auditory focus	Can hear students, can hear teachers, hear one another talking, asking
Academic success	Achieve tasks, learn well, allow time to engage in activity
Emergency	Know how to handle emergency situations, such as fire, flood, poison, choking, cutting, injury

Teachers have to arrange the contents of the classroom to meet professional and legal standards. Table 6.2 lists criteria for consideration when designing a positive learning environment. Keep in mind that the classroom is a formalized place where children can engage in different kinds of learning.

As Table 6.2 indicates, teachers can set up tables for science learning centers to allow students easy access for conducting inquiry activities, including hands-on and minds-on activities. Students can rotate from one center to another during scientific processes. Teachers have the option of putting students into small groups of three or four for each center or pairing them up to work on specific science activities. Another option is to group students and assign each group to a center to complete given tasks within the time allocated. In other words, teachers can assign students to groups and direct them to a center for appropriate investigation or experimentation.

Teachers can prescribe the same inquiry activity for all students and allow students to conduct their own investigations or experiments individually at their desks. For instance, teachers may give each student a rock to examine and observe and ask students to jot down their own descriptions of the rocks' characteristics. Science lesson plans can be taught in different formats: large group, small group, pairs, or individual student. The format depends on the lesson plan design. Remember, creating a positive learning environment that engages children in science promotes student learning and is especially important in a multicultural setting.

ORGANIZE SCIENCE MATERIALS

Being organized is a top priority for teachers. It gets lessons off to a good start and saves time. Finding time to prepare instruction can be challenging because teachers have so many things on their plates; they have administrative responsibilities, staff meetings, conferences, professional development, planning, and testing and they must provide discipline and classroom management, make copies, and grade papers. These requirements consume approximately 20% of teachers' personal time and at least two months of work each year. Organizing science materials, such as cutouts, premade props, rocks, minerals, charts, blocks, clocks, beakers, flasks, measuring cups and tapes, tweezers, droppers, balloons, plates, cups, rubber bands, solutions, brushes, telescopes, microscopes, masks, magnifying glasses, magnets, beads, coins, play dough, clay, crayons, scissors, rulers, gloves, goggles, children's books, handouts, chemicals, food colors, and more and labeling each box or container properly can take considerable time. If possible, teachers should also provide labels identifying types of inquiry activities or content standards. Although organizing takes time, it is time well spent because organized teachers are more effective than disorganized teachers; organization keeps teachers on track.

Besides keeping things organized, teachers need to label materials properly and make sure that all materials or supplies are clean and sterile, if necessary. Health and safety precautions are always number one considerations, and teachers are responsible for handling science materials properly. Also, they need to remind students of classroom rules and safety rules before and during science activities. Preventing injury is the highest priority, and all students have to be trained to be extra careful with any inquiry activities that require potentially dangerous materials such as sharp objects, chemical mixtures, dust, food ingredients, fire, candies, peanuts, and real animal tissues.

One cautionary note for teachers: when storing science materials under lock, latch, or combination locker, teachers must not ask students to remove materials from the shelves, cabinets, or boxes when the materials are needed; this will avoid accidental injuries. Teachers have to prepare materials for each inquiry activity prior to the delivery of instruction. It is poor professional judgment to ask classroom helpers to pass out science materials to students; however, students may help pass out common items such as papers, crayons, rulers, and balloons.

Cleaning up after inquiry activities is very important. Teachers often run out of time for cleanup and rush students to put science materials on their desks, on a counter top next to a sink, or on tables. Students sometimes rush to get in line for lunch or recess and do not wash their hands properly with soap. Keep in mind that hand sanitizers may kill germs, but they do not remove chemicals, stains, or dangerous substances. Hand sanitizers are chemicals, too, and children need to wash their hands after sanitizing. The bottom line is that teachers need to make sure all students clean their hands properly—no exceptions.

PREPARE INQUIRY INSTRUCTION

Teachers need to find their comfort zone in science in order to teach it effectively. Many do not believe they can deliver science instruction well for a variety of reasons. No doubt upper-grade science teachers know real science—biology, chemistry, botany, physics, and geology. Teaching science to K-6 students, however, mostly requires an understanding of science concepts, and how science works in the preliminary grades confuses some teachers. Others are fearful to teach science because it is their academic weak area, but that is perfectly all right. What teachers need to do is to start teaching science with their strengths.

To prepare inquiry instruction, teachers definitely need to do some ground work. They need to read the teacher's manual to make sure that each chapter or unit covers exactly what they want to teach and the content standards are included. Teachers need to evaluate every detail to make sure they understand how to implement the processes. If there are any confusing terms, meanings, or phrases, teachers should supplement the material with clear and concise details to make it appropriate for the grade level of their students.

Prepping includes checking science materials, supplies, equipment, handouts, and copies for independent practice in class, as presented in Figure 6.4. Teachers can organize the content of the lessons to fit the time allotted for each. Whether prior knowledge is there should be taken into account to make the scientific processes flow smoothly from the beginning all the way to the end. Prepping is part of planning, and teachers need to organize lesson plans so they connect to previous ones. Primary-grade teachers are required to teach three different areas of science content: life, earth, and physical. Planning helps teachers refocus on these standards.

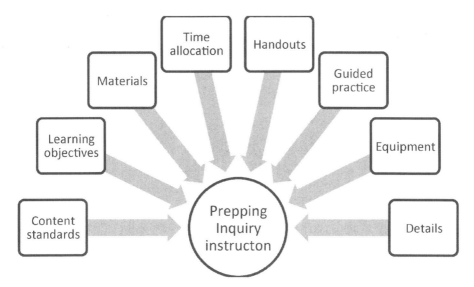

Figure 6.4 *Elements of prepping for inquiry instruction*

The number one cause of ineffective science teaching is the lack of practice. Not taking time to practice inquiry activities before teaching them is a costly mistake because it results in loss of time as due to disruptions, confusion, frustration, or fragmentation. These pitfalls can be avoided when teachers practice inquiry activities, making sure they are clear and the teachers have mastered the basic concepts and principles.

DESIGN INQUIRY LESSON PLANS

Today's teachers teach science concepts straight from the book because everything has been scripted for them. Nearly 80% of teachers use the direct instruction model to teach all academic subject matter to all students. This one-model-fits-all approach is not always conducive to learning, especially for science, because students do not learn by listening, but by doing. Some school districts have switched from direct instruction to the Sheltered Instruction Observation Protocol (SIOP) to include intervention strategies. Ideally, SIOP has the same mechanics as ELD and SDAIE lesson plan formats; however, the way SIOP is implemented requires much time and teachers do not have the luxury to allocate 45 to 60 minutes for each SIOP lesson. A normal inquiry lesson plan should last 30 to 45 minutes or less, depending on the nature of the lesson.

Table 6.3 Comparison of Direct Instruction, Guided Inquiry, and Five- and Three-Step Lesson Plan Formats

Direct Instruction	Guided Inquiry	Five-Step Lesson Plan	Three-Step Lesson Plan
Basic components:	Basic components:	Basic components:	Basic components:
1. Learning objectives	1. Learning objectives	1. Anticipatory set	1. Into
2. Materials	2. Materials	2. Instruction	2. Through
3. Engagement or motivation	3. Engagement or motivation	3. Guided practices	3. Beyond
4. Learning procedures: scripted presentation, guided practice, independent practice, evaluation and closure	4. Learning procedures: inquiry activities, observation, data collection, data analysis, conclusion, evaluation, and closure	4. Closure/ evaluation/ assessment	
5. Assessment	5. Assessment	5. Independent practice	

The essential ingredients of a science lesson plan are the title, content standards, learning objective, anticipatory set, instruction, guided practices, closure/evaluation/assessment, and independent practice, as shown in Table 6.3. In California the most common lesson format is the five-step lesson; however, teachers can use the three-step model or other models as well. Tables 6.4 and 6.5 present the formats for ELD and SDAIE, and Table 6.6 illustrates the SIOP format.

Keep in mind that teaching science as inquiry requires that teachers include inquiry processes for hands-on and minds-on activities. Without firsthand experiences, science can be difficult to explain to young children in primary grades; therefore, teachers must always allow students to discover, explore, and conduct investigations or experiments. In addition, science lesson plan design must be appropriate for the cognitive development of all learners at the particular grade and age.

ORGANIZE HANDS-ON MATERIALS

Teachers need to organize all materials needed for hands-on activities ahead of time to get ready for inquiry teaching. Hands-on materials might include samples, premade objects, charts, posters, rocks, magnets, crayons, owl pellets, skeleton, cutouts, placards, and more. Hands-on activities are designed to elicit scientific engagement and practice firsthand experience. Students should engage in hands-on activities to build their inquiry skills of observation, comparison, contrasting, classification, measurement, prediction, recording, communication,

Table 6.4 ELD Lesson Plan Format

Procedural Process	Key Concepts	Examples of Activity
Title:	Volcano Eruption	What causes volcanoes to erupt?
Grade level:	4th grade	
ELD levels:		Lesson is appropriate for grade level and learning ability level of ELD students.
__ Beginning	Choose an ELD level	
__ Early intermediate		
__ Intermediate		Instruction is in English without primary support (L1).
__ Early advanced		
__ Advanced		Use thematic unit or 2–3 day lesson plan.
Date:	December 10, 2009	
Time:	15–30 minutes	
ELD standards	4th grade, ELD 1.2 or 4.1	Choose one appropriate language arts standard.
Content area standards	Link to other content area standards.	Science or language arts.
Learning objective	List one specific objective or outcome.	Students will learn about volcano eruptions.
Key concepts or vocabulary:	Magma, lava, eruption, explosion, temperature, fire, burning, gas.	List all vocabulary on the board and recite words and definitions with students.
Materials or resources	Video, handouts, worksheet, transparencies, books, crayons, markers, and posters.	Prepare hands-on and minds-on activities for students to do in class.
Prior knowledge	Engagement, prompt, props, and intriguing questions.	Ask students to share about volcano eruptions before tapping into lesson.
Reflection or reteaching	What is fun? What do students like best? Any changes?	Revise lesson plan and include new ideas for next time.

Table 6.5 SDAIE Lesson Plan Format

Procedural Process	Key Concepts	Examples of Activity
Title:	Create or choose a title for the lesson	Where do animals find food to eat?
Subject area:	Science	Life science.
Grade level:	4th grade	
Date:	December 12, 2009	
Time:	15–30 minutes	
Grade-level content area standard	4th grade life science, standard 2a. Food chain or food web.	Introduce students to food chain or food web.

(Continued)

Procedural Process	Key Concepts	Examples of Activity
ELD levels: __ Beginning __ Early intermediate __ Intermediate __ Early advanced __ Advanced	Choose ELD level to focus on, even though not all students are at the same level.	For 4th grade science, the lesson should be appropriate for intermediate level; however, take the lesson from concept to concrete.
ELD standards linkage	4th grade, ELD 1.2 or 4.1.	Vocabulary building and writing sentences.
Learning objective	List one specific objective or outcome.	Students will learn about basic food chain or food web and create a food chain using plants, animals, and people.
Key concepts	Herbivores, carnivores, omnivores, decomposers, producers, and consumers	Ask students to give examples for each group or write a sentence about each group.
Materials or resources	Video, handouts, work-sheet, transparencies, books, crayons, markers, and posters.	Prepare hands-on activity for students to do in class with these materials.
Prior knowledge	Engagement, prompt, props, and intriguing questions.	Tap background knowledge into lesson and learning objective.
Procedures or steps	List specific steps for instruction: preview, review, share, and then move into lesson plan.	What is food chain? What is food web? What is the difference between the two?
Scaffolding activities: 1. Modeling 2. Bridging 3. Contextualization 4. Schema building 5. Representation of text 6. Metacognitive development 7. Summative assessment 8. Alternative assessment	Follow scaffolding techniques and procedural process.	Give students examples according to each step and follow through.
Independent practice	Use book or computer for in-class assignment and use worksheet for homework assignment.	Select a specific area for further practice: creating a more complex food chain.
Reflection or reteaching	What is fun? What do students like best? Any changes?	Revise lesson plan and include new ideas for next time.

Table 6.6 SIOP Lesson Plan Format

Procedural Process	Key Concepts	Examples of Activity
SMART	Acronym for SIOP	Specific or strategic, measurable, attainable, results-oriented, time-bound
School	Name of school	Lincoln Elementary School
Team	Specify SIOP team	Life science team
Date	Start date	July 4, 2012
Learning objective	What the team wants to achieve	Implement one or two specific learning needs, such as writing, reading, math skills
Language objective	Include steps, processes, resources, approaches	Short-term, long-term, systematic approach, implementation
Implementation team	Set up steps for implementation	Identify site team members
SIOP facilitator	Name a teacher	Mrs. Brown or Mr. Smith
Core teacher group	Consultation, support, resources	SIOP team includes teachers and school administrators
Resources	Books, paraprofessionals, time, room, equipment, parents	Identify resources to carry out the SIOP plan
Timeline	How long?	Steps need to be taken to reach the goal
Data analysis	Measure, collect data	Timeline to keep all data up to date
Team objectives	Action steps, who, timeframe, results	The findings or final outcomes for SIOP plan
Administrative comments	Principal, coordinator, lead teacher, team members	Review, evaluate, discuss, and reflect
RTI	Acronym for response to instruction or response to intervention	Accommodations, modifications, interventions

Note. Information from *Response to Intervention (RTI) and English Learners: Making it Happen,* by J. Echevarria and M. Vogt, 2011, Boston, Pearson Education.

making inferences, drawing conclusion, explanation, analysis, investigation, and experimentation. For instance, teachers can demonstrate a volcano eruption with a premade model of a volcano constructed out of clay or play dough, baking soda, vinegar, liquid soap, and food color or ketchup; they can explain each step of the eruption with these materials. After showing the model, teachers can pass out premade models to each group so students can recreate the experiment. Any hands-on activity requires specific written or verbal instructions or guidelines for students to follow. Teachers need to go over the processes of the activity with students and make sure all students follow every step in conducting the hands-on experiment—no exceptions. The correlation between active engagement and retention of information from instruction is high (see Table 6.7), and teachers need to make sure that students are actively taking part in the hands-on activity.

Table 6.7 Correlation Between Active Role in Learning and Retention

Role	Retention	Possible Explanations
Reading	10%	Students retain only what is relevant to their real-life experiences or interests.
Listening or hearing	20%	Students retain only what is interesting or exciting.
Seeing	30%	Students retain only the highlights of scenes, actions, and episodes that they like.
Combining listening and seeing	40%	Students retain only their favorite parts of the story that are relevant to their personal life experiences and what they can remember by encoding and decoding the messages.
Engaging in discussion or saying	70%	Discourse, conversation, or discussion allows students to retain more information by engaging in critical thinking and analysis of situations.
Experiencing, practicing, or doing hands-on activity	90%	Experiencing, doing, practicing, engaging in hands-on activity or firsthand experience enhances students' knowledge, skills, critical thinking, analysis, and logical application.

Note. Information from *Elementary Classroom Management* (3rd ed.), by C. M. Charles and G. W. Senter, 2002, Boston: Allyn and Bacon.

In the lower grades, written instruction is not as effective as verbal instruction because students cannot read well. However, students need to practice reading written instructions, so teachers should post them on the board, the overhead projector screen, or on the ELMO screen. With the verbal instructions in the lower grades, teachers have to model every single step with students. In the higher grades, written instructions are appropriate, but teachers must make sure no step is skipped and all procedural steps are followed carefully and strictly.

Hands-on activities require ongoing close monitoring and supervision to alleviate health and safety concerns. Teachers need to make sure students do not mishandle any samples and precautions are given before starting activities. For lower grades, teachers need to remind students that they cannot taste, sniff, or eat any samples unless doing so is completely safe, as might be the case with candies or fruits. Also, teachers need to make sure that no children get hurt while handling sharp or hard objects. Prevention is the key to safety and security.

Teachers are the ones who need to pass out hands-on materials to students to make sure nothing is broken or misplaced. Classroom helpers should be used sparingly and carefully unless the helpers are adults. Before passing anything out, teachers need to inspect all materials to ensure the safety of all learners. Teachers must instruct students on how to handle materials before, during, and after completing inquiry activities. Students are usually excited to do hands-on activities and they can easily forget to follow the rules. Therefore, teachers need to remain in control and facilitate the process at all times.

Furthermore, teachers need to make sure safety devices are available for students to use during inquiry activities, such as gloves, goggles, masks, brushes, sticks, toothpicks, plastic bags, construction paper, washing liquid, towels, wipes, hand sanitizers, cups, plates, and clocks. If teachers do not have the budget to purchase these materials, they can ask parents for donations to help with science activities. Often teachers have to provide these items themselves from home or other places, such as dollar stores, discount stores, or craft suppliers. Teachers need to avoid expensive inquiry activities unless they are absolutely necessary or the school can afford them.

USE MINDS-ON ACTIVITIES

Besides hands-on activities, teachers need to include minds-on activities to help students focus on learning scientific knowledge and acquiring skills. Minds-focused activities are thought-provoking tasks that engage students in critical thinking about their inquiry activities to improve their inquiry skills. For instance, after allowing students to observe different kinds of rocks for ten minutes, teachers ask them to jot down in their notebooks what they have just observed. Teachers can specifically ask students to use adjectives to describe the rocks, such as *coarse, round, smooth, angled, jagged, shiny, uneven, sharp, big, small, red, blue, white, black, yellow, green, white, dark,* or *brown.* These adjectives help students understand the characteristics of the rocks.

Moreover, teachers can ask for volunteers to describe the rocks verbally or to give details about the rocks. To engage all, teachers can take a little time to ask each student to explain the rocks in his or her own words. For the higher grades, teachers can use closed or open-ended questions to lead the inquiry processes and ask students to respond to these questions in writing.

In an earlier chapter, the scientific processes of the 5-E and 8-E models were discussed in detail; teachers can us these models to guide them in designing minds-on activities. These models follow a systematic approach; however, overusing them could result in boring and tedious lessons. Teachers need to prescribe lessons appropriately. Throughout the inquiry lesson, teachers must consistently implement these criteria: checking for understanding; monitoring student work; adjusting any difficulty problems; providing feedback; encouraging active participation at all times; stressing the importance of using kinetic, touch, auditory, and visual (KTAV) modes of learning; and applying appropriate strategies to meet diverse learners' needs. Minds-on activities promote science literacy, construction

Table 6.8 Engagement Level by Activity Type

Activity Type	Engagement Level	Sample of Tasks
Minds-on activities with concrete materials	High	Writing/jotting down thoughts and reflections in journal after conducting an experiment.
Hands-on activities with concrete materials	High	Firsthand experience, observing an experiment, or conducting an investigation in a group.
Visiting school garden	High	Observing different plants or vegetables, picking some leaves for experiment, or harvesting some fruits.
Computer lab activities	Medium to high	Logging onto websites to find out more about a specific topic or finding answers from computer.
Guided discussions	Medium to high	Participating in learning activities, asking questions, listening to peers, taking a role in the learning process, and working responsibly. Teacher is a guide or facilitator, not the leader and controller.
Reading activities	Low to medium	Reading aloud, silent reading, or teacher reads and students listen.
Listening and watching the teacher	Low	These types of activities barely engage students or hold their interest.
Listening only	Very low	These types of activities are considered disengaging.
Lecturing or preaching	Very low	These types of activities are not academically appropriate for Grades K-12.

of new knowledge and skills, and the development of inquiry skills. For this reason, Howe (2002) stressed that hands-on and minds-on activities engage students in science at any level of learning. Table 6.8 shows the level of engagement of various types of activities.

USE SENSIBLE ACTIVITIES

Even if teachers have the academic freedom to design any hands-on and minds-on activities they would like to see in class, they should think twice about the cost of the activity before implementing the lesson plan. Ideally, teachers do not have to do expensive hands-on and minds-on activities that require many materials. Teachers must try to be conservative in order to save money because resources for inquiry activities are scarce unless the school has a good-sized budget for science supplies and materials. This is especially important for new teachers, who are beginning from scratch. However, teachers can find science materials everywhere—at home, in the garage, in the school cafeteria, in the school supply room, and in the classroom. If the teacher's manual has a lesson plan that requires items teachers do not have and cannot afford, they can think creatively to modify the activity. Let's try a life science activity, for example, that measures heart beats. The manual calls for students to use stethoscopes to listen to their heartbeats, but few teachers have even one stethoscope. So teachers need to change the activity so they can measure heart beats without stethoscopes.

First, teachers ask students to find an area on their bodies where they can detect their own pulses, such as the wrist, the neck, the big thumb, or the clavicle. Once students locate the pulse on their bodies, teachers demonstrate how to count the beat for 30 seconds; they count their heartbeats and give the result to the students. Then teachers administer the inquiry activity, giving students specific instructions to follow. Everyone tries it together for 30 seconds.

After 30 seconds have elapsed, the teachers ask their students to jot down the total count of their heartbeats on paper and multiply that number by two to get the total number of heartbeats per minute. To engage students in scientific learning, teachers explain that the normal heartbeat rate for children is 130–160 whereas for adults the normal number of heartbeats per minute is 40–80; however, the number at any given time depends on the life situation. For instance, fear may cause the heartbeat to go up or stop, medication can slow down or increase the heartbeat, and relaxation could slow down the heartbeat as well. The adapted activity is as good as the real medical activity that requires the stethoscope.

As in this example, teachers need to think about ways to make their inquiry activities cheap, fun, and reasonable; otherwise, they may need a large science budget to purchase materials and supplies for hands-on and minds-on activities.

DEVELOP TECHNIQUES FOR IMPLEMENTING ACTIVITIES

Once teachers have organized inquiry instruction with careful planning and preparation, they need to figure out exactly how to implement their science activities in class. Even if they know how to use the lesson plan formats, sometimes things do not fall into place as planned. Developing techniques to engage students, to tap students into the learning objective, and to implement planned activities requires consistent and ongoing planning and preparation. Each teacher is unique, so lesson plan designs will differ. The way teachers introduce key concepts to students could determine how the process will go and how the teaching and learning will take place. Teachers should practice their art to find meaningful techniques for implementing science activities as inquiry.

Besides following the lesson plan format, answering the following questions about how they plan to introduce science concepts to their students will help teachers choose or develop appropriate and effective implementation techniques:

1. *Teacher planning and preparation*—Is the teacher ready to teach the lesson plan as designed? What needs to be changed, included, or excluded? Is there enough time to do all the parts?

2. *Student preparation*—Are students ready for the content in the lesson plan? How can students be prepared for instruction? Is the learning objective appropriate for the students? How should it be taught? How should the students learn?

3. *Preview and review of lesson plan*—What concepts should be previewed or reviewed with students? How can prior knowledge and skills be engaged in the lesson plan? What might students not already know?

4. *Set clear expectations for learning*—What is expected of students? What key concepts are important? How should each key concept be taught? What instruction is appropriate? What guided practice is needed?

5. *Science materials*—Are there enough science materials for all? How should materials be distributed or shared in group? How will student work be collected? What should be done during this activity?

6. *Implementing activities*—What is required first, second, third, and so on? What instructions or directions should be given to students? How should the activities be explained? What steps do all students need to know?

7. *Monitoring and supervising activities*—What should teachers do during the activity? What should be done if students do not understand the activity? Can adjustment be made accordingly? How can teachers facilitate the process? How can teachers keep things flowing smoothly? What happens if some students take too long? How can students be kept focused or engaged in the task?

8. *Providing support or assistance*—When is it necessary to provide support? What kind of assistance might students need? What could be too complicated or too easy for students to do? What should teachers do if many students have the same problems? How will management and discipline problems be addressed? How should students be praised or commended for doing hard work? How should student progress be affirmed and reaffirmed?

9. *Dealing with low and high achievers*—How should teachers prepare to deal with students who need more time? How should teachers deal with students who finish early? What adaptations, modifications,

accommodations, and interventions might be needed? How much time is needed for low achievers?

10. *Finishing up the activities*—When should the activity be concluded? What happens if many do not finish on time? When should students be given a signal to speed up the process? How can the teacher help students manage their time effectively? What should students do after the activity? What is next? How should this activity be brought to a close? How much time should be allowed for clean up?

11. *Putting things away*—When is it time to tell students to stop working? When is it time to tell students to clean up, wash hands, or to put everything away? How much time is needed for clean up?

12. *Assigning independent work*—Should independent work be required? How much homework should be required? How long is the independent work? When is it due? What chapter or pages in the book should students complete?

If grades are required, teachers also need to develop rubrics for grading or create grading scales for each assignment or activity. For science, most teachers do not use grading as motivation, but they use inquiry activities as tools for developing inquiry skills. However, some teachers use science vocabularies for quizzes or review tests. Teachers usually practice new concepts and terminologies with students through word banks or cloze techniques. Keep in mind that teachers are responsible for science literacy, and one of the ways to ensure students understand science language is through the inquiry approach with hands-on and minds-on activities.

USE A GROUP PROCESS

Teachers can implement hands-on and minds-on activities in class in different ways depending on the nature of each lesson; however, teachers have to decide what ways will benefit students the most, not what way is easiest for teachers to control. As mentioned earlier, the classroom environment has to be suitable for individual learning, group activity, and whole-class teaching. A typical classroom has desks, tables, centers, or stations for different academic activities. Sometimes, teachers want to group students to work together but space limits student engagement and participation. Sometimes, teachers may want to conduct a model experiment but cannot find appropriate space where all students can see. These are examples of academic hindrances inside the classroom that teachers need to overcome by determining ways to make teaching and learning science effective.

Using scientific processes is effective with the right prescriptions for inquiry activities. Not all activities require grouping. For K-6 science, teachers need to consider using student grouping in one of these formats:

1. *The whole-class format*—teachers lead, control, administer, lecture, demonstrate, guide, model, or facilitate instruction to the whole class.
2. *The individual format*—each student is on his or her own to conduct investigations and experiments using the scientific processes, or each student is working independently.
3. *The pair-up or think-pair-share format*—Two students work together to share, observe, analyze, classify, or compare objects or perform another inquiry activity together, or a pair of students works on an activity together and presents the findings to the class.
4. *The small-group format*—students are assigned to small groups for cooperative learning tasks and work through the scientific processes together, or a group of three or more students works collectively and cooperatively on a single task.
5. *The large-group format*—half of the class is assigned to work together cooperatively and collectively as a team; large-group teamwork is often used for big projects that require a lot of manpower, such as plowing land to make a garden.

In collaborative group structures or formats, each group member has a specific role; otherwise, not all students would receive the benefit of being in the group. Teachers need to make sure each member has a role; role assignments should be determined by the group members and must be rotated every once in awhile to allow different students to play different roles, as depicted in Figure 6.5. Also, teachers need to diversify groupings; otherwise, the same students will group themselves because they are friends. Teachers can assign students to groups randomly or orderly.

Remember, teachers have to facilitate learning for all students regardless of whether they are in a group. Conflict may occur in groups and without knowing it teachers cannot always intercept it in a timely manner. Students are children and sometimes they have attitudes that bother other members in the group. Teachers need to make sure all members have responsibilities and show respect for one another. To help students be productive in groups, teachers need to stress that building a learning community promotes student learning and scientific discourse, and moreover, collaboration makes learning science fun, enjoyable, and exciting.

As effective as grouping is, teachers should know the pitfalls of grouping. Some students could become dependent on the group for learning science

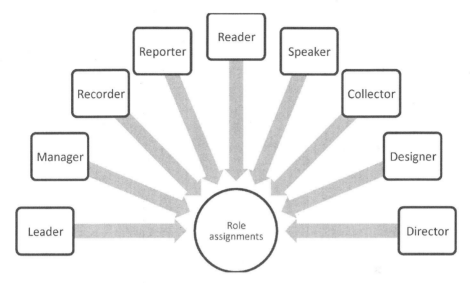

Figure 6.5 *Sample of role assignments*

concepts, and teachers need to educate students on the place of cooperation and competition in education. Cooperation takes place when they have to work collaboratively, collectively, and cooperatively in a group with others to get things done. Competition happens when students must learn how to compete within the cooperative process to get things done.

PLAN MANAGEMENT WELL

The key to providing students with quality instruction is classroom management. Without management, it does not matter how well teachers have planned to teach, engage, or implement strategies; teaching is nearly impossible. Teachers have to have a well-structured and well-organized classroom for teaching and learning to occur. The structure of the class determines how rules, consequences, and disciplinary actions are applied to academic tasks and student behaviors. For instance, inquiry activities can be messy, slimy, dirty, exciting, and loud; without strong classroom management, students could be out of control during science activities, compelling teachers to stop the lesson. Teachers need to plan classroom management well at all times in order to allow students to enjoy learning science.

During a science activity, having a noisy class is not necessarily bad because students are excited about or having fun with the inquiry processes. For instance, if teachers take out some insects or bugs, such as tarantulas, scorpions, worms, spiders, snails, grasshoppers, and dragonflies, the classroom could be loud or silent. Having a well-behaved classroom does not mean that students are learning or not learning; learning depends on how the teachers engage students in the lesson.

Most importantly, for teaching science, teachers need to pay close attention to these areas: individual student work, group activity, and independent practice. For individual student work, teachers need to provide students with clear and concise instructions and procedural processes or guidelines and make sure all students are on the same page. For group activity, teachers make sure each student has an assigned responsibility and all participants are clear about their roles. Students without a role in a group will not engage in the group activity. If teachers cannot find students roles to play in a group, it is better to do independent practice. Remember, teachers have to monitor, supervise, facilitate, and guide the processes and not leave students to conduct experiments or investigations themselves. Management and discipline is an ongoing process.

Teachers must take classroom management seriously in order to prevent incidental injuries to children in the classroom. Precaution is the key to making the learning environment safe for all. Intervention measures are good, but they are implemented after something has happened and sometimes they are too late. Here is an old saying about careful planning and prevention: "An ounce of prevention is worth a pound of cure." Teachers must plan management well to prevent health and safety problems.

SUMMING UP

This chapter covered a variety of ways to ensure that teachers are adequately prepared to teach inquiry science. Classroom management and student discipline are number one on teachers' must-have lists because without strong management, teaching is nearly impossible. Student behaviors are unpredictable, and teachers have to be ready to handle the unexpected. Rules, consequences, and procedural guidelines must be clear and must be implemented consistently in a way that is fair, firm, logical, flexible, meaningful, and purposeful.

Today's science education is taught mostly with scripted instruction and students are left to fend for themselves without firsthand experience. Not all teachers engage students in inquiry activities, such as hands-on and minds-on activities, experimentation, and investigation. Time constraints have limited teachers in being creative with their teaching passion; however, creativity is what makes the greatest educators. Even if teachers use scripted instruction, they can still include creative inquiry activities to help students learn science through the scientific processes and so sharpen their inquiry knowledge and skills.

Teachers can prepare, plan, design lesson plans, craft activities, and implement science in a variety of ways as long as the ways benefit all students. There are different lesson plan formats teachers can use; however, without hands-on and minds-on activities and inquiry processes, much teaching is meaningless. Children learn not by listening, but by doing. Teachers must find ways to engage children in science. Firsthand experience is as important as the quality of instruction. Inquiry instruction should be based on content standards as mandated.

CHAPTER SEVEN

Engage All Children IN Science

The universe is full of magical things patiently waiting for our wits to grow sharper.

—EDEN PHILLPOTTS *A SHADOW PASSES*

INTRODUCTION

The increasing diversity of the student population in U.S. schools has increased the need for finding appropriate inquiry instruction to address the academic challenges teachers face each and every day in the classroom. Cultural diversity should not be viewed as a weakness, but as a strength. Students of diverse backgrounds bring different prior knowledge, skills, and experiences to the classroom, and the more diverse the student population is, the more diverse will be classroom performance. The teaching and learning challenges that come from diversity are not all that new to this nation's schools. Today's teachers may feel overwhelmed or somewhat frustrated with all the challenges, but nothing is too difficult to overcome if teachers embrace student diversity as a good thing.

Most classrooms today are multicultural, like a rainbow, and contain students from at least three different ethnic backgrounds. The multicultural challenges are real; for this reason, teachers have to learn to become multicultural educators. This chapter explores how teachers can engage all learners in science as inquiry despite cultural diversity, learning disabilities, diverse needs and abilities, and exceptionalities.

To overcome multicultural challenges, teachers have to believe that every single child can learn science concepts. Moreover, teachers have to know that children will learn at different speeds regardless of the teachers' expectations.

CHILDREN ARE UNIQUE

Teachers were once children themselves, and now they teach children of others. Many teachers are parents and have children in school as well. They should easily recognize that children are unique people who think differently and similarly. Children have beautiful minds and understand the world differently from adults in so many ways, and teachers need to correct them academically and help them through conceptual changes. Understanding the uniqueness of each child should help teachers plan their teaching. Teaching children as though they are adults will not work well, and teachers have to adjust their teaching to children's levels of comprehension instead of expecting children to understand their higher-order thinking. Teachers who understand children's behaviors and development can work well with children.

Children will achieve academic progress, success, and understanding in different ways. In learning inquiry science concepts, children of diverse backgrounds learn at different speeds and depths as they explore questions and answers about their surroundings and the natural world. Some children are not as fortunate as others; they have learning limitations that require accommodations, adaptations, and interventions. For these students' special needs, teachers may be required to adapt or adjust inquiry instruction and science activities. Teachers' professional commitment to the students is to make science accessible and relevant for all students regardless of race, gender, cultural/ethnic background, learning disability, personal aspirations, interests, and motivation. No children should be left behind in science; all should have the same opportunity to learn science concepts in order to attain the highest level of scientific literacy of which they are capable.

As the numbers in Table 7.1 indicate, every classroom is likely to have children with challenging learning needs and special learning requirements. For instance, students of color who have language barriers and lack the linguistic skills needed for science may require bilingual materials written in their primary languages so that someone who speaks their primary languages can assist them. High achievers or children who are gifted and talented may require teachers to give them more challenging tasks to keep them from becoming bored. As they prepare science experiences, teachers need to address multicultural issues related to the overall academic needs of all learners in the classroom to make sure all children receive the same quality of instruction.

As indicated in an earlier chapter, students with special needs, such as ELLs and SNs, may pose instructional challenges to teachers. Students may

Table 7.1 California and National Student Demographics

Characteristic	California	Nation
White	31.9%	58.0%
Black	8.0%	16.9%
Asian/Pacific Islander	11.0%	4.4%
Hispanic	45.2%	19.5%
American Indian/Alaska Native	0.8%	1.2%
Economically disadvantaged	47.9%	36.7%
English language learners	24.9%	7.8%
Students with disabilities	10.6%	12.8%
Migrant students	2.5%	0.6%
LEP students	1.5 million	5.2 million

have differences in cognitive development, intellectual ability, learning styles, and writing styles. They may have diverse experiences; physical, social, and emotional differences; or challenging attitudes and personalities. Public Law 94-142 requires that teachers do their very best to adapt or adjust science lesson plans to meet the needs of these students. The Individuals with Disabilities Education Act (IDEA), formerly known as Public Law 94-142, legally mandates educational services to special needs students and provides federal funds to states and local education agencies (LEA) to assist in the education of students with disabilities. Table 7.2 gives an idea of the numbers of students in

Table 7.2 Numbers of Students in U.S. with Selected Disabilities

Types of disability	Approximate Total Number	Percentage
1. Specific learning disability	2,800,000	55.5%
2. Speech or language impairment	1,000,000	19.0%
3. Mental retardation	614,000	10.8%
4. Emotional disturbance	470,000	8.2%
5. Other health impairments	254,000	4.5%
6. Multiple disabilities	113,000	2.0%
7. Hearing impairment	72,000	1.3%
8. Orthopedics impairment	71,000	1.3%
9. Autism	65,000	1.3%
10. Visual impairment	27,000	0.6%
11. Developmental delay	19,000	0.38%
12. Traumatic brain injury	14,000	0.24%
13. Deaf-blindness	2,000	0.03%

Note. Information from *To Assess the Free Appropriate Education of All Children with Disabilities: Twenty-First Annual Report to Congress on the Implementation of the Individuals with Disabilities Education Act (IDEA),* US Department of Education, 1999, Washington, DC. Some numbers are rounded.

Table 7.3 Six Principles of IDEA Mandates

Principle	Meaning
1. Zero rejection	No student with disabilities can be excluded or rejected from a free, appropriate education.
2. Nondiscriminatory evaluation	Schools are required to evaluate students fairly to determine if they have a disability, identify what kind of disability the student has, and identify how extensive it is.
3. Appropriate education	School must design IEP based on nondiscriminatory evaluation for individual students.
4. Least restrictive environment	Schools are required to educate students with disabilities alongside students who have no disabilities and students should not be removed unless they cannot be educated successfully in that environment.
5. Procedural due process	IDEA (PL 94-142) safeguards students' right to receive education and to sue school in court.
6. Parental and student participation	Schools are required to collaborate with parents, guardians, and students in designing and carrying out special education programs.

the country with identified disabilities. Table 7.3 lists the six principles upon which the IDEA mandates are based. As an old saying says, "the hardest job in teaching all children is to properly manage the time to give every child an opportunity to learn."

Regardless of how teachers may feel about special-needs students, the bottom line is that diverse experiences, prior knowledge and skills, capabilities, abilities, needs, limitations, and cognitive abilities of students will influence how teachers prepare, plan, implement, and teach science as inquiry.

RECOGNIZE CHILDREN'S CHALLENGES

Teachers must recognize challenges their students face early in order to accommodate them by modifying and adapting lesson plans or intervening during instruction. Teachers leave many students behind by ignoring, neglecting, overlooking, or simply not recognizing their basic needs. Figure 7.1 presents some of the basic needs all students have. Teachers may not realize how important these needs are, but meeting these needs should be included in instructional processes. Ignoring these fundamental needs and challenges can hinder students' engagement in inquiry activities.

Take, for example, *primary language*, which is known as L1 in education. Nearly 10 million U.S. students speak a language other than English at home. Teachers are asked to identify students whose primary languages are not English; however, the identification process does not help teachers deal with their needs.

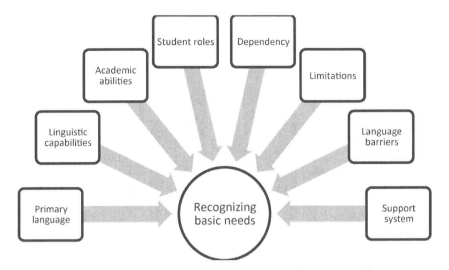

Figure 7.1 *Recognizing Basic Needs*

What teachers need to do is understand that children who speak their native language may have special learning needs and may require instructional assistance before they feel as though they are drowning and fall through the cracks.

Students with language barriers may or may not have an adequate academic *support system* at home because their parents are monolingual in languages other than English. Involving their parents may be helpful if language assistance is available; otherwise, students whose cultural backgrounds do not match the dominant culture at the school may not fare well academically without the extra support teachers can provide to them. As Vang (2006) wrote, LEP students face tremendous challenges in learning science as in another other academic subject areas because they need to develop academic language and scientific knowledge and skills needed for inquiry processes.

Teachers also need to recognize the characteristics of low and high achievers in class. Heacox (1991) questioned whether the teacher, the student, or someone else was responsible for the academic success or failure of students with special needs. Perhaps everybody is, but in most cases, student failure is related to the system that fails to provide teachers, parents, and students with adequate resources and proper tools to help students learn, especially in science. To help all children achieve in science as well as in other academic areas, teachers must understand cultural diversity and the diverse needs, different abilities, limited capabilities, and characteristics of high achievers, shown in Table 7.4, and low achievers, given in Table 7.5.

Table 7.4 Characteristics of Various Types of High Achievers

Type	Characteristics
Goal-oriented	Know how to set up short-term and long-term academic goals and work toward them.
Positive thinkers	Expect to be successful because of prior experiences or have intrinsic and extrinsic motivation.
Confident	Have strong, positive, and believable feelings about personal abilities to achieve.
Resilient	Are not afraid to make mistakes and do not let failure get them down.
Self-disciplined	Can resist distractions and diversions and stay focused to concentrate on learning tasks.
Have pride	Develop a sense of inner satisfaction, proud of accomplishments, believe in self, and independent rather than dependent.
Proficient	Develop skills to cope well, have necessary skills to be successful, and have what is required to do well.
Risk taker	Work on the edge, push the limit to learn new things, and have courage and confidence in self to achieve.

Note. Information from *Up from Under-Achievement: How Teachers, Students, and Parents Can Work Together to Promote Student Success*, by D. Heacox, 1991, Minneapolis, MN: Free Spirit.

Table 7.5 Characteristics of Various Types of Low Achievers

Type	Characteristics
The rebel	See no relevance in classroom assignment and activities: Why do we have to do this anyway? This is a total waste of time.
The conformist	Decide doing well in school is just not worth it: I don't notice that I am smart.
The stressed learner or perfectionist	Have self-esteem that rises and falls depending on academic performance: It's not good enough.
The struggling student	Lack the basics of how to learn, how to manage, and how to organize schoolwork: I just don't get it.
The victim	Do not want to accept responsibility for the lack of success: It's not my fault.
The distracted learner	Have personal problems that affect school performance, such as influences, stress, life situations, and poor organizational skills: I just can't handle it all.
The bored student	Need more challenging tasks, have difficulties with tasks, or have advanced abilities: There is nothing new and exciting to learn in class.
The complacent learner	Content with the status quo, believe things to be normal, and go with the flow: I'm doing just fine.
The single-sided learner	Pick and choose subject matter to learn based on personal interests: It doesn't interest me.

Note. Information from *Up from Under-Achievement: How Teachers, Students, and Parents Can Work Together to Promote Student Success*, by D. Heacox, 1991, Minneapolis, MN: Free Spirit.

SCIENCE FOR ALL STUDENTS

National and state standards require that teachers teach inquiry science concepts inclusively to all students regardless of who they are because every single child has to have the opportunity to learn science in the least restricted environment. To make science appropriate and suitable for all students, teachers have to take into account the multiple intelligences; these help teachers understand how different children behave, learn, interact, and develop academically and intellectually. Gardner (1993) listed the characteristics of multiple intelligences that are essential for teachers to consider when working with students of diverse abilities and needs in the multicultural setting (see Table 7.6).

To engage all children in inquiry science, teachers can use these characteristics as a guide to help them develop meaningful and inclusive science lesson plans that are appealing to students, and teachers can plan ahead of time to make sure that the content of all inquiry instructions benefit students because students do not learn the same way. If teachers include the academic components of hands-on and minds-on activities, as illustrated in Table 7.7, in teaching science as inquiry, most students will learn regardless of their learning styles.

These components—simplification, contextualization, comprehension, and lesson plan design—should work for all students regardless of the lesson plan format; however, scripted instruction may prevent teachers from using these components. Teachers need to find ways to incorporate these four areas into their daily practice in order to design inquiry science for all kinds of learners with diverse needs, abilities, and challenges.

SCIENCE FOR NEWCOMERS

How do teachers teach students who may not speak a word of English? *Newcomer* is a term for a student who has little or no English skills at all. Teaching inquiry science concepts to these students can be quite challenging.

Each school district has transient students who move out or come in to the schools throughout the year. The transient student population is growing in some metropolitan and rural areas and declining in others. Transient students may be resettled refugees, visitors from other countries, sponsored aliens, or foreign students. Transiency rates depend on socioeconomic factors, such as job security, family reunion, housing, employment opportunities, and family relocation. Teachers must be ready to welcome newcomers to their classrooms. Newcomers are comprised of all ages, both genders, diverse academic backgrounds, and diverse socioeconomic statuses.

Table 7.6 Multiple Intelligences

Type of Intelligence	Basic Definition	Areas of Interest	Areas of Strength	Possible Learning Styles
Linguistic	Word-smart or understand words and language easily.	Read, write, memorize, and tell stories.	Memorization and reading.	Reading, saying, hearing, or seeing words: The word player.
Logical/ mathematical	Logical-smart, number-smart, or understand logical connections among different ideas, concepts, and theories.	Do experiments, work with numbers, ask questions, explore patterns or relationships between objects, and infer results.	Math, reasoning, logic, problem solving, analogy, and details.	Categorizing, ordering, sequencing, classifying, abstracting, and explaining patterns or relationship: The questioner.
Spatial/ visual	Picture-smart or understand the expressions of arts, visual images, or mental images.	Draw, build, design, look at pictures, examine objects, and create images.	Imagination, visualization, sensing, reading maze, interpret charts, and solving puzzles.	Visualizing, dreaming, mental imaging, drawing pictures, creating photographs: The visualizer.
Musical/ audio	Music-smart, sound-smart, rhythm-smart, or understand the patterns of sound systems.	Sing, hum tunes, listen, play to music, write songs, respond to music, or create rhythm.	Memorization, picking sounds, understanding rhythms, or sensitivity to sounds.	Sound, rhythm, melody, music, voices, or artful: The music lover.
Bodily/ kinesthetic	Hand-smart, body-smart, sports-smart, physical fitness, agility, or understand patterns of body movement.	Move, use body language, gesture, touch and talk, or act out.	Perform physical activities, dance, sports, acting, crafts design, drafting, or hands-on.	Touching, moving, interacting, processing, sensations of body movement, or feeling the physical appearance: The mover.

Interpersonal	People-smart, friends-smart, social-smart, or understand grouping and social relationships.	Make friends, like people, talk to people, join groups, share with people, depending on, or player of team.	Sharing, understanding, socializing, leading, following, organizing, communicating, listening, mediating, showing, or manipulating.	Sharing, comparing, relating, cooperating, socializing, communicating, following, or leading: The socializer.
Intrapersonal	Self-centered, self-smart, self-propelled, or understand own ways.	Be a loner, be isolated, pursue own interests, set up personal goals, or independent.	Focusing on self, dealing with inward feelings, pursuing personal interests more, like own ways of doing things, choose own goals, or follow instincts.	Being a loner, working alone, being very independent, being self-centered, having own space, creating own turf, liking individualized project, or being introvert: The individual.
Natural	Flexible, adaptable, accommodating, considerate, or understand diverse needs and differences.	Have flexible and adaptable patterns of thinking, feeling, understanding, or communicating with people.	Focusing on all forms of learning, interests, considering all things as important, adjusting to needs, or being able to manage change well.	Having the ability to adapt to different learning environment or subject matter, adjusting to needs, or controlling changes with flexibility: The flexible learner.

Note. Information from *Multiple Intelligences: The Theory in Practice*, by H. Gardner, 1993, New York: Basic Books.

Table 7.7 Academic Components of Hands-on and Minds-on Activities

Simplification	Contextualization	Comprehension	Lesson Plan Design
1. Simple words or word choice appropriate for grade level	1. Meaningful clues and cues to engage	1. Previews	1. Five-step format
2. Slower speech rate to communicate or interact	2. Hand gestures or body language	2. Question checks	2. Three-step format
3. Clear enunciation or slow reading approach	3. Pleasant facial expressions or smiling approach	3. Key concepts checks	3. ELD format
4. Controlled vocabulary or new words	4. Act out meaning or total physical response	4. Understanding checks	4. SDAIE format
5. Controlled sentence length or syntax structure	5. Academic props, aids, supports, or perks	5. Comprehension checks	5. Direct instruction format
6. Use of cognates or similar words, like antonyms or synonyms	6. Graphics, tables, arts, KWL, or charts	6. Clarification checks	6. Inquiry-based instruction
7. Limited use of idioms, riddles, slang, and implicit words	7. Realia, pictures, arts, posters, placards, or drawings	7. Reviews	7. Guided inquiry
8. Parts-to-whole or whole-to-parts approach	8. Overheads, ELMO, Smart boards, clickers, or small boards	8. Reflections	8. ESL,TESOL, SIOP, or RTI
9. Wait time for response or delay for processing	9. Maps, idea web, concept mapping, charts, tables, or atlas	9. Repetitions	9. PQ5Rs
10. Plenty of examples or samples	10. Manipulatives, coins, beans, sticks, cubes, or blocks	10. Readings	10. 5Ws+H
	11. Visuals, pictures, posters, or Pictionary	11. Recitations	11. Inquiry skills approach or scientific processes
	12. Samples or examples or hands-on activities	12. Expansions	12. Hands-on and minds-on approach
		13. Words and definitions	13. Whole-class approach
		14. Cooperative learning, pairing, or small group	14. Large-group approach
		15. Adaptations, modifications, accommodations, and interventions	15. Small-group approach
		16. Guided practices and independent practices	16. Pairing up approach
			17. Individual approach

Teachers can engage newcomers in inquiry science with hands-on and minds-on activities described in Table 7.7, using accommodations, modifications, adaptations, and interventions as necessary. Teachers should reject the "sink or swim" approach that leaves students to fend for themselves. Academic saturation may work for some, but not all. Some students may need minimal instructional guidance and others may need in-depth assistance because they lack academic skills, language skills, or interpersonal skills. Teachers need to find academic resources to help individual students.

SCIENCE FOR MIGRANT STUDENTS

What can teachers do to help students who appear or disappear periodically? Migrant families move from place to place to find work to feed their families. Their children move along with them. Education for migrant students is sporadic; it has been interrupted many times. For most migrant families, frequent movement is not a choice, but a way of life.

Migrant students make up a large proportion of the transient students in the south and west, especially in California, Arizona, Texas, and New Mexico. Federal and state mandates are in place to provide these unique students equal opportunity in public schools. Most counties in the southern and western states have migrant education programs for these students. Most of the migrant students are in rural schools rather than inner-city schools.

Unlike the newcomers, most migrant students have been enrolled in public schools; therefore, learning science is not a strange idea to them. Teachers need to recognize the needs of individual students and prescribe the academic components listed in Table 7.7 to help them learn science concepts. A majority of migrant students are Spanish speaking, and bilingual resources should be available to help them, including bilingual materials and bilingual staff or paraprofessionals. Usually, teachers can get help for migrant students from their school district or the county office of education.

SCIENCE FOR IMMIGRANT/REFUGEE STUDENTS

How do teachers teach immigrant and refugee children who are new to the United States? They generally do not speak a word of English, nor do their parents. Should they be treated like ghost children in the classroom, present but ignored? Should they be merely seat warmers?

Immigrant and refugee students are newcomers, and they continue to arrive in U.S. schools because of warfare in other countries. Some families immigrated to the U.S. for economic opportunities and others came for safe haven, fleeing their homelands in order to survive. The children of these war-displaced families are refugees; everything in U.S. schools is new to them. In 1975, a large influx of Hmong refugees entered the U.S., and their children were refugee students who faced tremendous academic challenges as the result of refugee resettlement programs. Other immigrant students are children of people who entered the U.S. for a variety of reasons, such as reunification with their families, job opportunities, educational opportunities, or tourism.

To help newcomers, like migrant students, learn science concepts, teachers can implement hands-on and minds-on strategies listed in Table 7.7. These children of diverse backgrounds may not be able to express their science knowledge and skills in verbal or written forms because their English skills are still under construction; however, their cognitive development in learning science concepts is similar to that of any other students of the same age.

SCIENCE FOR LEP STUDENTS

Does the academic label schools put on children determine how teachers should help them? Who are the true English-language learners? Why do schools call these children by different names? What can teachers do to include them all in science education?

Of the 50 states, California appears to have the largest number of English-language learners (ELL), or nonnative speakers (NNS), both limited English proficient (LEP) and fluent English proficient (FEP) (see Table 7.1). LEP students may be newcomers, migrant students, immigrant students, or refugee students; many children who were born in the U.S. are also designated as LEP because their English proficiency is limited. In other words, LEP students could be either U.S. born or foreign born. Most LEP students are not new to the school system, and learning science concepts is not all that strange to them. Their academic classification and label may not have anything to do with what they are capable of in school. Sometimes these labels are put on them for fiscal reasons. Therefore, teachers must not assume that all LEP students have the same needs and limitations as newcomers, immigrant students, or refugee students.

As Table 7.7 demonstrates, teachers have many options for implementing inquiry-based science instruction for LEP students. If all concepts in simplification and contextualization work for newcomers, immigrant students, and refugee students, they should also work for the majority of LEP students. Keep in mind that LEP students make up a very diverse group of students who speak different dialects and have different cultural backgrounds. Over 425 dialects are spoken in U.S. schools, and over 100 different dialects are spoken in California's K-12 schools. Meeting all these challenges appears impossible; however, it is important to try to make science education available to everyone regardless of the primary language (L1) of a student.

A number of instructional methods, including ELD, SDAIE, ESL, TESOL, SIOP, and RTI, should work for all students; however, direct instruction may not benefit LEP, migrant, immigrant, and refugee students because it is a scripted approach with little or no hands-on and minds-on activities. Moreover, direct instruction is teacher-centered and may not lead students into inquiry activity.

SCIENCE FOR SPECIAL-NEEDS STUDENTS

Who are the special-needs students in the classroom? What is so special about them? What do teachers need to know in order to help them learn? What are their limitations and special needs? Can regular teachers understand them?

Many scientists and inventors had disabilities and limitations. The list includes Isaac Newton (epilepsy and stuttering), Alexander Graham Bell (learning disability), Thomas Edison (learning disability and partial deafness), Henry Ford (dyslexia), Albert Einstein (Asperger syndrome or autism), and Stephen Hawking (motor neuron disease). This fact and these names should make teachers optimistic about helping children with exceptionalities, disabilities, and limitations learn science concepts.

The Teacher Performance Expectation (TPE) Standards and Teacher Performance Assessment (TPA) mandated in California require teachers to use instructional adaptations to meet the learning needs of ELL and special-needs students (SN). To help teachers recognize the learning needs of these students, Table 7.8 presents some of the characteristics of students with language-learning disabilities. As mentioned in an earlier chapter, the widely used definition for learning disabilities presented by Kirk (1962, as cited in McNamara, 2007) is as follows:

> A learning disability refers to retardation, disorder, or delayed development in one or more of the processes of speech, language, reading, writing, arithmetic, or other school subjects resulting from a psychological handicap caused by a possible cerebral dysfunction and/ or emotional or behavioral disturbance. It is not the result of mental retardation, sensory deprivation, or cultural and instructional factors.

According to McNamara, the 10 most common characteristics of students classified as having a learning disability are (a) hyperactivity; (b) perception impairments; (c) emotional lability; (d) general coordination deficits; (e) disorders of attention, short attention span, distractibility preservation; (f) impulsivity;

Table 7.8 Behavior Characteristics of Students with Language-Learning Disabilities

Behavior Area	Characteristic	Possible Cause
Peer relations	Poor	Being a loner or playing alone
Adjustment to change	Poor	Easily upset or confused
Perseveration	Persistent	Spending too much time on a task
Emotional control	Poor	Easily angered or emotional
Dealing with frustration	Poor	Stamping foot or sulking
Asking for assistance	Poor	Sitting quietly or delaying assistance
Communication in general	Poor	Reserved, quiet, or self-centered
Physical comfort	Excessive	Need hugs, touches, or comfort from others
Hyperactivity	Excessive movement	Problems settling down
Learning style	Variable performance	Doing well on one task and poorly on another
Task completion	Poor	Starting a task but cannot finish it on time
Maturity level	Immature	Behaving below age level
Learning new concepts	Poor or reduced vocabulary	Understanding issues and prefers the use of object labels
Responding to questions	Delay or need wait time	Requiring extra time to process thought
Situational behaviors	Inappropriate and funny	Laughing or talking to self
Dealing with dysnomia	Unable to recall words	Difficult time recalling needed words
General attitude	Impulsive	Responding without thinking through
Following directions	Poor, unable to follow	Need to be told to behave

Note. Information from *Students with Learning Disabilities* (6th ed.), by C. D. Mercer and P. C. Pullen, 2005, Upper Saddle River, NJ: Merrill/Prentice Hall.

(g) disorders of memory and thinking; (h) specific learning disabilities—in reading, arithmetic, writing, spelling; (i) disorders of speech and learning, and (j) equivocal neurological signs and EEG irregularities.

The most commonly known conditions present in special-needs students are attention deficient disorder (ADD), attention deficient hyperactivity disorder (ADHD), and autism. In teaching inquiry science, teachers need to consider the characteristics presented in Table 7.8 and the academic components listed in Table 7.7 as they design appropriate inquiry instruction for these students. For instance, an autistic boy may prefer to work on an inquiry activity alone; however, teachers need to monitor and supervise him closely in case he gets frustrated with the activity or easily gives up on the task. For ADD and ADHD, teachers need to keep students with these conditions busy and constantly remind them to finish tasks. Perhaps teachers can use appropriate reinforcement to keep these students engaged in tasks. The problem is that these students may not finish their tasks on time; therefore, teachers should do whatever is necessary to encourage them to complete academic tasks. Ideally, teachers need to keep these students actively engaged in learning the inquiry activities.

Special-needs students may present other problems, such as behavioral, emotional, psychological, conduct, mental, and medical conditions. Teachers may not be able to deal with these effectively without seeking outside professional assistance. These conditions may contribute to the overall learning disabilities of the students. As a safety precaution, teachers should prescribe appropriate inquiry activities that will not put these students in harm's way. Teachers should not allow students to conduct any scientific experiment or investigation that will cause harm to them or others due to their limitations, disabilities, or cognitive development levels.

Furthermore, today's teachers are not properly trained to handle students with orthopedic, visual, and hearing impairments or severe mental conditions. Dealing with these medical and physical impairments requires professional training and special accommodations in a classroom that is equipped with tools, devices, and machines to help teachers meet the needs of these students. In rare situations when teachers have to deal with such students, it is highly recommended that the classroom setting is suitable to include these students in the scientific processes. Parents of these students should be notified of their proposed participation in inquiry activities and teachers should be sure the activities are consistent with their legal IEP. Teaching science concepts to these students often requires extra effort to reach out to them at their level of learning. The bottom line is that teachers have to recognize each student's needs and must prescribe only those inquiry activities that are appropriate for the student's cognitive maturity and development level.

SCIENCE FOR GIFTED AND TALENTED STUDENTS

Who are students with exceptionalities? What is so special about them? How do teachers work with students who are super intelligent? How do teachers accommodate their high level of thinking? What can teachers do to make sure there are checks and balances in teaching and learning?

As discussed earlier, Gollnick and Chinn (2009) described gifted and talented students as individuals with very high intelligence or students who possess unusual gifts and talents in the arts. They need specially designed educational programs or curricula in order to reach their full potential. Similarly, Ryan and Cooper (2001) pointed out that gifted children usually have high intellectual ability, and talented children have creative or artistic abilities. Gifted and talented children give evidence of potential for high achievement or performance in academic, creative, artistic, or leadership areas. As with all other children, gifted and talented students have specific strengths and weaknesses.

More interestingly, Manning and Baruth (2009) observed that these students are exceptionally diverse and sometimes appear as antisocial, creative, high-achieving, divergent thinkers and perfectionists; they may have attention-deficit disorders, dyslexia, or other complex disorders. Like all students, they need to learn how to form personal identities, deal with independence, explore romantic relationships, and develop warm and loving interpersonal relationships. They need to identify and develop their personal values, attitudes, personalities, and belief systems. Some students with exceptionalities who are culturally different from the mainstream face very complex issues and challenges.

As indicated in Tables 7.6 and 7.7, teachers can engage all children in science by recognizing their strengths and weaknesses as well as their challenges, limitations, and disabilities, and take all factors into consideration before prescribing inquiry activities for them. Honestly, there is no perfect way teachers can deal with all problems or solve all learning needs; however, teachers who appreciate students' diverse learning needs are better at teaching and learning science concepts because engaging all children in science learning promotes academic equality. Teachers may have to make academic inclusion a goal for themselves and their students in the multicultural setting in order to embrace student diversity.

As bridge builders, teachers need to do the following to make inquiry science beneficial to all learners:

1. Teach science as inquiry.
2. Apply prior knowledge and skills to science concepts.
3. Bring science concepts to students' level of understanding.
4. Promote acquisition of social, logical, and physical knowledge in students.
5. Recognize multiple intelligences and challenges.
6. Create individualized education plans to meet the needs of specific students.
7. Use a barrier-free education approach to accommodate special learning needs.
8. Use hands-on and minds-on activities to help students focus on learning.
9. Select the most appropriate approach to make teaching and learning science fun.
10. Try to meet students' physical needs early.
11. Try to meet students' learning needs early.
12. Select an appropriate inquiry approach to engage students.
13. Prompt students with questions to get them active, excited, and curious.

14. Apply coaching and mentoring processes to help students learn concepts.
15. Use deductive and inductive approaches to make science predictable and stimulate debate.
16. Teach science learning strategies and techniques to boost student learning.
17. Use graphic organizers whenever necessary to accommodate student needs.
18. Engage students in short-term and long-term memorization exercises.
19. Teach mnemonics to specific students whenever necessary.
20. Use inquiry-based activity approaches to engage all in science.
21. Apply a system that employs behavior modifications with rewards for reinforcement.
22. Adapt or modify learning materials for LEP, ELL, and SN students.
23. Practice mobility orientation to help specific students with special needs.
24. Provide equal opportunity for learning and for doing activities.
25. Learn from students and their diverse needs, abilities, limitations, and disabilities.

Keep in mind that these are suggestions for teachers to consider when dealing with student diversity and all kinds of learning challenge that may appear in the multicultural setting. There is no panacea to all teaching obstacles; however, it is imperative to recognize some imminent challenges before they become large. Finally, in order to deal with the learning needs of students, teachers need to understand the controversy surrounding right- and left-brain learning, as illustrated in Table 7.9. Teachers need to apply this information with caution in regards to the practice of brain-based learning. Sometimes it is not ethical or professional to determine who belongs to the right- or left-brain learner group, and labeling students may cause complex controversies. Instead, teachers should create a positive learning environment for all.

BUILD POSITIVE RELATIONSHIPS

To include all students in learning science, teachers may need to build bridges between students and themselves. Maintaining good rapport with students creates a positive relationship that fosters teaching and learning; however, being able to reach out to every single student in the classroom requires persistent effort because each student is unique. Teachers have to be appreciative of who students are without trying to change their cultural identity. At the same time, they may need to try to modify their personalities and attitudes toward learning.

Teachers have their own cultural baggage, as do students. Teachers need to examine their cultural values carefully and professionally. Teachers may need to

Table 7.9 Contrast of Right- and Left-Brain Learners

Right-Brain Learners	Left-Brain Learners
• Visually oriented	Analytical
• Spatially oriented	Logical
• Demonstration	Concrete
• Experience	Sequential
• Open-ended questions	Lecture
• Nonverbal approach	Discussion
• Manipulation	Verbal cues
• Divergent thinking activities	Rules
• Flash cards	Short questions and short answers
• Maps	Yes or no approach
• Idea web	Texts
• Films	Word list or word bank
• Audiotapes	Workbook exercises
• Crafts	Readings
• Drawing activities	Drills
• Wholistic approach	Linear mode approach
• Broad thinking process	Meaning and retention
• Intuitive thinking	Question and answer exercises
• "Guess-timating"	Vocabulary and definitions
• Testing ideas and principles	Note taking
• Visual and spatial mode approach	Recitation
• Use non-sequential mode	Repetition
• Total physical response	Memorization
• Integrate performance arts	Review

examine their attitudes toward student diversity when preparing and planning science lessons for the multicultural classroom. Their expectations, perceptions, attitudes, acceptance, or rejection may influence how they teach, model, interact, react, grade student work, and value students' ways of learning.

Most importantly, their body language or tone of voice reveals how they feel about teaching students of color, and their psycho-social dimensions may have greater impact on student learning than they think. Students may react to their personalities and attitudes positively or negatively. For this reason, teachers must be trained to be cross-culturally competent in order to create a learning environment where students feel comfortable to cooperate, collaborate, express themselves, and engage in instructional processes without worrying about being treated differently and unfairly. Remember, teachers are life savers and bridge builders, and they coach and mentor students in learning science concepts.

A positive relationship with students promotes civility in the classroom and encourages students to work cooperatively and collaboratively. Most importantly, positive relationships help teachers manage the class and control student behaviors, and one goal of all teachers is to have effective classroom management and student discipline. Civility, cooperation, collaboration, and good classroom management all start with one thing: healthy student–teacher relationships.

SUMMING UP

This chapter gave an overview of the importance of inclusiveness and encouraged teachers to create a learning environment that includes all learners in science. It also discussed how teachers can deal with student diversity in the multicultural setting. Today's student population is very diverse and teachers face tough challenges in meeting students' learning needs. Teaching science as inquiry is a challenging task for many teachers because of the diverse learning needs of students.

For inquiry science, hands-on and minds-on activities are beneficial to nearly all learners; however, students with visual impairments, hearing impairments, orthopedic impairments, and mental retardation may not receive the benefits. Certain student groups, such as newcomers and ELL, LEP, FEP, migrant, immigrant, and refugee students, could be left out of some activities because they need additional resources. These types of barriers must be overcome so teachers can teach inquiry science effectively to all learners.

PART THREE

Integration OF Science WITH Academic Content Areas

CHAPTER EIGHT

Teach Integrated Inquiry Content

Science is built up of facts, as a house is built of stones; but an accumulation of facts is no more a science than a heap of stones is a house.

—HENRI POINCARÉ *SCIENCE AND HYPOTHESIS,* 1905

INTRODUCTION

As mentioned in earlier chapters, inquiry science is not an academic subject that teachers have to teach separately without making any connections with other academic subjects such as language arts, mathematics, and social studies. It is difficult to teach science concepts alone, and it is impossible for students to learn science concepts without conducting investigation and experimentation. The scientific processes involve other academic subjects, and science is actually a language arts subject itself. Teachers who believe that science is a separate subject need to overcome the misconceptions about science. Without mathematical skills, learning science would be difficult because students need to have logical skills to conduct experiments. Similarly, without language arts skills, learning science would be impossible because students need to be able to express their learning in verbal or written form or both. This chapter encourages teachers to integrate science content with the content of other academic subjects.

Students' abilities to use mathematical skills and language arts are practical tools in learning science concepts, and mastery of science knowledge and skills will lead students toward the development and construction of new knowledge and skills in other subjects.

WHY INTEGRATED CONTENT MATTERS

Students need to apply knowledge and skills learned in other academic disciplines to learn inquiry science concepts. Mainly, mathematical concepts and language arts skills play major roles in learning science. ELL, NNS, or LEP students who lack these skills lag behind in mastery of science literacy because they lack academic language skills. Learning inquiry science without making connections with other subjects will not advance student learning. Students need to have learning opportunities that enhance their math, reading, writing, and technological skills in order to conduct investigations and experiments to learn about their surroundings and the natural world.

Looking at the components of the 5-E and 8-E models of instruction (see Table 8.1) gives an idea of why integrating content across subjects is so important in teaching and learning. How can students *engage, explore, explain, elaborate,*

Table 8.1 The 5-E Model of Instruction

Components	Expectations	Examples
Engagement	Engage learners in inquiry-based instruction or asking questions about objects.	What do plants need to live? How many planets are in the solar system? What is the difference between insects and bugs?
Exploration	Observe, plan, or conduct simple investigation to gather data or information about objects.	Water, soil, light, space; study all the planets; compare and contrast insects and bugs.
Explanation	Use data and information to explain, use simple variables to label or sort out information, try to answer questions.	What would happen to plants if there is no light, water, soil, or space? Why are planets different in size? How are insects and bugs different?
Elaboration	Learn to apply new understanding to new questions, or connect learned experience to real life experience.	Use results to explain different plants with details. Use information to tell how planets are different. Use characteristics of insects and bugs to explain differences and similarities.
Evaluation	Engage in formal and informal learning by assessing science knowledge, understanding, application, and abilities.	What students have learned about planets, solar system, and insects and bugs.

evaluate, experiment, expect, and *enjoy* (components of the 8-E model) without practicing the inquiry skills of science: *observe, infer, compare, contrast, classify, measure, communicate, use numbers, predict, record data, analyze data, form a hypothesis, use variables, conduct experiments, launch an investigation,* and *make a model?* The knowledge and skills essential for learning science concepts are also useful in learning other academic subjects.

UNDERSTAND CONTENT AREA STANDARDS

Teachers need to adhere to the content area standards of all academic subjects in order to design integrated content for inquiry instruction, as shown in Tables 8.2 and 8.3. Keep in mind that content standards are broad based and teachers must know how to apply key concepts across the disciplines. As mentioned in earlier chapters, science standards are guidelines that teachers have to follow in designing inquiry science lesson plans with scientific learning objectives. Most importantly, learning objectives must be appropriate for the specific grade level or the age of students; otherwise, the contents of a lesson plan could be too high or too low for students. In applying content standards to everyday teaching of science concepts, teachers need to make sure the concepts are relevant and appropriate for students.

Teachers may try to align the content of academic subjects, shown in Tables 8.4; and the standards of the different academic subjects, shown in Table 8.5; however, there is no perfect alignment in teaching and learning. Teachers need to learn how to build bridges to connect academic subjects. For instance, teachers may require students to use measurement (math skills) to conduct an inquiry activity, or teachers can connect math concepts such as inch, square inches, foot, feet, or square feet with science concepts by measuring the perimeter or area of different shapes.

Understanding content area standards enables teachers to see the relevance of academic curricular activities based on content knowledge, as shown in Table 8.6. Acquiring mathematical and language arts skills gives students academic abilities and practical applications that bolster their learning in science if teachers consistently model to students how to apply inquiry skills. On the other hand, teachers can promote science concepts in social studies by prescribing inquiry activities that examine the relationships between science technology and societal change or investigate how technology has changed human activities. Today's students may be interested in exploring how life is evolving around technological devices when everyone has a cellular phone, iPad, iPod, laptop, and Internet service. Perhaps the science and technology make life easier but more expensive.

Table 8.2 National Science Educational Standards (NSES)

Grade level	Unifying concepts and Processes	Science as Inquiry	Physical Science	Life Science	Earth and Space Science	Science and Technology	Science in Personal and Social Perspective	History and Nature of Science
K-4	System, order, and organization; evidence, models, and explanation; change, constancy, and measurement; evolution and equilibrium; and form and function	Ability to perform, understand, or learn scientific inquiry	Properties, objects, position, motion, light, heat, electricity, or magnetism	Characteristics of plants and animals; life cycles; and ecosystems	Properties, earth's layers, objects in the sky, climate changes, and materials	Use technology, differences between natural objects and objects made by man	Health, relationships, people, society, resources, life challenges, and changes	Science as human endeavor, discovery, and invention
5-8	System, order, and organization; evidence, models, and explanation; change, constancy, and measurement; evolution and equilibrium; and form and function	Ability to perform, understand, or learn scientific inquiry	Properties, changes, matters, motions forces, and transfer of energy	Structure, function, ecosystem, food chain/web, reproduction, heredity, behavior, people, society, adaptations, survival, and differences	Earth layers/ structure, earth history, planets, solar system, and changes	Abilities, design, understand technology, and applications	Health, resources, people, society, hazards, risks, benefits, diseases, and environments	Science as human endeavor, nature of science, and history of science

Note. Information from *A Sample of National Science Education Standards,* by Joseph M. Peters, 2006, Upper Saddle River, NJ: Pearson Education.

Table 8.3 California Science Content Standards for Grades K–12

Grade level	Physical Science	Life Science	Earth Science	Investigation/ Experimentation
Kindergarten	Properties of materials (clay, cloth, paper, house, car, toys, objects), observe, measure, predict, color, size, shape, weight, texture, flexibility, attraction to magnets, floating, sinking	Types of plants and animals, differences, similarities, comparing, classifying, seed-bearing plants, birds, fish, insects, stems, leaves, roots, arms, wings, legs	Earth structures, air, wind, land, water, mountains, rivers, oceans, valleys, deserts, landforms	Observe, compare, classify, describe, communicate
First	Forms and states of matter, gases, liquids, solids, properties of substances, mixed, cooled, or heated	Plants and animals, needs, survival, adaptations, food, sharp teeth eats meat; flat teeth eats plants, shelter, nesting, physical needs	Weather patterns, wind vane, weather conditions, temperature, thermometer, observe, measure, light, rain, fog, snow, climate changes	Observe, predict, measure, describe, communicate
Second	Motions of objects, force, strength, push, pull, sound, vibration, pitch, noise, beat	Life cycles of plants and animals, germination, pollination, reproduction, growth, development, parents, offspring, characteristics	Earth is made of materials, soil, water, fossils, rocks, minerals, resources, energy	Predict, observe, measure, describe, communicate, experiment, test, record
Third	Forms of energy and matter, light, heat, water, wind, gas, fuel, food, solid, liquid, gas, evaporation, melting, substances, atoms, particles	Adaptations, behavior, survival, reproduction, growth, extinction, biomes, life forms, ecosystem	Objects in the sky, patterns, constellations, stars, planets, day, night, dark, light, seasons, lunar cycles	Predict, observe, measure, describe, communicate, experiment, test, record
Fourth	Electricity, magnetism, energy, light, motions, forces, charges, poles, compass, effects, circuits, design, motors, devices, generators, magnetic field	All organisms need energy and matter to live and grow, food chain, food web, herbivores, omnivores, carnivores, consumers, decomposers, producers, recycle of plants and animals	Properties of rocks and minerals, process of formation, igneous, sedimentary, metamorphic, rock cycles, earthquakes, landslides, erosion, volcanic eruption, landforms, weathering, transportation, deposition, wind, waves	Read, predict, observe, measure, describe, communicate, infer, formulate, experiment, test, record

(Continued)

Grade level	Physical Science	Life Science	Earth Science	Investigation/ Experimentation
Fifth	Types of matter, periodic table, chemical reactions, elements, metal, nonmetal, gas, solid, liquid, chemical properties, atoms, molecules, physical properties	Plant and animal structures, respiration, transpiration, waste disposal, digestion, functions of internal organs, metabolism, chemical breakdowns	Weather cycles, patterns, conditions, seasons, evaporation, condensation, precipitation, rain, hail, snow, fog, sleet, ice, lakes, oceans, rivers, underground water, convection currents, temperature	Conduct study, read, predict, observe, measure, describe, communicate, infer, formulate, experiment, test, record
Sixth	Heat and thermal energy, climate changes, heat waves, light, radiation, flow of energy, temperature, convection currents, transfer of energy, humidity, pressure	All organisms in ecosystem, exchange energy and nutrients, sunlight, photosynthesis, produce food, food web, abiotic factors, light, water, natural energy, material resources, air, soil, rocks, minerals, petroleum, fresh water, wildlife, forests, renewable energy, nonrenewable energy	Plate tectonics and earth's structures, geological events, earthquakes, tsunamis, shakes, motions, eruptions, layers, fossils, epicenter, faults, landforms, weather patterns, climate, shapes, topography	Conduct study, read, use technology, predict, observe, measure, describe, communicate, infer, formulate, experiment, test, record, science project
Seventh	Physical principles in living systems, light spectrum, light waves, reflection, refraction, electromagnetic light, wavelengths, lenses, eyes, magnify glass, telescope, microscope, camera, light colors, light travel	Cell biology, genetics, structure and function in living systems, cells, tissues, organs, muscles, joints, skeleton, genes, traits, heredity, recessive, dominant, mitosis, reproductive organs, sexual activity, pollens, seeds, fruit, fertilization, pregnancy, chromosomes, plant and animal cellular structures, species, natural selection, anatomy, fossils	Earth and life history, age of the earth, rock cycles, evolution of life on earth, geological processes, geological time scale, extinction, fossils, fire, flood, catastrophic events, eruptions, impacts of asteroids	Conduct study, read, use technology, predict, observe, measure, describe, communicate, infer, formulate, experiment, test, record, science project

| Eighth | Motions, forces, structure of matter, properties, density, buoyancy, forms of matter, velocity, speed, balanced, unbalanced, inertia, action, reaction, static, gravity, elastic, tension, compression, friction, atomic structure, proton, neutron, electron, properties, molecular motions, elements on periodic table, acidic, basic, neutral | Chemistry of living systems, carbon, carbohydrates, fats, proteins, DNA, principles of chemistry in living organisms | Earth in the solar system, structure and composition of the universe, milky way, stars, planets, galaxies, black hole, distance between planets, eclipse, shine, waxing, waning | Conduct study, read, use technology, predict, observe, measure, describe, communicate, infer, formulate, experiment, test, record, science project |

Note. Information from *Science Content Standards for California Public Schools: Kindergarten through Grade 12*, California Department of Education, 2003, http://www.cde.ca.gov/be/st/ss/documents/sciencestnd.pdf

Table 8.4 Selected Subject Content Related to Standards

Subject	Content According to Standards
English language arts	Reading, writing, speaking, listening, viewing, literature, grammar, conventions
Mathematics	Numbers and operations, algebra, geometry, measurement, data analysis, probability, problem solving, reasoning and proof, communication, connections, representations
Social studies	People, language, culture, time, continuity, change, places, environment, development, identity, individuals, groups, power, authority, governance, ruling, production, distribution, consumption, consumers, science, technology, society, global connections, civil ideals, practices, leaders, leadership, values, norms
Science	Life science concepts, earth science concepts, physical science concepts, earth and space science, connections, applications, hypothesis, thinking, processes, tools, technologies, communication, investigation, experimentation, properties

CREATE INTEGRATED SCIENCE

Creativity is what makes teachers the best artists. Teaching is an art, and teaching science is a creative art. There is no perfect way of integrating content for inquiry science; teachers may find their own unique ways of integrating science with other academic subjects. Some of these ways use graphic organizers, KWL charts, or scaffolding, and others may use concept mapping, thematic teaching, idea webs, and contextualization to connect key concepts across the academic discipline. Figures 8.1, 8.2, 8.3, and 8.4 give examples of some of these tools and techniques. Teachers do things differently depending on the individual teachers' prior knowledge and science backgrounds.

Science and mathematics can go hand in hand since math skills are great tools for science and mathematics is the language of science. Teachers can integrate science and mathematics by applying mathematical concepts or skills in scientific inquiry. For instance, students use numbers to label or classify objects during inquiry skills activities, or teachers ask students to make predictions about the number of strands of hair on top of their heads. These kinds of inquiry activities make connections between science and mathematics, as presented in Figure 8.5. Integrating content makes teaching and learning science fun, intriguing, and entertaining; without integration, teachers and students may perceive science to be a difficult subject to teach and to learn, and that is an inaccurate perception for inquiry science.

Table 8.5 Standards for Science, Math, Social Studies, and Language Arts Content

Science Content Standards	Math Content Standards	Language Arts Content Standards	Social Studies Content Standards
Standard A: Science as inquiry: 1. Develop ability to do scientific inquiry 2. Understand about scientific inquiry *Standard B: Physical science:* 1. Understand properties, changes of properties in matter 2. Motions and forces 3. Transfer of energy *Standard C: Life science* 1. Structure and function in living system 2. Reproduction and heredity 3. Regulation and behavior 4. Populations and ecosystems 5. Diversity and adaptations of organisms *Standard D: Earth and space science:* 1. Structure of the earth system 2. Earth's history 3. Earth in the solar system *Standard E: Science and technology* 1. Abilities of technological design 2. Understand about science and technologies	*Standard A: Numbers and operations:* 1. Understand numbers, ways of representing numbers, relationships among numbers and number systems 2. Meanings of operations and how they relate to one another 3. Compute fluently and make reasonable estimate *Standard B: Algebra:* 1. Patterns, relations, and functions 2. Represent, analyze, use algebraic symbols 3. Math models, quantitative relationship 4. Analyze changes in various contexts *Standard C: Geometry:* 1. Analyze characteristics, properties, shapes, arguments, and relationships 2. Locations, spatial relationship, coordinate, and representation systems 3. Transformation, symmetry 4. Visualization, spatial reasoning, and modeling	*Standards:* 1. Read a wide range of print and non-print texts for multiple purposes 2. Read a wide range of literature from many periods and genres to build understanding of human experience 3. Apply a wide range of strategies to comprehend, interpret, evaluate, and appreciate texts 4. Adjust spoken, written, and visual language to communicate effectively for different purposes 5. Employ a wide range of strategies in writing for a variety of purposes 6. Apply knowledge of language structure, conventions, and genre to create and discuss print and non-print texts 7. Conduct research, generate questions, gather data, and communicate discoveries	*Standards:* 1. Have experiences that provide for the study of culture and cultural diversity 2. Provide for the study of the ways human beings view themselves in and over time 3. Provide for the study of people, places, and environments 4. Provide for the study of individual development and identity 5. Provide for the study of interactions among individuals, groups, and institutions 6. Provide for the study of how people create and change structures of power, authority, and governance 7. Provide for the study of how people organize for the production, distribution, and consumption of goods and services

(Continued)

Science Content Standards	Math Content Standards	Language Arts Content Standards	Social Studies Content Standards
Standard F: Science in personal and social perspectives: 1. Personal health 2. Populations, resources, and environments 3. Natural hazards 4. Risks and benefits 5. Science and technology in society *Standard G: History and nature of science:* 1. Science as human endeavor 2. Nature of science 3. History of science	*Standard D: Measurement:* 1. Measurable attributes, units, systems, and processes 2. Techniques, tools, and formulas for measuring *Standard E: Analysis and probabilities:* 1. Formulate questions, collect data, analyze data, and answer questions 2. Statistical analysis of data 3. Evaluate, infer, and conclude based on data 4. Concepts of probability	8. Use various technologies, information sources to gather data and communicate knowledge 9. Respect for diversity in language use, patterns, and dialects 10. Use first language to develop competency in English 11. Participate as knowledgeable, reflective, creative, and critical members of diverse literacy communities 12. Use spoken, written, and visual language to accomplish own purposes	8. Provide for the study of relationships among science, technology, and society 9. Provide for the study of global connections and interdependence 10. Provide for the study of the ideals, principles, and practices of citizenship in a democratic republic

Note. Information from *National Science Education Standards*, Center for Science, Mathematics, and Engineering Education, 1996, Washington, DC: National Academies Press, http://books.nap.edu/html/nses/html/overview.html#content and *A Sampler of National Science Education Standards*, by Joseph M. Peters, 2006, Upper Saddle River, NJ: Pearson Education.

Table 8.6 Overview of NSES Science Content Knowledge

Science Education Program Standards	History/Nature of Science Standards	Science Teaching Standards	Assessment Standards	Content Standards
1. The program of study in science should connect to other school programs	1. Science as human endeavor	1. Plan an inquiry-based program	1. Assessments must be consistent with the decisions they are designed to inform	1. Ask a question about objects, organisms, and events in the environment
2. Science content must be embedded in a variety of curricular programs that are developmentally appropriate, interesting, and relevant to students' lives	2. Nature of science	2. Guide and facilitate learning	2. Achievement and opportunity to learn science must be assessed	2. Plan and conduct a simple investigation
3. The science program should be coordinated with the mathematics program	3. History of science	3. Recognize and respond to student diversity and encourage all students to participate fully in science learning	3. The inferences made from assessment about student achievement and opportunity to learn must be sound	3. Employ simple equipment and tools to gather data and extend the senses
4. Collaborative inquiry requires adequate and safe space		4. Engage students in ongoing learning		4. Use data to construct reasonable explanations
5. The most important source is professional teachers		5. Design and manage learning environments that provide students with the time, space, and resources needed for learning science		5. Communicate investigations and explanations
		6. Develop community of learners		

Note. Information from *National Science Education Standards*, Center for Science, Mathematics, and Engineering Education, 1996, Washington, DC: National Academies Press, http://books.nap.edu/html/nses/html/overview.html#content and *A Sampler of National Science Education Standards*, by Joseph M. Peters, 2006, Upper Saddle River, NJ: Pearson Education.

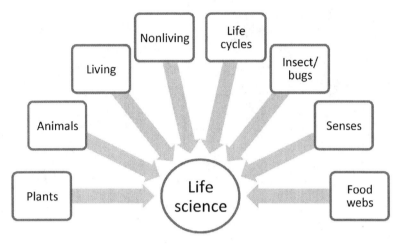

Figure 8.1 *Idea web for life science*

Integrating content serves many meaningful purposes in learning science, including the following:

1. It creates instructional activities that enhance knowledge and skill construction and comprehension in different content areas.
2. It uses reading, writing, and literacy to enrich the learning of science concepts.
3. It applies social studies concepts and skills to connect science concepts with real-life experiences, issues, and events.

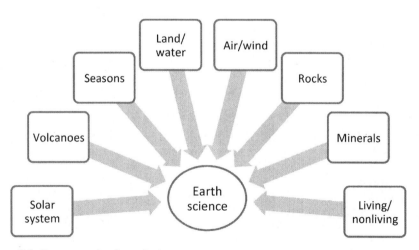

Figure 8.2 *Concept mapping for earth science*

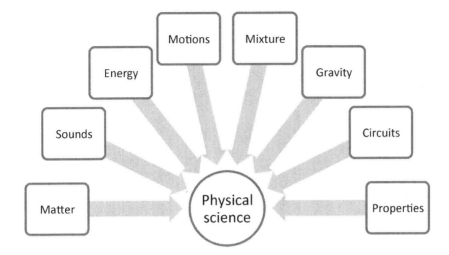

Figure 8.3 *Concept mapping for physical science*

4. It enriches understanding of the key concepts in academic subjects and content areas.
5. It enhances development of academic language across academic subjects.
6. It promotes effective teaching and learning of science.
7. It increases students' abilities, interest, and curiosity
8. It promotes flexible teaching and learning across academic subjects.
9. It enhances pedagogical skills.
10. It improves lesson plan design and identification of learning objectives.

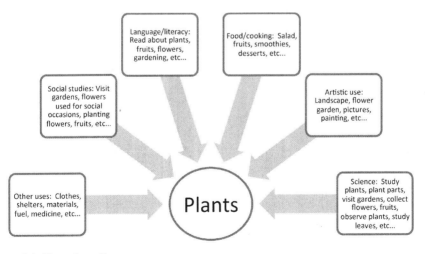

Figure 8.4 *Thematic teaching concept*

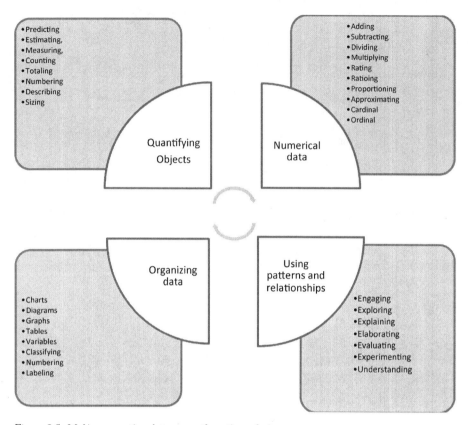

Figure 8.5 *Making connections between mathematics and science*

Teachers can do more to make integrated content appropriate, relevant, and suitable for any grade level, as long as the content of a lesson plan is based on inquiry standards. Keep in mind that teaching other academic subjects may not require inquiry approaches, and teachers may need to make instructional adjustments, modifications, accommodations, and adaptations in order to include inquiry.

PROMOTE SCIENCE LITERACY

As mentioned in earlier chapters, many children of diverse backgrounds do not lack science concepts, but they do lack science literacy. Science literacy is crucial in learning science, and teachers need to promote it throughout the course of inquiry instruction. ELL, LEP, FEP, NNS, and SN students frequently are not as literate in science as their classmates; however, lower science literacy should not preclude them from learning science. Hands-on and minds-on activities require less literacy and promote the understanding of science concepts as well as the development of science literacy. What teachers need to do is design inquiry activities that will enhance students' understanding of science concepts along with literacy. In other words, teachers need to integrate reading and writing with science, and as part of learning, teachers should explore ways to help students learn key concepts as well as science terminology. Some of those ways are creating word banks, defining new vocabulary for students, using guided practices to connect concepts, using new words in simple sentences, including cloze exercises for practice, using spelling tests to promote literacy, and asking students to write key words in science journals.

In science, literacy means different things to different teachers. Literacy is more than the ability to read and write; it means students are able to comprehend, apply, and understand science words in scientific contexts. To help teachers understand science literacy, Bybee (1997) defined the different types as follows:

1. *Illiteracy in science* means that students are unable to understand a question or locate the question in a given disciplinary domain.
2. *Nominal literacy in science* means that students understand the disciplinary basis of a question or topic but display misunderstanding in response.
3. *Functional literacy in science* means that students have the knowledge of scientific vocabulary in a specific context, such as using a new word in a sentence, identifying a new word on a test, recognizing the definition of a new word, or connecting concepts to the meaning of a new word.
4. *Conceptual literacy in science* means that students understand the way that disciplinary concepts relate to the whole discipline; they know the parts-to-whole of the discipline and have the knowledge of both the parts and the whole of that discipline.
5. *Procedural literacy in science* means that students understand the process of inquiry and the knowledge and skills required to complete this process successfully, such as following written instructions or step-by-step directions, and are able to link concepts to the scientific methods and procedural processes of inquiry used to develop new knowledge and skills within a specific discipline.
6. *Multidimensional literacy* means that students understand science as a cultural enterprise, as interconnected with society, and are able to incorporate the history and nature of science in practical use.

These six definitions are similar to the notions of how teachers define academic language in children. According to Cummins (1981), they use the term *basic interpersonal communication skills* (BICS) to describe students who are able to express their views or opinions verbally with some limitations in second-language development, and they apply the term *cognitive academic language proficiency* (CALP) to

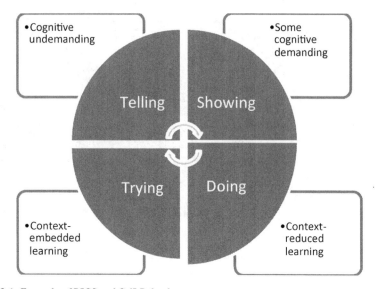

Figure 8.6 *Examples of BICS and CALP development*

Source: An educational psychology of methods in multicultural education, C.T. Vang, 2010, New York: Peter Lang Publishing.

students who can perform academic tasks with little or no assistance from teachers (see Figure 8.6). Students of diverse backgrounds will need to more time to learn new science words and develop science literacy. Without instructional adaptations, these children will lag behind, and teachers need to promote literacy in all children in spite of their different capabilities in academic subjects.

The top two quadrants of Figure 8.6, telling and showing, illustrate BICS; students who are limited in ability are able to perform at this level. The two lower quadrants, trying and doing, are considered to be CALP because they describe students that are able to perform academic tasks.

According to the national Benchmarks for Science Literacy Project 2061 (American Association for the Advancement of Science, 1993), students in Grades K-8 are expected to learn, know, and understand specific science concepts, as shown in Tables 8.7 and 8.8. These benchmarks are good guidelines for promoting science literacy in children in Grades K-5.

MATHEMATICS IN SCIENCE

As Figure 8.5 illustrates, mathematics is the language of science. Math skills serve many uses in science and they are inextricable parts of science education. For elementary science, mathematical concepts, knowledge, and skills are limited in

Table 8.7 Grades K-2 Benchmarks for Science Literacy

K-2 The Nature of Science	K-2 The Physical Setting	K-2 The Living Environment	K-2 The Human Organism	K-2 Common Themes
When a science investigation is done the way it was done before, we expect to get very similar results.	There are more stars in the sky than anyone can easily count, but they are not scattered evenly, and they are not all the same brightness or color.	Some animals and plants are alike in the way they look and in the things they do, and others are very different from one another.	People have different external features, such as the size, shape, and color of hair, skin, and eyes, but they are more like one another than like other animals.	SYSTEMS
Science investigations generally work the same way in different places.	The sun can be seen only in the daytime, but the moon can be seen sometimes at night and sometimes during the day. The sun, moon, and stars all appear to move slowly across the sky.	Plants and animals have features that help them live in different environments.	People need water, food, air, waste removal, and a particular range of temperatures in their environment, just as other animals do.	MODELS
People can often learn about things around them by just observing those things carefully, but sometimes they can learn more by doing something to the things and noting what happens.	The moon looks a little different every day, but looks the same again about every four weeks.	Stories sometimes give plants and animals attributes they really do not have.	People tend to live in families and communities in which individuals have different roles.	CONSTANCY AND CHANGE
Tools such as thermometers, magnifiers, rulers, or balances often give more information about things than can be obtained by just observing things without their help.	Some events in nature have a repeating pattern. The weather changes from day to day, but things such as temperature and rain (or snow) tend to be high, low, or medium in the same months every year.	There is variation among individuals of one kind within a population.	All animals have offspring, usually with two parents involved. People may prevent some animals from producing offspring.	SCALE
	Water can be a liquid or a solid and can go back and forth from one form to the other. If water is turned into ice and then	Offspring are very much, but not exactly, like their parents and like one another.	A human baby grows inside its mother until its birth. Even after birth, a human baby is unable to care for itself, and its survival depends on the care it receives from adults.	
		Magnifiers help people see things they could not see without them.	The human body has parts that help it seek, find, and take in food when it feels hunger—eyes and noses for detecting food, legs to get to it, arms to carry it away, and a mouth to eat it.	

(Continued)

K-2 The Nature of Science	K-2 The Physical Setting	K-2 The Living Environment	K-2 The Human Organism	K-2 Common Themes
Describing things as accurately as possible is important in science because it enables people to compare their observations with those of others.	the ice is allowed to melt, the amount of water is the same as it was before freezing.	Most living things need water, food, and air.	Senses can warn individuals about danger; muscles help them to fight, hide, or get out of danger.	
When people give different descriptions of the same thing, it is usually a good idea to make some fresh observations instead of just arguing about who is right.	Water left in an open container disappears, but water in a closed container does not disappear.	Animals eat plants or other animals for food and may also use plants (or even other animals) for shelter and nesting.	The brain enables human beings to think and send messages to other body parts to help them work properly.	
Everybody can do science and invent things and ideas.	Chunks of rocks come in many sizes and shapes, from boulders to grains of sand and even smaller.	Living things are found almost everywhere in the world. There are somewhat different kinds in different places.	People use their senses to find out about their surroundings and themselves.	
In doing science, it is often helpful to work with a team and to share findings with others.	Change is something that happens to many things.	Plants and animals both need to take in water, and animals need to take in food. In addition, plants need light.	Different senses give different information. Sometimes a person can get different information about the same thing by moving closer to it or further away from it.	
	Animals and plants sometimes cause changes in their surroundings.	Many materials can be recycled and used again, sometimes in different forms.	Some of the things people do, like playing soccer, reading, and writing, must be deliberately learned. Practicing helps people to improve. How well one learns sometimes depends on how one does it and how often and how hard one tries to learn.	
	Objects can be described in terms of the materials they are made of (clay, cloth, paper, etc.) and their physical properties (color, size, shape, weight, texture, flexibility, etc.).	Different plants and animals have external features that help them thrive in different kinds of places.	People can learn from each other by telling and listening, showing and watching, and imitating what others do.	
	Things can be done to materials to change some of their properties, but not all materials respond the same way to what is done to them.			

All team members should reach their own individual conclusions, however, about what the findings mean.

A lot can be learned about plants and animals by observing them closely, but care must be taken to know the needs of living things and how to provide for them in the classroom.

The sun warms the land, air, and water.

Things move in many different ways, such as straight, zigzag, round and round, back and forth, and fast and slow.

The way to change how something is moving is to give it a push or a pull.

Things that make sound vibrate.

Things near the earth fall to the ground unless something holds them up.

Magnets can be used to make some things move without being touched.

Some kinds of organisms that once lived on earth have completely disappeared, although they were something like others that are alive today.

Eating a variety of healthful foods and getting enough exercise and rest help people stay healthy.

Some things people take into their bodies from the environment can hurt them.

Some diseases are caused by germs, some are not. Diseases caused by germs may be spread by people who have them. Washing one's hands with soap and water reduces the number of germs that can get into the body or that can be passed on to other people.

People have many different feelings—sadness, joy, anger, fear, etc.—about events, themselves, and other people.

People react to personal problems in different ways. Some ways are more likely to be helpful than others.

Talking to someone (a friend, relative, teacher, or counselor) may help people understand their feelings and problems and what to do about them.

Table 8.8 Grades 3–5 Benchmarks for Science Literacy

3-5 The Nature of Science	3-5 The Physical Setting	3-5 The Living Environment	3-5 The Human Organism	3-5 The Common Themes	FOSS
Results of similar scientific investigations seldom turn out exactly the same. Sometimes this is because of unexpected differences in the things being investigated, sometimes because of unrealized differences in the methods used or in the circumstances in which the investigation is carried out, and sometimes just because of uncertainties in observations. It is not always easy to tell which.	The patterns of stars in the sky stay the same although they appear to move across the sky nightly, and different stars can be seen in different seasons. Telescopes magnify the appearance of some distant objects in the sky, including the moon and the planets. The number of stars that can be seen through telescopes is dramatically greater than can be seen by the unaided eye. Planets change their positions against the background of stars. The earth is one of several planets that orbit the sun, and the moon orbits around the earth. Stars are like the sun, some being smaller and some larger, but so far away that they look like points of light. Things on or near the earth are pulled toward it by the earth's gravity.	A great variety of kinds of living things can be sorted into groups in many ways using various features to decide which things belong to which group. Features used for grouping depend on the purpose of the grouping. Some likenesses between children and parents, such as eye color in human beings, or fruit or flower color in plants, are inherited. Other likenesses, such as people's table manners or carpentry skills, are learned.	Unlike in human beings, behavior in insects and many other species is determined almost entirely by biological inheritance. Human beings have made tools and machines to sense and do things that they could not otherwise sense or do at all, or as quickly, or as well. Artifacts and preserved remains provide some evidence of the physical characteristics and possible behavior of human beings who lived a very long time ago. It takes about 9 months for a human embryo to develop. Embryos are nourished by the mother, so substances she takes in will affect how well or poorly the baby develops. Human beings live longer than most other animals, but all living things die.	SYSTEMS MODELS CONSTANCY AND CHANGE	Human Body Measurement Magnetism and Electricity Environments Levers and Pulleys. Water Solar Energy Landforms Variables Models and Design. Ideas and Inventions Structures of Life Mixtures and Solutions Environments Levers and Pulleys.

Measurement
Earth
Materials
Landforms
Food and
Nutrition
Solar Energy

SCALE

Scientific investigations may take many different forms, including observing what things are like or what is happening somewhere, collecting specimens for analysis, and doing experiments.

Investigations can focus on physical, biological, and social questions.

Results of scientific investigations are seldom exactly the same, but if the differences are large, it is important to try to figure out why.

One reason for following directions carefully and for keeping records of one's work is to

Like all planets and stars, the earth is approximately spherical in shape. The rotation of the earth on its axis every 24 hours produces the night-and-day cycle. To people on earth, this turning of the planet makes it seem as though the sun, moon, planets, and stars are orbiting the earth once a day.

When liquid water disappears, it turns into a gas (vapor) in the air and can reappear as a liquid when cooled, or as a solid if cooled below the freezing point of water. Clouds and fog are made of tiny droplets of water.

Air is a substance that surrounds us, takes up space, and whose movements we feel as wind.

Waves, wind, water, and ice shape and reshape the earth's land surface by eroding rock and soil in some areas and depositing them in other areas, sometimes in seasonal layers.

For offspring to resemble their parents, there must be a reliable way to transfer information from one generation to the next.

Some living things consist of a single cell. Like familiar organisms, they need food, water, and air; a way to dispose of waste; and an environment they can live in.

Microscopes make it possible to see that living things are made mostly of cells. Some organisms are made of a collection of similar cells that benefit from cooperating. Some organisms' cells vary

There is a usual sequence of physical and mental development among human beings, although individuals differ in exactly when they learn things.

People are usually able to have children before they are able to care for them properly.

From food, people obtain energy and materials for body repair and growth. The indigestible parts of food are eliminated.

By breathing, people take in the oxygen they need to live.

Skin protects the body from harmful substances and other organisms and from drying out.

The brain gets signals from all parts of the body telling what is going on there.

The brain also sends signals to parts of the body to influence what they do.

(Continued)

3-5 The Nature of Science	3-5 The Physical Setting	3-5 The Living Environment	3-5 The Human Organism	3-5 The Common Themes	FOSS
provide information on what might have caused the differences.	Rock is composed of different combinations of minerals. Smaller rocks come from the breakage and weathering of bedrock and larger rocks. Soil is made partly from weathered rock, partly from plant remains, and also contains many living organisms.	greatly in appearance and perform very different roles in the organism.	Human beings have different interests, motivations, skills, and talents.		
Scientists' explanations about what happens in the world come partly from what they observe, partly from what they think.	Heating and cooling cause changes in the properties of materials. Many kinds of changes occur faster under hotter conditions.	For any particular environment, some kinds of plants and animals survive well, some survive less well, and some cannot survive at all.	Human beings can use the memory of their past experiences to make judgments about new situations.		
Sometimes scientists have different explanations for the same set of observations. That usually leads to their making more observations to resolve the differences.	No matter how parts of an object are assembled, the weight of the whole object made is always the same as the sum of the parts; and when a thing is broken into parts, the parts have the same total weight as the original things.	Insects and various other organisms depend on dead plant and animal material for food.	Many skills can be practiced until they become automatic. If the right skills are practiced, performance may improve.		
Scientists do not pay much attention to claims about how something they know works unless the claims are backed up	Materials may be composed of parts that are too small to be seen without magnification. When a new material is made by combining	Organisms interact with one another in various ways besides providing food. Many plants depend on animals for carrying their pollen to other plants or for dispersing their seeds.	Human beings tend to repeat behaviors that feel good or have pleasant consequences and avoid behaviors that feel bad or have unpleasant consequences.		
			Learning means using what one already knows to make sense out of new experiences or information, not just storing the new information in one's head.		
			Food provides energy and materials for growth and repair of body parts.		

(Continued)

with evidence that can be confirmed and with a logical argument.

Science is an adventure that people everywhere can take part in, as they have for many centuries.

Clear communication is an essential part of doing science. It enables scientists to inform others about their work, expose their ideas to criticism by other scientists, and stay informed about scientific discoveries around the world.

Doing science involves many different kinds of work and engages men and women of all ages and backgrounds.

two or more materials, it has properties that are different from the original materials. For that reason, a lot of different materials can be made from a small number of basic kinds of materials.

Things that give off light often also give off heat. Heat is produced by mechanical and electrical machines, and any time one thing rubs against something else.

When warmer things are put with cooler ones, the warm ones lose heat and the cool ones gain it until they are all at the same temperature. A warmer object can warm a cooler one by contact or at a distance.

Some materials conduct heat much better than others. Poor conductors can reduce heat loss.

Changes in speed or direction of motion are caused by forces.

Changes in an organism's habitat are sometimes beneficial to it and sometimes harmful.

Most microorganisms do not cause disease, and many are beneficial.

Almost all kinds of animals' food can be traced back to plants.

Some source of "energy" is needed for all organisms to stay alive and grow.

Over the whole earth, organisms are growing, dying, and decaying, and new organisms are being produced by the old ones.

Vitamins and minerals, present in small amounts in foods, are essential to keep everything working well.

As people grow up, the amounts and kinds of food and exercise needed by the body may change.

Tobacco, alcohol, other drugs, and certain poisons in the environment (pesticides, lead) can harm human beings and other living things.

If germs are able to get inside one's body, they may keep it from working properly. For defense against germs, the human body has tears, saliva, skin, some blood cells, and stomach secretions. A healthy body can fight most germs that do get inside. However, there are some germs that interfere with the body's defenses.

3-5 The Nature of Science	3-5 The Physical Setting	3-5 The Living Environment	3-5 The Human Organism	3-5 The Common Themes	FOSS
	The greater the force is, the greater the change in motion will be. The more massive an object is, the less effect a given force will have on it.	Individuals of the same kind differ in their characteristics, and sometimes the differences give individuals an advantage in surviving and reproducing.	There are some diseases that human beings can catch only once. After they've recovered they don't get sick from them again. There are many diseases that can be prevented by vaccination, so that people don't catch them even once.		
	How fast things move differs greatly. Some things are so slow that their journey takes a long time; others move too fast for people to even see them.	Fossils can be compared to one another and to living organisms according to their similarities and differences. Some organisms that lived long ago are similar to existing organisms, but some are quite different.	Different individuals handle their feelings differently, and sometimes they have different feelings in the same situation.		
	The earth's gravity pulls any object toward it without touching it.		Often human beings don't understand why others act the way they do, and sometimes they don't understand their own behavior and feelings.		
	Without touching them, a magnet pulls on all things made of iron and either pushes or pulls on other magnets.		Physical health can affect people's emotional well-being and vice-versa.		
	Without touching them, material that has been electrically charged pulls on all other materials and may either push or pull other charged materials.		One way to respond to a strong feeling, either pleasant or unpleasant, is to think about what caused it and then consider whether to seek out or avoid similar situations.		

Table 8.9 Math Content Standards

Category	Standard
A: Number and operations	• Understand numbers, ways of representing numbers, relationship among numbers and number systems
	• Meanings of operations and how they relate to one another
	• Compute fluently and make reasonable estimates
B: Algebra	• Patterns, relationships, and functions
	• Represent, analyze, use algebraic symbols
	• Math models, quantitative relationships
	• Analyze changes in various contexts
C: Geometry	• Analyze characteristics, properties, shapes, arguments, and relationships
	• Locations, spatial relationships, coordinates, and representations systems

their use; otherwise, the complexity of math could hinder students' understanding of scientific inquiry. Measurement, however, is very useful for learning science concepts in the K-6 grades, and high achievers may be able to use math skills to solve complex problems or to conduct a series of tests for a science project.

To incorporate math skills in science, teachers need to know the math content standards, as shown in Tables 8.9 and 8.10. Keeping these basic mathematical concepts in mind enables teachers to easily link their science education to the content standards in accordance with the recommendations of the National Council of Teachers of Mathematics (1989).

Table 8.10 Math Standards for Measurement

Standards for measurement activities

K-4 students should:
1. Understand length, width, capacity, weight, mass, volume, area, time, temperature, angle, and height of objects
2. Apply and develop the scientific processes of measuring objects
3. Apply and develop the concepts of measuring related to the units of measurement
4. Predict, make, and use estimates of measurement
5. Apply, make, and use measurement in problems
6. Apply, make, and use measurement in everyday life situations or events

5-8 students should:
1. Observe, compare, contrast, and solve problems
2. Predict, estimate, make, and use measurement to describe and compare phenomena (objects)
3. Select and use appropriate units and tools to measure to the degree of accuracy required in a particular situation

Mathematical measurements are made according to the customary system (standard system) in inches, feet, yards, and miles; according to the metric system (SI), in kilometers, millimeters, centimeters, or meters; and on other scales, such as degrees (Celsius or Fahrenheit). Mathematics has useful tools for illustrating scientific concepts, information, and data in a variety of forms, as shown in Figure 8.7. Graphing is a good way to explain, organize, and interpret data; however, elementary students may not be able to use complex graphs. Even though only bar or column graphs appear to be used commonly at the elementary level, standardized tests require students to be able to read many different kinds of graphs. For this reason, teachers may need to introduce students to different graphs, as illustrated in Figures 8.8, 8.9, and 8.10.

In the higher grades, teachers may want to familiarize students with the differences between quantitative and qualitative data. Quantitative data refers to the amounts of something (how much or how many) rather than the quality or standard of something; qualitative data relates to the quality or standard of something rather than amounts or numbers. An example of an investigation that examines qualitative is having students gather information about who voters plan to vote for in an election. The students will need to determine how many people they will interview and record how many choose one candidate and how many choose another. Teachers have time constraints that might render these types of studies impossible at the elementary level; however, they cannot be ruled out completely because some students may want to accept the challenge of doing one.

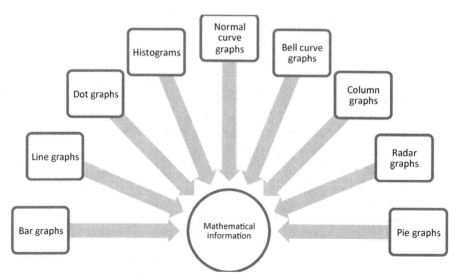

Figure 8.7 *Examples of mathematical information*

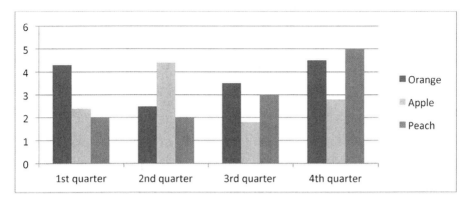

Figure 8.8 *Sample of bar or column graph*

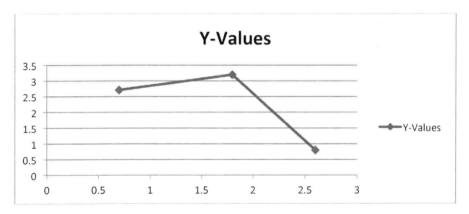

Figure 8.9 *Sample of XY graph*

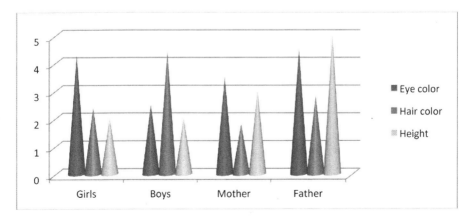

Figure 8.10 *Sample of bar or cone graph*

LANGUAGE ARTS IN SCIENCE

Math is the language for science, but language arts are necessary for both math and science because without language no teaching or learning is possible. Students learn academic language before they learn anything else. Language is the most powerful tool in communication; it is the prime vehicle of communication in written and verbal forms. Language is the channel by which people share information.

For elementary students, language is defined as a system of words, phrases, and grammar use by people who live in a country or a geographical location to communicate with one another. The English language is used for communication in the U.S. and is now a universal language around the world because many people in many countries can speak English.

In school teachers need to stress the importance of literacy, which refers to the ability to read, write, speak, and listen. Reading, writing, speaking, and listening skills promote science literacy and enhance student learning of science concepts. Teachers need to promote reading and writing in science as much as possible. The fact that some students are limited in their ability to speak English in class does not mean that they cannot read, write, spell, or listen to others. Academic performance should be based on the ability to read and write, not on speaking and listening abilities. In other words, teachers need to recognize that some students are not as outspoken as others, but they could be proficient in reading and writing. On the other hand, some students are verbally proficient but do not read and write well. Teachers need to take these factors into account when teaching science concepts in the multicultural classroom.

Language experiences are important for academic performance across the whole curriculum. The 5-E and 8-E models require linguistic skills for each process. Teachers may need to engage the prior knowledge of students to learn more about their reading and writing abilities. Table 8.11 lists the standards for language arts content; these are important in science education because students need to have language skills to communicate and reason as they perform inquiry investigations and experiments in science. As Table 8.12 illustrates, reading and writing skills are keys to achieving science literacy. In fact, the reading and writing standards contain the tools that appear to be the most value for children to have in order for them to be competitive anywhere in the academic arena; without these tools, students struggle to read directions, instructions, and procedural steps in conducting inquiry investigations and experiments.

Teachers should require students to practice writing short investigative reports to document their findings throughout the inquiry processes. For part of this writing, students need to record their daily learning of science concepts in a journal for reflective purposes. Teachers should make their own journal entries as

Table 8.11 Language Arts Content Standards

1. Read a wide range of print and non-print texts for multiple purposes.
2. Read a wide range of literature from many periods and genres to build understanding of the human experience.
3. Apply a wide range of strategies to comprehend, interpret, evaluate, and appreciate texts.
4. Adjust spoken, written, and visual language to communicate effectively for different purposes.
5. Employ a wide range of strategies in writing for a variety of purposes.
6. Apply knowledge of language structure, conventions, and genre to create and discuss print and non-print texts.
7. Conduct research, generate questions, gather data, and communicate discoveries.
8. Use various technologies and information sources to gather data and communicate knowledge.
9. Demonstrate respect for diversity in language use, patterns, and dialects.
10. Use first language to develop competency in English.
11. Participate as knowledgeable, reflective, creative, and critical members of diverse literacy communities.
12. Use spoken, written, and visual language to accomplish own purposes.

a best professional practice as well. Toward the end of each semester or progress report period, teachers need to collect students' science journals and grade them. Expressions in student journals may help teachers reflect on their overall pedagogical skills and knowledge, science pedagogical skills and knowledge, science conceptual bridges, science conceptual changes, and science critical thinking.

Table 8.12 Examples of Reading and Writing in Science

Examples of Reading in Science	Examples of Writing in Science
Students should:	*Students should:*
1. Read a wide range of print or texts to build an understanding of texts to acquire new information to respond to the needs and demands of society and the workplace and for personal fulfillment.	1. Apply a wide range of strategies in the writing process to communicate with different audiences for a variety of purposes.
2. Apply a wide range of strategies to comprehend, interpret, evaluate, and appreciate text.	2. Apply knowledge and skills of language structure, language conventions, media techniques, figurative language, and genre to create, critique, and discuss print or writings.
3. Understand prior experience, interactions with other readers and writers, word meanings, word identification, and knowledge of textual characteristics and features.	3. Conduct research on issues and interests by generating ideas, questions, and problems.
4. Adjust spoken, written, and visual language to communicate effectively for different purposes.	4. Gather, evaluate, organize, observe, and synthesize data from a variety of sources.
	5. Use gathered information to communicate with audiences for a variety of purposes.

Perhaps the feedback would help teachers to reexamine whether they are teaching science as inquiry, focusing on skills, or focusing on instruction. Remember, science standards prefer that science concepts be taught through inquiry.

SOCIAL STUDIES IN SCIENCE

As with mathematics and language arts, social studies has a significant role to play in science. In the elementary grades, social studies is a social science and examines history, politics, economics, and people. It is a humanity that promotes civic competence, civility, and peace. Table 8.13 lists the social studies content standards that connect science and humanities together to help students create a more complete picture of their surroundings and the nature of the world of people. Teachers should encourage students to inquire to learn about social studies topics such as the extinction of animals, endangered species, animal migrations, drought, global warming, world population, famine, democracy, elections, warfare, the global economy, housing crises, and disease epidemics or pandemics. These social issues affect life and people in the world.

Social studies lesson plans could also examine the history of science or scientists. As a foundation for such plans, Table 8.14 lists some scientists in different categories of interest.

Another great way to connect science and social studies is to examine how food and cultures help people connect, live, socialize, and survive in the world. Each culture has traditional foods: Thai, Mexican, Japanese, Hmong, American, Korean, Chinese, Italian, Greek, Indian, and Vietnamese, to name a few. Simple dishes could be made to highlight different cultures, such as tacos, sausages,

Table 8.13 Selected Social Studies Content Standards

1. Have experiences that provide for the study of culture and cultural diversity.
2. Provide for the study of the ways human beings view themselves in and over time.
3. Provide for the study of people, places, and environments.
4. Provide for the study of individual development and identity.
5. Provide for the study of interactions among individuals, groups, and institutions.
6. Provide for the study of how people create and change structures of power, authority, and governance.
7. Provide for the study of how people organize for the production, distribution, and consumption of goods and services.
8. Provide for the study of relationships among science, technology, and society.
9. Provide for the study of global connections and interdependence.
10. Provide for the study of the ideals, principles, and practices of citizenship in a democratic republic .

Table 8.14 Selected Scientists in Selected Categories

Scientists by Science Discipline	Female Scientists	African-American Scientists	Hispanic Scientists	Scientists/ Inventors with Disabilities
1. Albert Einstein—physics	1. Marie Curie	1. Benjamin Banneker	1. Narciso Monturiol	1. Isaac Newton
2. Charles Darwin—evolution	2. Florence Rena Sabin	2. Rebecca Cole	2. Carlos Finlay	2. Alexander Graham Bell
3. Michael Faraday—electricity	3. Maria Goeppert	3. Edward Alexander Bouchet	3. Severo Ochoa	3. Thomas Alva Edison
4. Marie Curie—Radioactivity	4. Dorothy Crowfoot Hodgkin	4. Daniel Hale Williams	4. Luis Walter Alvarez	4. Henry Ford
5. William Harvey—anatomy	5. Edith Hinckley Quimby	5. George Washington Carver	5. Baruj Benacerraf	5. Albert Einstein
6. Dmitri Mendeleev—Chemistry	6. Jane Goodall	6. Charles Henry Turner	6. Mario Molina	6. Stephen Hawking
7. James Watson—DNA structure	7. Rebecca Cole	7. Archibald Alexander	7. Ellen Ochoa	
8. Frederick G. Hopkins—vitamins		8. Roger Arliner Young		
9. Jonas Salk—vaccination		9. Charles Richard Drew		
10. Alexander Fleming—penicillin				

hamburgers, hot dogs, fried chicken, French fries, smoothies, barbeque, salads, soups, and desserts. Cultural foods bring people and the world together, as do the Olympic Games and the World Cup soccer tournament.

Children today are accustomed to fast food menus and have little knowledge and skills about culinary dishes. Of course, they can see television programs and entertainers that describe various dishes, but cooking is great science because it is a hands-on and minds-on activity. Usually, good cooks are good scientists who can mix foods and drinks to create great tastes. Students may be good scientists themselves without realizing it because they can make a sandwich, mix simple drinks, brush their teeth, take a shower or a bath, wash and clean their belongings, and keep themselves clean (hygiene). These examples of common activities indicate how social studies is connected to everyday science.

SUMMING UP

This chapter emphasized the use of integrating content across the whole curriculum to help students develop a more complete understanding of their surroundings and the natural world. Science can be taught along with other subjects, such as mathematics, language arts, and social studies.

Mathematics is the language for science. Students use numbers and other math concepts to organize data. Measurement and counting are practical math tools used in science. Students measure objects and interpret the results using either the metric or the standard system.

The subject of language arts contains the language of all academic subjects. Without a system of communication, learning science or any other content is extremely difficult. Language arts literacy involves reading, writing, speaking, and listening skills. These skills are absolutely essential in teaching and learning science as well as other subjects. Science processes, such as those in the 5-E and 8-E models, require language skills. Teachers can integrate mathematical skills with science and apply language skills to communicate information. The inquiry processes always involve math and language skills.

Furthermore, social studies can be connected with science in many ways. Foods and cultures can be used to explain the concept of science as human endeavor. Each culture is unique, as are the people of any culture. Culinary science has changed the way people cook and eat. Different cultures bring a variety of tastes from different parts of the world. Without question, social studies, like mathematics and language arts, is an inextricable part of science.

CHAPTER NINE

Use Technology AS Inquiry Support

Every great advance in science has issued from a new audacity of imagination.

— JOHN DEWEY *THE QUESTV FOR CERTAINTY*, 1929

INTRODUCTION

Today educational technology is abundant and available at home and in school. Teachers and students have easy access to electronic multimedia devices, such as television, cellular phones, iPads, iPods, ELMOs, and SMART Boards; however, not every classroom is equipped with up-to-date technology. Many schools do not have the fund to purchase computers for students, but most schools do have computer labs where students can surf the Web to get the information needed to support their learning of inquiry science concepts. Nearly every teacher has a personal computer in the classroom for professional use, such as checking email messages, looking for instructional support materials, and accessing online resources. This chapter explores the benefits of educational technology in the classroom because technology has a tremendous influence on everyday life, teaching, and learning and the powerful influence of the technological devices has changed instructional practices so much that teachers need to be selective about the type of electronic devices that best support and enhance teaching and learning science in the multicultural setting.

THE ROLE OF MASS MEDIA

Teachers and students have joined the information age of technological exploration and exploitation. Technology is changing rapidly, and media are being used as a major source of information, exposing people to a variety of communications. Sometimes, what is seen can be believed, but other times, what is seen is disturbing. Electronics has changed the world over the last century in many ways, some good and some not. Teachers need to protect their students and themselves when it comes to the use of mass media and electronic multimedia technology in the classroom.

Today teachers and students are exposed to numerous forms of public and private communication, and these communications can reach a large number of people around the world. Mass media, including television, radio, movies, newspapers, magazines, books, and electronic devices (cellular phones, videotapes, computers, computer discs, music tapes, iPad, iPod, ELMO, SMART boards, and computer chips), have tremendous influence on lives, teaching, and learning inside and outside the classroom. Teachers need to be selective about the type of media and technological applications to which students are exposed in class, and they should be concerned about the amount of time teachers and students spend with such supportive technological devices. Just as good parents control their children's television watching at home, teachers should control how much technology is used in the classroom in place of instruction from teachers. Most importantly, the role of media and technological devices is to support instructional practices; media and technology should never replace human instruction.

Both teachers and students are living in an electronic world and the influence of mass media will increase rather than lessen. Some of the influence is negative as it sometimes portrays violence, perversity, falsehood, and immorality as normal or good. For this reason, teachers as well as parents need to be constantly alert to the influences of mass media and technology on their lives, on teaching, and on learning.

The flip side of the pervasiveness of mass media is that technology is now part of everyday life and everyone has to learn how to live with or without it.

POWERFUL INFLUENCE OF TECHNOLOGY

Millions of children in the world today are affected by mass media and technological devices. Many children spend hours watching television shows or browsing the Web for personal gratification. The way the media and technology influence lives, teaching, and learning is psychologically destructive in some cases. For instance, some teenagers have to seek professional assistance for Internet addiction. This is as bad as substance abuse or drug addiction. On the other hand, media and technology have advanced life, teaching, and learning exponentially.

Many teachers today are dependent on technology for resources, such as online lesson plans, animations, and video clips. These online resources may not necessarily have the quality that enables teachers to meet science content standards. Teachers need to evaluate their sources to make sure they are academically sound and support the education standards; they may need to modify or adapt what they find online to make it academically sound. Teachers should use technology only to enhance teaching, not replace it; they should not depend on technology to be the main source of instruction. Students will not benefit from such a practice, and gluing students to a computer screen will not facilitate inquiry-based instruction. Science knowledge and skills are developed and constructed through hands-on and minds-on activities, not by simply watching and listening, no matter how clever or appealing the technology is.

If technology is used as part of everyday classroom routine, students will become dependent on it, as will teachers. The powerful influence of technology should be limited; otherwise, the negative influences on teaching and learning could damage the inquiry processes as teachers and students are not able to function academically without the use of technological devices to guide instruction. In other words, a psychological addiction to technology could result, leading to poor-quality instruction and eventual instructional failure, especially for science concepts and inquiry instruction. Therefore, inquiry science should be taught with limited technological support to maintain the authenticity of guided inquiry instruction. Too many technological applications will prevent children from socializing together, being creative in learning, reading textbooks, paying attention to teachers, interacting with group members, and engaging in inquiry activities.

TECHNOLOGY CAN'T BE THE TEACHER

Teachers know well that students do not learn concepts and skills directly from computers; however, students can be taught to enhance their learning with the information stored in computers if they are guided properly. That is why parents need to sign consent forms to allow their children to browse the Web in the classroom. Online resources are not designed to be used in place of a teacher; that is, technology cannot be the teacher. Think about this: If computers could be the teachers, why must teachers be trained academically, professionally, and ethically before becoming licensed by the state? If technology is used wisely, it can be an effective tool providing good support for instructional practices, making inquiry activities conducive to learning. If is used ineffectively, however, it can be a double-edged sword that distorts information. Teachers should consider using technology to help their students acquire some knowledge and skills, to introduce key science concepts, and to enhance the learning of science concepts through inquiry-based approaches.

Effective use of technology can help teachers and students learn *about*, *from*, and *with* technological devices that will enhance the inquiry processes. Learning *about* technology gives students the ability to use the components of the computer systems to define scientific vocabulary words, to operate the procedures required for computers, and to access Internet services. Learning *from* technology has to do with the ability to use computers to enhance teaching or learning; to operate computer applications such as CD-ROMs, digital images, arts, designs, simulations, data, and visual aids; and to extrapolate useful information to help in learning science concepts. Learning *with* technology enhances learning through using databases; collecting data; writing reports; storing data or information for future use; and using tools such as Microsoft Outlook, spreadsheets, graphing software, power point presentations, and word processing.

Even though these are good uses of technology, teachers are the prime source of teaching and learning. Computers can be much better than older tools for many uses, but teaching is still best done by a teacher.

USE EDUCATIONAL TECHNOLOGY

The National Science Education Standards (NSES) provides a basic standard for science and technology for Grades K-4 and a basic standard for Grades 4-8 (see Table 9.1). The International Society for Technology in Education (1999) proposed six broad guidelines for planning technology-based activities that would help students achieve academic progress, succeed in learning, and develop basic communication and life skills; these standards are listed in Table 9.2. The two sets of standards should be used as guidelines for teachers on how to include technology as part of instructional practice.

Table 9.1 NSES Science and Technology Standards

Expectations for Grades K-4: Use computers or technology to conduct inquiry activities, understand differences between natural objects and objects made by man
Expectations for Grades 5-8: Abilities, design, understand technology and applications; use computers to access, gather, store, retrieve, and organize data

Table 9.2 Examples of International Society for Technology in Education Technology Standards

Basic operations and concepts	Social, Ethical, and Human Issues	Technology Productivity Tools	Technology Communication Tools	Technology Research Tools	Technology Problem-solving and Decision-making tools
1. Demonstrate a sound understanding of the nature and operation of technology systems	1. Understand the ethical, cultural, and societal issues related to technology	1. Use technology tools to enhance learning, increase productivity, and promote creativity	1. Use telecommunication to collaborate, publish, and interact with peers, experts, and other audiences	1. Use technology to locate, evaluate, and collect information from a variety of sources	1. Use technology resource for solving problems and making informed decisions
2. Be proficient in the use of technology	2. Practice responsible use of technology systems, information, and software	2. Use productivity tools to collaborate in constructing technology-enhanced models, preparing publications, and producing other creative works	2. Use a variety of media and formats to communicate information and ideas effectively to multiple audiences	2. Use technology to process and report results	2. Employ technology in the development of strategies for solving problems in the real world
3. Know how to use technology or apply to everyday life	3. Develop positive attitudes toward technology uses that support lifelong learning, collaboration, personal pursuits, and productivity	3. Apply to everyday life situations	3. Apply to everyday life situations	3. Evaluate and select new information resources and technological innovations based on the appropriateness to specific tasks	3. Apply technology knowledge and skills to everyday life situations
	4. Apply technology to everyday life			4. Apply to everyday life needs or situations	

Note. Information from *National Educational Technology Standards for Students: Connecting Curriculum and Technology*, International Society for Technology in Education (ISTE), 1999, Eugene, OR: Author.

Because technology changes rapidly, teachers need to keep up with it in order to take advantage of the latest innovations to support instruction and enhance student learning. For inquiry science, teachers need to know the software, simulations, online resources, productivity tools, data collection tools, analysis tools, multimedia tools, and telecommunications resources that can enhance the teaching and learning of science concepts. State mandates require that teachers be computer or technologically literate; otherwise, using educational technology would be problematic. Teachers need to know what hardware is needed in the classroom and how the hardware or software can be arranged and managed to take advantage of the educational technology resources available to support inquiry science instructions.

Staying at the cutting edge of learning technology throughout their teaching career is challenging for teachers; however, teachers always have the opportunity to take advantage of technology innovations through professional development courses or trainings. Companies, schools, and school districts offer these trainings because not knowing the latest advancements in technological applications would limit teachers' abilities to connect technology to the science curriculum.

To make the classroom technology oriented for computer applications, teachers should do the following:

1. Have access to basic Internet services.
2. Promote technology literacy in children.
3. Embed science concepts with technology.
4. Use computer-assisted instruction approaches.
5. Limit lengthy computer use for inquiry activities.
6. Use quality software and hardware.
7. Use computer simulations and animations.
8. Use process skills for inquiry activities.
9. Use databases, or Microcomputer-based laboratory (MBL) and Calculator-based laboratory (CBL) to collect, store, and process data.
10. Use multimedia presentations to support inquiry activities.
11. Keep meaningful websites and science materials handy:
    a. CD-ROMs (electronically stored information discs)
    b. DVD players
    c. Wild Project
    d. National Geographic
    e. NASA
    f. Children books

    g. Geographic information system (GIS)

    h. Global Learning and Observations to Benefit the Environment (GLOBE)

    i. Student's Cloud Observations On-Line activities (S'COOL)

    j. Clouds and the Earth's Radiant Energy System (CERES)

12. Maintain a list of science programs and projects.

Teachers need to incorporate the six areas of the International Society for Technology in Education standards described in Table 9.2 into their science teaching to help students understand the importance of knowing how to operate a computer. However, young children in Grades K-1 may have limited access to computers; they may be ready to begin to learn the skills required in these standards. Teachers should include technology with inquiry science to show these students how to enhance their learning. For example, a teacher can show a 5-minute video clip on the life cycle of a butterfly to students. This kind of simulation or animation should be conducive to learning; however, the hands-on and minds-on activities should not be replaced with simulations.

If a computer lab is available or there are enough computers in the classroom for small-group activities, teachers can put students in pairs and assign them to a computer to check out the simulations online. In this way students can learn how to use the computer at the same time they are learning about the life cycle of a butterfly.

USE TECHNOLOGY IN CLASS

As mentioned earlier, teachers have to be extra careful about allowing students to browse the Web on computers in class. The Web is a super highway that gives students access to a lot of information, good and bad, even if the server is blocked. Parents need to be informed about the nature of technology used in class and parents must sign the consent forms for their children to use the technology. Teachers must keep the consent forms up to date to avoid any potential misunderstanding with parents.

Most teachers today use ELMOs, overhead projectors, SMART Boards, iPads, iPods, and laptop or desktop computers for assisting instructions. These devices are good tools for inquiry instruction as well as creative teaching. However, too much technology is a bad teaching practice because children do not learn from computers, and parents do not send their children to school to be taught by computers. Good teachers would agree that computers should be used for meaningful purposes and not for convenience to get the teacher or the students through the day. In other words, well-organized teachers usually plan to teach; however, disorganized teachers usually plan to depend on computers for survival. Teachers can find online resources that teach science concepts without considering the content standards and the learning objectives. This is not an acceptable practice. Moreover, the direct instruction approach allows teachers to teach science concepts straight out of the book, and this technique involves little or no inquiry process skills. For effective use of technology in teaching science, teachers should remember three key phrases: How are students going to learn about technology, from technology, and with technology in the classroom (see Figure 9.1). Teachers should also evaluate how technology is being used or applied in class.

Preparing for electronic instruction takes time, and teachers need to be efficient about using technology in class. Sometimes teachers take too much time getting the computer ready, and sometimes the computer is down because the system is not working. Such unanticipated situations may disrupt electronic teaching. Teachers need to prepare their computers before time for the lesson to make sure the system is working properly. Otherwise, solely depending on the use of technology in the classroom could be a hassle with a headache because time is easily lost.

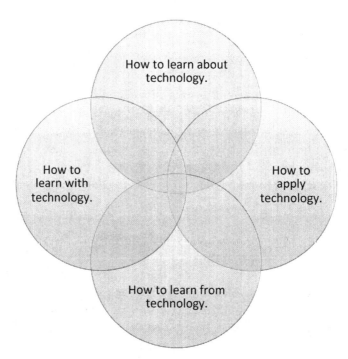

Figure 9.1 *How to use technology in class*

USE TECHNOLOGY LAB

Depending on where the school is located, teachers start using computers very early to facilitate instruction at all grade levels. Some classrooms have a few computers available for a lab, and others have none. In some schools, there is a computer lab where teachers can sign up and take the whole class for academic activities, such as math, language arts, computer skills, science, social studies, and research.

If the classroom has a lab, teachers need to make sure all children have equal opportunity to use the computer for inquiry science. Monitoring the lab is time consuming when there are not enough computers for everyone to use at once; however, teachers can choose to display the lesson on the ELMO or big screen to help all students learn. If teachers want to allow students to use the classroom computers, specific procedural guidelines should be given to all students. All students must understand the conditions in order to make smooth transitions. Taking turns does not always work well with students. But it is necessary to rotate 20, 25, or 30 students so they can have equal access to the computers. Sufficient time must be allocated for computer lab so it does not become a waste of time.

Teachers can take the whole class to the lab for any prescribed activities, but travel to and from the lab takes time. Scheduling must be flexible to make the most use of the lab. Teachers need to determine when the best time to use the lab is. Instead of stopping instruction to take students to lab, it may be better to go early in the morning, before recess, after lunch, or just before school ends. Picking the right time slot can save time. However, the ideal time slots may not be available and teachers may need to adjust their instructional routines to accommodate computer lab schedules.

For classrooms without a lab, teachers can use PowerPoint presentations with laptops or desktop to present information. Keep in mind that technology is used as an instructional supplement to enhance teaching and learning and not as the primary source of academic instruction.

Regardless of what kind of lab is available, teachers need to make sure that the room is set up appropriately for educational technology activities. As shown in Figure 9.2, the classroom should be organized with designated centers for students to enjoy, process, and rotate through while conducting inquiry activities.

CORRECT SCIENCE MISPERCEPTIONS

Today's children are confused about what is true and what is not until they reach adulthood. Before enrolling in school, children watch many television programs. Children's programming such as *Sesame Street*, the Sprout channel, the Disney

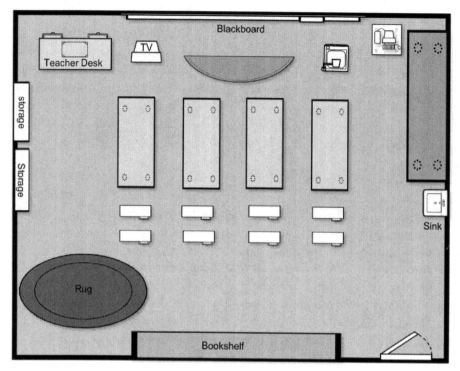

Figure 9.2 *Example of centers for inquiry activities*

World channel, Cartoon Network, and Walt Disney movies do not always depict the right attributes of animals, plants, people, and life. Children are also socially and culturally influenced in their understanding of life events by their parents, siblings, and friends. Their perceptions and conceptions of their surroundings and the natural world undoubtedly have at least some unrealistic thoughts, misperceptions, and falsehoods. Some of the advanced computer animated movies coming out of Hollywood make children fantasize about life without knowing how much technology can change and affect their lives negatively and positively. Children tend to believe what they see in the movies.

The computer simulations, video clips, CD-ROMs, and animations used in the classroom will do the same to students if teachers should fail to notice and correct their misperceptions and misconceptions. Children do not know whether some things are real or illusions, and all they think about is how it appears to be. One example is the controversy surrounding the debate over creation and intelligence design. How can teachers explain the controversy and elicit reasoned discussion about it with students who refuse to believe that the world was created by a supreme being or students who insist that it was? These perceptions need to be addressed within their academic and scientific contexts so that students can understand science separately from religious values. Otherwise, students will grow up with their misperceptions, some introduced by technology.

Teachers need to suspend their personal values and beliefs while engaging children in inquiry science. Teachers' values may not have much influence on young children because they do not catch everything that is said in class, but older children are influenced by what they hear from their teachers. For instance, a teacher asks students to roll their tongues and touch the tongue to the tip of their nose, saying anyone who cannot perform this feat is dumb. Such an exercise and derogatory remark does not constitute inquiry science at all; rather, it is bigoted science. Teachers cannot expect all students to be able to roll their tongues to touch their noses. This is a clear example of negative reinforcement of misperceptions.

Technology can correct some science misperceptions in children if it is used as a conceptual bridge. A conceptual bridge facilitates conceptual change in students by connecting or helping create meaningful linkage between their life experiences and an explanation of those experiences that arises in the inquiry process. In other words, the inquiry process helps students link learned experience with prior knowledge to develop or construct clearer and better understandings. Technology can be a conceptual bridge if it engages students in the process of learning that involves making changes in their knowledge and skills schemas toward the development or construction of concrete concepts. Use of technology with a spiraling science curriculum that builds from year to year helps teachers facilitate conceptual change, correcting students' misperceptions.

USE TECHNOLOGY AS INQUIRY

As mentioned in earlier chapters, inquiry refers to the scientific process of investigation and experimentation. Inquiry involves the strategies, methods, approaches, and processes of developing generalizations and constructing scientific meanings by asking and answering questions. Technology, if used correctly, can be a tool that supports the inquiry processes. Teachers and students can use computers to explore any science concept to learn more about it, to collect data, to store data collected, to conduct investigations and research, to process the inquiry skills step-by-step, and to analyze data through multimedia presentations.

Teachers can also use open-ended questions, closed questions, and focus questions to guide the technological inquiry processes. As shown in Table 9.3, teachers can use inquiry questions for descriptive investigation, classification investigation, and experimental investigation. They can also design basic procedural guidelines

Table 9.3 Sample Questions for Various Types of Scientific Investigations

Science Concept	Questions for investigations	Descriptive Investigation	Classificatory Investigation	Experimental Investigation	Basic Procedural Guidelines
Animals	What are farm animals? What are domesticated animals? What do cats and dogs have in common?	✓			Name what animals live on the farm, at the zoo, or at home. Compare and contrast cats and dogs.
Plants	What do plants need to live? What are plants used for? Plants include what?	✓			Learn about sun, water, soil, space; talk about things made from plants; and show a variety of plants.
Static electricity or magnetism	What causes static? Do magnets attract or repel? What things are attracted to magnets and what things are repelled?	✓	✓		Collect or gather different things for testing, test south and north poles, and use balloons for static electricity.
State of matter	What are the four states of matter? What is density? What is the chemical property of each type of matter? How does heat affect matter?	✓	✓	✓	Ice cube for solid, water for liquid, and dry ice for gas; melting process, heat transfer, density, and molecular structure.
Friction, motion, reaction, and energy	What is inertia? What causes things to move? What is the cause and effect of action and reaction?	✓		✓	Use pulling or pushing to show motions; show action and reaction experiment; talk about kinetic and potential energy.

Table 9.4 Samples of Closed and Open-Ended Inquiry Questions

Question	Closed	Open-Ended	Inquiry Purposes
Do you like the taste of fortune cookies?	✓		
How do you describe the taste in your mouth?		✓	
What are the animals doing?	✓		Observing
What are the objects doing?	✓		Observing
Have you seen different animals or plants before?	✓		Observing, engaging
What do you see the animals doing in the picture?	✓		Observing, analyzing
How can you tell if animals are the same or different?		✓	Observing, comparing, contrasting, inferring,
What can you tell about the objects in the picture?		✓	Observing, inferring, concluding
What have you just observed?		✓	Explaining, inferring, concluding, elaborating,
What objects do you think will float or sink in water?		✓	Analyzing, observing, inferring, explaining, elaborating, concluding
How do you describe each animal?		✓	Observing, communicating, explaining, elaborating, analyzing, inferring, concluding,
Where do these animals stay at night?		✓	Observing, predicting, hypothesizing, inferring,
How can you tell if the object is moving or not moving?		✓	Observing, analyzing, explaining, elaborating, experimenting, inferring, concluding

for using technology support to guide investigations to help students focus on answering the questions, as illustrated in Table 9.4.

Teachers must engage students in the inquiry process even when technology is used to support the teaching and learning of science concepts. Without utilizing inquiry skills, such as observing, communicating, inferring, classifying, comparing, contrasting, predicting, or measuring, technology-assisted instructions could be meaningless and fruitless. However, using technology to support inquiry science can make students curious, eager, and excited to learn new concepts. Teachers can use focus questions to guide students and show a simulation or video clip about the newly introduced concepts to engage students' prior knowledge in the investigation process.

RETRIEVE INFORMATION FROM COMPUTERS

Teachers need to carefully evaluate and select computer programs that will best fit the needs of their students. Remember, there are top, middle, and bottom students in each class. The information students retrieve from computers could be obsolete, too difficult to understand, too hard to read, and not appropriate for the grade level or the age of students. For instance, K-1 students will not be able to read texts on the computer screen; however, the artifacts, simulations, pictures, visual aids, and animations may be helpful to them. In the other grades, some students, especially ELL, NNS, and SN students, may not be able to read all the instructions step-by-step; therefore, they may not be able to follow what is shown on the screen. Computer programs have to be academically sound and standards-based.

To help find appropriate science software and Internet sites, teachers need to do their homework and compile a list of resources for their specific grades. These resources must meet the content standards; otherwise, inquiry science is being taught with improvised or impoverished content. Teachers may want to ask themselves these questions when looking for a computer program to assist in inquiry science activities:

1. Can students operate the computers?
2. Can students understand the software?
3. Can students read the directions or instructions?
4. Can students understand the menu?
5. Is the program appropriate or suitable for the grade level?
6. Is the program easy or hard for students to use?
7. Does the program have audio instructions?
8. Is the program flexible for students to use?
9. Is the program designed for science learning?
10. Is the program's content relevant to standards?
11. Does the program have appropriate graphics, artifacts, illustrations, and pictures?
12. Has the program been used by other teachers or schools?
13. Is the program compatible with PC, Mac, or other computer formats?
14. Is the program organized and aligned with inquiry science?
15. How long does each section take?

Students may not be able to retrieve all the information they need from the computer in a short time. Teachers need to allow sufficient time for students to extract the information. In many cases, students copy the information word by word on paper, and that takes a long time unless teachers model how to cut and paste on Word documents. Also, printing could pose a problem because it is costly. Many times students are shown the information on the screen but are told not to print out anything to take with them. Teachers should preview the information and allow students to print out some of it to save ink. However, students will learn more easily if they can have access to hard copies of information because they cannot remember everything they have seen on the screen. For this reason, teachers may need to print out samples and make copies available for everyone to practice from.

PROMOTE TECHNOLOGY LITERACY

Now as always, educational technology is going to be a big part of education and can enhance the quality of inquiry science teaching and learning. Computer knowledge and skills are essential for everyday use today. To help students meet this academic challenge, teachers need to promote technology literacy in children early. They can use programs or websites such as *Kid Pix, Hyper Studio, PowerPoint, Inspiration, Walt Disney, ABC.com, Crayons.com, kids.com,* and others to promote the appropriate use of technology. Many kindergarteners today know how to play video games and how to log on to home computers using a login I.D. and a password. Teachers can enhance technology literacy by incorporating key concepts or words as part of their science lessons. Children need to become very familiar with words such as mouse, keyboard, screen, monitor, icon, space bar, menu, desktop, World Wide Web (www), start button, and shutdown. Teachers can also promote computer skills by talking about the following activities or concepts:

- How to start a computer
- Log in or log on
- Login ID and password
- Checking emails
- Accessing the Internet
- Files and documents
- Saving files or documents
- Opening a file or document
- Printing a file or document
- Closing a file or document
- Shutting down the computer
- Saving files or documents on hard drive, USB, or discs
- Restarting or rebooting a computer
- Crashes, blue screens, error messages, and frozen screens
- Searching for information online

Children need to learn technological skills as they advance through the grades; they need to know *PowerPoint, RAMs, microbyte, megabyte, gigabyte, byte, and memory.* Promoting computer knowledge and skills early may inspire students' interests in technology science as well. Table 9.5 illustrates what it means to be technologically literate. Computers and electronic multimedia technology advance

Table 9.5 Knowledge and Skills That Constitute Technological Literacy

Technology Area	Knowledge or Skill
Basic operations and concepts	1. Demonstrate a sound understanding of the nature and operation of technology system 2. Be proficient of the use of technology 3. Know how to use technology or apply to everyday life
Social, ethical, and human issues	1. Understand the ethical, cultural, and societal issues related to technology 2. Practice responsible use of technology systems, information, and software 3. Develop positive attitudes toward technology uses that support lifelong learning, collaboration, personal pursuits, and productivity. 4. Apply technology to everyday life
Technology productivity tools	1. Use technology tools to enhance learning, increase productivity, and promote creativity 2. Use productivity tools to collaborate in constructing technology-enhanced models, prepare publications, and produce other creative works. 3. Apply to everyday life situations
Technology communication tools	1. Use telecommunication to collaborate, publish, and interact with peers, experts, and other audiences 2. Use a variety of media and formats to communicate information and ideas effectively to multiple audiences. 3. Apply to everyday life situations
Technology research tools	1. Use technology to locate, evaluate, and collect information from a variety of sources 2. Use technology to process and report results 3. Evaluate and select new information resources and technological innovations based on the appropriateness to specific tasks . 4. Apply to everyday life needs or situations
Technology problem-solving and decision-making tools	1. Use technology resources for solving problems and making informed decisions 2. Employ technology in the development of strategies for solving problems in the real world 3. Apply technology knowledge and skills to everyday life situations

Note. Information from *National Educational Technology Standards for Students: Connecting Curriculum and Technology,* International Society for Technology in Education, 1999, Eugene, OR: Author.

faster than education reforms and curriculum development; both teachers and students need to keep up with the latest technology in order to make teaching and learning science as inquiry fun and effective.

SUMMING UP

This chapter discussed how computers and electronic multimedia technology can be used effectively in the classroom to enhance the teaching and learning of science concepts. Educational technology provides good tools for teaching and learning; however, overuse of technology may have negative influences on teaching and learning. Teachers should not depend solely on electronic instruction and neglect the design of appropriate science lesson plans for inquiry instruction.

Computer simulations are supplementary materials and should not be used in place of the main instructional processes; computers and electronic devices cannot replace a good teacher. Teachers need to evaluate any computer programs used in the class to make sure the contents reflect the needs of students and meet science standards. Teachers also need to take into consideration that electronic lesson plans require preparation just as other lesson plans do; otherwise, electronic instruction would be improvised and impoverished teaching that is not conducive to learning.

Promoting technology literacy in children early is a must. Computer knowledge and skills are essential in today's world. Students need to learn basic computer skills as they advance through the grades. By the end of their senior year in high school, students should know how to operate a computer for basic use. Overall, technology is very influential and will affect the way teachers teach and the way students learn. Therefore, educational technology can be used to support the teaching and learning of inquiry science.

PART FOUR

Promoting Independent Learning

CHAPTER TEN

Assess Inquiry Science Learning

It is characteristic of science that the full explanations are often seized in their essence by the percipient scientist long in advance of any possible proof.

—JOHN DESMOND BERNAL *THE ORIGIN OF LIFE,* 1967

INTRODUCTION

Assessment plays a vital role in the teaching and learning of all academic subjects and is an integral part of teaching quality and effectiveness. Teaching accountability is huge; without academic assessment, no one knows how well teachers are teaching, where learners are going, whether teaching and learning are taking place, and how teachers can help students reach their learning goals. Teachers need to ponder these types of issues as they teach inquiry science concepts. To consistently deliver quality teaching, teachers, at the very least, must know how to assess students' academic progress and success. If teachers do not assess their students regularly, they may find them behind at the end of the term and discover that it is very difficult to catch them up. This chapter presents a variety of ideas of how teachers can assess science learning. Ongoing assessment is challenging, but it is also necessary. The only way teachers will know how much of the science concepts they are teaching their students have or have not learned and how well their students have mastered the inquiry processes is through academic assessment. Many forms of assessment are available to teachers.

WHY THE NEED TO ASSESS SCIENCE LEARNING

Simply, assessment is needed to improve the quality of teaching and learning. Without proper assessment, teaching could be anything, and not necessarily of any quality. Ongoing assessment is extremely important, and teachers must at the very least understand why students fail tests. They may fail for any number of reasons other than lack of knowledge or competence, such as inadequate language skills, language barriers, poor study skills, low comprehension level, and cognitive factors. Teachers may be responsible for some student test failures if (a) the test is poorly designed, (b) the students are poorly prepared, or (c) the instructional practices were poor. If teachers can fix these three items, their students will perform better on tests.

Assessing is time consuming. However, without knowing how students are faring in class, teachers can easily be off target and therefore not align instruction with learning needs. That would leave students who are falling behind to fend for themselves. Many of the students who fall through the cracks cannot help themselves—they are victims of disservice. Just as crops will grow where water flows, students will learn where teachers teach, show, and involve them. Quality assessment sets the foundation for teaching and learning for the rest of the year and beyond. Teachers who fail to assess their students are no better than students who fail to learn in class. Both national and state standards require teachers to do assessments on science learning just like any other academic subjects.

WHAT IS SCIENCE ASSESSMENT?

For inquiry science, academic assessment is an ongoing process of collecting or gathering information on student learning through inquiry activities (hands-on and minds-on activities). The information can come from performance on tests, completion of inquiry performance tasks, data collection worksheets, information checklists, participation in formal and informal discourses, group processes, acquisition of inquiry process skills, and performance of scientific processes (investigation and experimentation). In short, academic assessment is a process of retrieving information retained by students. As specified in the national standards for inquiry science, assessment and learning are two sides of the same coin; assessment determines the quality of learning as well as the quality of teaching. It provides practical information about the effectiveness of the teaching and learning that takes place in the classroom.

Table 10.1 Different Forms of Assessing Student Learning

Assessment	Measurement	Evaluation
Assessment is an integral part of the instructional process that gathers data or information for the specific purposes of gauging student learning.	*Measurement* is the process of collecting data or information about student learning.	*Evaluation* is the process of using data or information gathered from assessment or other sources to interpret or make judgments about student learning.
Types: Formal, informal, diagnostic, formative, summative, tasks, tests, paper-and-pencil tests, checklists, work samples, journal entries, discourses, observations, multiple choice, short-answer quiz, essay questions, surface assessment, norm-referenced tests, criterion-referenced tests	**Types:** Formal, informal, diagnostic, formative, summative, tasks, tests, paper-and-pencil tests, checklists, work samples, journal entries, discourses, observations, multiple choice, short-answer quiz, essay questions, surface assessment, norm-referenced tests, criterion-reference tests	**Types:** Formal, informal, diagnostic, formative, summative, tasks, tests, paper-and-pencil tests, checklists, work samples, journal entries, discourses, observations, multiple choice, short-answer quiz, essay questions, surface assessment, norm-referenced tests, criterion-reference tests

Academic assessment may not be the same as evaluation and measurement; Table 10.1 illustrates the distinctions among the three. These terms can be confusing because people use them interchangeably in the academic arena. *Evaluation* is the process whereby teachers use data and information from a variety of sources to arrive at a value judgment or discussion about student learning; it is based on measurement data, test results, formal and informal evaluations, answers to questions, interviews, and checklists. *Measurement,* similar to assessment, is a process used by the teachers to obtain data or information about student learning. *Assessment* is a measurement of student learning based on norm-referenced tests or instruments not designed by school districts or teachers.

The distinctions are slight, but the main thing teachers need to know is that science assessment involves the four knowledge areas (physical, logical, social, and arbitrary), inquiry process skills or scientific processes, and the development and construction of new knowledge and skills. Teachers who understand these areas can design meaningful measures to assess student learning of inquiry science concepts.

FORMAL AND INFORMAL PROCESSES

Teachers need to know the formal and informal processes of assessment, evaluation, and measurement. Some examples of formal and informal assessments are given in Table 10.2. *Formal processes* are systematic approaches to assessing,

Table 10.2 Examples of Formal and Informal Assessment Processes

Formal Processes	Informal Processes
Diagnostic, formative, summative, tasks, tests, work samples, journal entries, paper-and-pencil tests, multiple choice, short-answer quiz, essay questions, norm-referenced tests, high-stakes tests, criterion tests, scales, rubrics, points, reading skills, writing skills, math skills	Verbal, oral, checklists, discourses, observations, surface assessment, SOLOM, conversations, colloquium, facial expressions, BICS, speaking ability, participation, involvement, interest, social skills, interpersonal skills

evaluating, and measuring student learning with consistent use of performance tests. *Informal processes* involve inconsistent assessing, evaluating, and measuring based on facial expressions, interactions, checklists, observations, surface information, visual cues, work samples, engagement, participation, and involvement in group activities. Informal assessment is useful for diagnostic purposes because it can be used any time to gather needed information about student learning. The downside of using informal processes is that they appear to be and can be biased, prejudicial, and unreliable.

Teachers can use both formal and informal processes to assess science learning as long as the processes are used correctly to obtain information about student learning throughout the course of the inquiry processes. For instance, teachers may assess formally how students apply their inquiry skills during hands-on and minds-on activities, or teachers may informally assess how students engage in the group process during hands-on and minds-on activities to learn more about specific students' interests in learning inquiry science.

STANDARDS FOR ASSESSMENT

California Science Standards for Grades K-12 do not include specific standards for assessment of student learning; however, the national standards include some guidelines for teachers in assessing student learning of inquiry science concepts; these are listed in Table 10.3. Normally, teachers do not design performance tests to assess science knowledge and skills until students are in higher grades and learning concrete science, such as biology, chemistry, botany, geography, and physics. In the lower grades, teachers usually prescribe hands-on and minds-on activities to allow students to conduct their investigations and experiments. Performance on these inquiry activities are evaluated with formal and informal assessments. In some cases, teachers use science vocabulary for spelling tests, unit review tests with multiple-choice questions, tests that match words with definitions, true or false statements, or short-answer tests.

Table 10.3 Assessment Standards

1. Assessments must be consistent with the decisions they are designed to inform:
   a. Assessments are deliberately designed.
   b. Assessments have explicitly stated purposes.
   c. The relationship between the decision and data is clear.
2. Achievement and opportunity to learn science must be assessed:
   a. Achievement data should focus on the science content that is most important for students to learn.
   b. Equal attention must be given to the assessment of opportunity to learn and the assessment of student achievement.
3. The inferences made from assessment about student achievement and opportunity to learn must be sound:
   a. Assessments tasks are authentic
   b. Students have adequate opportunity to demonstrate their achievement.

Teachers generally must design and write their own tests to assess student learning of science in Grades K-6. Most teachers do not have time to design their own instruments, so they use whatever tests are included in the book they are using. Sometimes, these tests are not inclusive enough to measure student learning; teachers need to review these tests before using them and assuming they will provide adequate assessment. Also, tests premade by curriculum publishers may not meet science standards; therefore, it is better to use teacher-made tests that assess learning of what has actually been covered in class.

Furthermore, today's teachers have so many things on their plates they have little or no time for doing creative work. Chapter review tests and unit review tests are common tools for assessment, and teachers use them for performance tests because they are convenient. However, these tests are meaningful and good only if teachers have taught and thoroughly covered the contents of the entire chapter or unit. Otherwise, giving a review test on content that was not taught does not accurately assess student learning. In other words, teachers need to make sure that what is tested is what was taught.

ASSESS STUDENTS' PROGRESS

Science teachers must know three main types of assessments: *diagnostic, formative, and summative assessments*, as presented in Table 10.4. *Diagnostic assessment*, also known as *pre-assessment*, is a preview/review tool used *before* inquiry instruction to allow teachers to learn or discover students' prior knowledge, curiosity, interests, abilities, background information, experiences from previous lessons, and preferences. Diagnostic assessment can be conducted with formal or informal processes

Table 10.4 Three Types of Assessment

How to Apply	Diagnostic	Formative	Summative
Purpose	Pre-assessment of students' knowledge and skills prior to or before giving instruction	Ongoing assessment of student learning during or throughout instruction to permit adjustments	Assessment of student learning following the conclusion of a taught lesson, unit, or chapter to retrieve learned concepts and retention of information
When	Prior to inquiry instruction	During or throughout inquiry instruction	After inquiry instruction
Rationale	Assessing student needs, prior knowledge, learning experiences, interests, curiosity, preferences, perceptions, conceptions, prepping, tapping, and engaging	Assessing challenges, difficulties, comprehension, clarifications, adaptations, modifications, accommodations, interventions, conceptual bridge, idea map, concept mapping, contextualization, schematic building, and reframe focus	Assessing comprehension, retention, recall of facts, conceptual bridge, conceptual change, what is known, what is learned, what is improved, reteaching, reflective practices, four areas of knowledge, scientific literacy, constructivism, and inquiry process skills
Formats or designs	Formal, informal, diagnostic, formative, summative, tasks, tests, paper-and-pencil tests, checklists, work samples, journal entries, discourses, observations, multiple choice, short-answer quiz, essay questions, surface assessment, norm-referenced tests, criterion-referenced tests, projects, journals, reports	Formal, informal, diagnostic, formative, summative, tasks, tests, paper-and-pencil tests, checklists, work samples, journal entries, discourses, observations, multiple choice, short-answer quiz, essay questions, surface assessment, norm-referenced tests, criterion-referenced tests, projects, journals, reports	Formal, informal, diagnostic, formative, summative, tasks, tests, paper-and-pencil tests, checklists, work samples, journal entries, discourses, observations, multiple choice, short-answer quiz, essay questions, surface assessment, norm-referenced tests, criterion-referenced tests, projects, journals, reports
Reflective teaching	Adjust inquiry instruction to meet student needs, use appropriate approaches, prep students for instruction, and engage prior knowledge and skills	Give feedback, modify instruction, make adjustment, use differentiating instruction, understand challenges and difficulties, bridge concepts, connect key points, provide clarifications, check for understanding, and guide instruction and practices	Learn from students, give feedback, progress, success, failure, reflection, evaluation, What works well and what does not, what should be included or excluded, what should be improved next time, strengths and weaknesses, and how to grow and glow.

depending on the nature of the lesson plan learning objective. For instance, teachers may ask thought-provoking questions about animals or plants to get students ready for inquiry activities, or teachers can put up three to five questions about animals or plants on an ELMO or overhead projector and ask students to answer them before going over the answers with them.

Formative assessment is used *during* inquiry instruction primarily to provide meaningful information on student learning that teachers can use to adjust their instructional practices and enhance student learning. Formative assessment can be done either formally or informally. Informal assessment consists of practices such as questioning during instruction, thumbs up or down, yes or no answers, check lists, and simple observation. On the other hand, formal assessment is conducted through paper-and-pencil tests, quizzes, small white board drills, exercises, independent practice, and homework assignments. Both formal and informal assessments can be done during the phases of instruction and guided practice.

Summative assessment is used *after* inquiry instruction to evaluate student learning, progress, and acquisition of content knowledge from the lessons taught to them. The purpose of summative assessment is not to give teachers information to help them improve instruction, but rather to measure students' learning of the material the teachers delivered in class. Summative assessment focuses on student retention of information. Traditional methods of assessment—giving a quiz at the end of the period, having a test every Friday, having a chapter review test every other week, or requiring midterm and final exams—are examples of summative assessments.

Summative assessments could be challenging to students because students think they have to absorb all the information they received and repeat it for the tests. It is wise to test students regularly and frequently to reduce the amount of information they need to study or review for summative tests. Also, frequent testing allows teachers to conduct all three types of assessments more efficiently and effectively to address the needs of students. There are other kinds of tests teachers can use to improve the teaching and learning of science.

OTHER FORMS OF ASSESSMENT

As stated in earlier chapters, teachers need to ask themselves these three guiding questions before they start teaching inquiry science: What should students learn? How should they learn the contents? How should students be taught?

Science teachers should be familiar with different instruments used in assessments, particularly *authentic assessments* and *alternative assessments*.

Basically, *authentic assessments* have to with activities associated with real-life content or experiences. A student may be asked to perform a task that demonstrates acquisition of a skill. *Academic alternative assessments* are measures that are not traditional tests; they include portfolios, journals, holistic grading, student products, performances, group tests, presentations, peer evaluations, self-evaluations, case studies, individual projects, and extracurricular activities.

Regardless of what assessment is used, teachers cannot lose sight of the importance of a strong knowledge and skills base, and they must go beyond traditional learning to promote inquiry-based learning that emphasizes students' understanding of science concepts, principles, theories, and processes; their acquisition of inquiry skills; and their construction of new knowledge and skills. In other words, teachers must be able to guide students through and beyond the inquiry process to help them develop science knowledge and cognitive processes that foster lifelong learning of science.

ASSESS SPECIFIC KNOWLEDGE

Teachers need to devise appropriate tools or tests to be used during the formative and summative processes to carefully assess students' science knowledge and skills in order to determine what students have actually learned in science. Otherwise, the instructional methods may not achieve the learning objectives.

One goal of teaching is for students to gain knowledge, and there are different ways of looking at knowledge. Howe (2002) described four kinds of knowledge in science: logical, physical, social, and arbitrary. Another approach to science knowledge is to look at factual, conceptual, and procedural knowledge. *Factual knowledge* is an understanding of details, attributes, concrete representations, and real meanings of scientific phenomena. *Conceptual knowledge* is an understanding of scientific concepts, principles, ideas, hypotheses, theories, laws, and investigative procedures. *Procedural knowledge* is knowing how to use scientific processes to conduct investigation and experimentation to improve inquiry skills as well as science knowledge and skills.

Acquiring any kind of knowledge involves *cognitive processes* as well as knowledge. Cognitive processes have to do with the ways in which students know, understand, apply, and ascribe meaning to inquiry science. For instance, teachers may prescribe a hands-on and minds-on activity for students to do that requires that they follow procedural guidelines to conduct an investigation or experiment; the activity can be completed only as the students employ the cognitive processes of formulating a hypothesis, using variables correctly, and applying inquiry process skills. Howe (2002) distinguished between science learning objectives, which he called cognitive content objectives (knowing what), and cognitive process objectives (knowing how). Teachers should assess both content knowledge and process skills in students as early as possible, realizing that both are measured in standardized testing.

HIGH-STAKES TESTS

Teachers should not confuse science assessment in the classroom with high-stakes tests. Classroom assessments are usually designed by teachers; high-stakes tests are norm-referenced tests or criterion-referenced tests, or instruments. Most state tests assess reading, writing, speaking, and math skills. Very few national and state tests require school districts to assess students on science skills. Interestingly, as Table 10.5 indicates, the scores on science tests are used to determine the English language proficiency of students who speak languages other than English at home.

Teachers must be familiar with the CELDT scores for ELL, LEP, NNS, and FEP students. Tables 10.6, 10.7, and 10.8 show the scores used by school districts in California to determine the proficiency levels of these students in

Table 10.5 CST Proficiency Level Scores

Proficiency Level	Language Arts	Mathematics	History	Science
Advanced	392–600	418–600	400–600	399–600
Proficient	350–391	350–417	350–399	350–398
Basic	300–349	300–349	300–349	300–349
Below basic	263–299	247–299	275–299	269–299
Far below basic	150–262	150–246	150–274	150–268

Table 10.6 CELDT Listening and Speaking Proficiency Level Scores, Grades K-12

Proficiency Level	Grade K	Grade 1	Grade 2	Grades 3–5	Grades 6–8	Grades 9–12
Beginning	220–408	220–419	220–452	220–437	220–437	220–433
Early intermediate	414–456	424–467	456–491	442–479	441–480	438–481
Intermediate	460–504	471–515	495–535	483–522	484–521	484–522
Early advanced	509–544	521–555	544–568	529–558	528–557	526–562
Advanced	556–710	587–710	587–710	571–710	571–710	571–710

Source: *California English Language Development test (CELDT): Explaining and Using 2010–2011 Summary Results*, California Department of Education, 2011, pp. 14–16.

Table 10.7 CELDT Reading Proficiency Levels, Grades 2–12

Proficiency Level	Grade 2	Grades 3–5	Grades 6–8	Grades 9–12
Beginning	340–434	340–460	340–459	340–455
Early intermediate	440–474	466–496	487–498	466–498
Intermediate	479–509	501–529	503–529	502–532
Early advanced	515–538	536–554	534–560	537–563
Advanced	556–630	567–640	567–650	569–650

Source: California English Language Development test (CELDT): Explaining and Using 2010–2011 Summary Results, California Department of Education, 2011, pp. 14–16.

Table 10.8 CELDT Writing Proficiency Levels, Grades 2–12

Proficiency Level	Grade 2	Grades 3–5	Grades 6–8	Grades 9–12
Beginning	280–405	280–441	280–439	280–441
Early intermediate	418–462	448–486	447–483	448–483
Intermediate	468–506	492–528	488–522	488–528
Early advanced	512–536	537–571	530–572	536–568
Advanced	544–640	587–690	588–700	587–700

Source: California English Language Development test (CELDT): Explaining and Using 2010–2011 Summary Results, California Department of Education, 2011, pp. 14–16.

the tested areas of listening and speaking, reading, and writing at the different grade levels. The CELDT scores for each proficiency level are much higher than the STAR scores for the corresponding level; however, the constructs of the two tests are different.

School districts use different sources to evaluate student learning and language proficiency levels; often the tests they use were not designed for assessment in these areas because the reliability and validity of the tests have not been established. For instance, the summative assessment CST prepping and testing are quite common in today's schools, especially in California. The Academic Performance Index (API), with its rankings based on students' total scores on the CST, drives school curricula. Normal API rankings range from 200 to 1,000 with the median being 800. STAR program results, which are reports of results from California standardized tests, indicate a student's academic standing and success and the student's language proficiency level—far below basic, below basic, basic, proficient, or advanced. Scores that indicate these proficiency levels in the different content areas of the CST are shown in Table 12.9. New teachers must learn how to interpret these psychometrics; otherwise, the results could be misleading to teachers as well as students and parents.

WAYS TO ASSESS SCIENCE LEARNING

As indicated in Tables 10.1, 10.2, and 10.4, science teachers may want to find out what assessment approaches or techniques they should use to determine where students are in science learning. Keep in mind that there is no perfect way of assessing science knowledge in students. Teachers must find ways to meet all students' needs because student diversity may influence how teachers assess student learning. Teachers must take multicultural factors and issues into consideration when assessing student learning. For instance, verbal skills or communication skills in English may be absent in students who speak English as a second language, and ELL, NNS, and SN students should not be subject to the same criteria for group interaction because their limited English speaking ability could make them timid in a group. In other words, teachers should look at the bigger picture when assessing students who may have language barriers.

One approach to assessing student learning in science is to use *traditional assessments*. This means paper-and-pencil tests with true or false questions, short-answer questions, multiple choice questions, and short essay questions. This approach has advantages and disadvantages. Short-answer questions and essay questions are designed for constructed-response whereas multiple-choice and true-false questions are based on the forced-choice approach. To make these tests appropriate and effective, teachers need to construct the content of the tests carefully so they target the needs of students. Teachers need to pay attention to the construct of each question and its answer to determine what it really measures. In other words, does the whole test measure science knowledge, skills, concepts, reading comprehension, science literacy, language ability, and science vocabulary?

Moreover, teachers need to make sure these instruments assess learning in ELL, NNS, and SN students who may not be able to write well or read directions. How will teachers explain the results if students guess correctly on multiple-choice questions? What will teachers do if students leave all essay and short-answer questions blank? Most importantly, what are teachers going to do about teaching and learning if teachers should receive poor feedback from the traditional assessment? Remember, assessment serves two main purposes: formative assessment of the effectiveness and quality of teaching and self-assessment of the teachers. Of course, teachers should think about different ways of assessing student learning; otherwise, the feedback they receive is going to be the same.

Another approach is to use performance assessment to assess student learning. Performance assessments could be paper-and-pencil tests as well; however, in science, teachers can require students to perform tasks instead of taking traditional tests. Performance approaches are effective in assessing inquiry process skills: observing, communicating, measuring, inferring, predicting, collecting data, analyzing data, hypothesizing, concluding, investigating, and experimenting. Requiring students to present their tasks could be challenging, but adjustments can be made to accommodate diverse learning needs and abilities. Demonstrating proficiency in these tasks requires more process work than producing products. To facilitate the process, teachers need to provide all students with the following: *A focus; context; directions; time allocation; submission deadline for all work; quality criteria; opportunity to revise draft; and scoring guides, grading scales, or rubrics.* Keep in mind that performance assessment is based on hands-on and minds-on inquiry activities, and teachers should strategize effective ways to administer it. Examples of science assessments are presented in Table 10.9.

Table 10.9 Comparison of Traditional and Performance Science Assessments

Inquiry Purpose	Traditional Approach	Performance Approach
Recalling science knowledge, retention, memory, skills, and construction	Multiple-choice, short-answer, true-false, or matching games; prior knowledge and learned experiences	Observing, measuring, organizing, sorting, classifying, communicating, predicting
Conceptual knowledge, comprehension, application, and inference	Multiple-choice, short-answer, true-false, or matching games; prior knowledge and learned experiences; experiment, investigation; data analysis; and presentation	Observing, measuring, organizing, sorting, classifying, communicating, predicting, data collection, analysis, writing, reporting, presenting, charting, graphing, concept mapping, idea web, idea map, variables
Inquiry process skills, science process, inquiry procedures, inquiry attitudes, investigative processes, and experimentation	Multiple-choice, short-answer, true-false, essay, or matching games; prior knowledge, and learned experiences; experiment, investigation; data analysis; and presentation	Observing, measuring, organizing, sorting, classifying, communicating, predicting, data collection, analysis, investigating, experimenting, writing, reporting, presenting, charting, graphing, concept mapping, idea web, idea map, variables, concluding, making models, project, further study
Cognitive content objective, cognitive process objective, learning objective, and content knowledge objective	Multiple-choice, short-answer, true-false, essay, or matching games; prior knowledge, and learned experiences; experiment, investigation; data analysis; presentation; making, modeling; demonstrating, competing; judging	Observing, measuring, organizing, sorting, classifying, communicating, predicting, data collection, analysis, writing, reporting, demonstrating, presenting, charting, graphing, concept mapping, idea web, idea map, variables, concluding, investigating, experimenting, making models, project, further study, competing, creating portfolio

Table 10.10 Criteria and Expectations for Task Performance Processes

Task Process	Verbal Criteria	Written Criteria	Performance Expectations
Individual process	Ask individual student to volunteer to share data or information with the class.	Ask individual student to jot down or write what he or she just observed.	Individual students make final reports to share their findings with the class.
Group process	Students can reach a consensus on given topic and share data or information with the class.	Students collaborate with group members to write down what the group has agreed on or concluded from what they just observed.	Students work in group to prepare a final report to share their findings to the class.
Class process	All students prepare to ask and answer questions.	All students write down what they just observed and share with the class in orderly or random fashion.	All students have equal opportunity to prepare their final report to share with the class.

It could be difficult for teachers to monitor, supervise, and control all students at once if each student is doing his or her task independently unless teachers prescribe the same task for everyone to do. However, teachers may be able to manage and control their classroom better if they put students to work in small groups at centers. The group process is challenging but not difficult if teachers provide specific guidelines and tasks for each group member to do. Table 10.10 illustrates some of the differences in criteria and expectations for individual, group, and whole-class task assignments. Each model has advantages and disadvantages. Teachers need to select criteria for performance tasks and make sure that the construct of such tasks includes at least the following:

- Prior knowledge and skills
- Grade-level appropriateness
- Student-centered approach
- Clear guidelines and procedural processes
- Connections with prior experiences
- Inquiry process and inquiry skills
- Diagnostic, formative, and summative criteria
- Science content standards as a basis
- Engagement of students in science knowledge, cognitive processes, and construction
- Materials, supplies, equipment, and data

- Inquiry-based approach
- Investigation and experimentation
- Sufficient time allocation
- Adaptations, modifications, accommodations, and interventions
- Cooperative learning or group process
- Individual or independent practices
- Science literacy promotion
- Involvement of reading, writing, and communication skills
- Use of mathematical skills
- Presentation of products

Both traditional and performance approaches serve meaningful purposes in learning science concepts. Some teachers prefer to use traditional methods for assessing retention of information or recalling of learned experiences, and others choose to use performance assessment to measure science as inquiry. Many use both methods to assess student learning of science concepts. It all depends on what was taught to the students.

USE PERFORMANCE CRITERIA

To make performance assessment challenging and academically sound, teachers need to develop their own rubrics, scales, criteria, and guidelines for assessing science knowledge. These performance criteria that guide students to complete given tasks are referred to as *scoring guides, rubrics, performance criteria, or performance levels*. Students must understand these scoring criteria and teachers must make sure they are appropriate for the grade level; otherwise, high expectations may not be attainable because students may be unable to meet the learning expectations. Also, teachers should carefully evaluate these criteria prior to assigning the task and make necessary changes to accommodate individual students' needs.

Teacher-made checklists can be used as scoring guides in assessing science performance. A checklist is an easy, convenient, quick, handy, useful, and timesaving tool that works well in the early grades. However, as with other assessments, checklists have disadvantages as well as advantages. For instance, checklist criteria are surface measures that involve little or no inquiry process skills. Students could be judged unjustly because of teachers' biases and preferences. Checking Yes or No statements or putting check marks in front of something that is well done, good, or not good is a personal call. Table 10.11 is an example of a completed checklist for judging a performance task. Table 10.12 presents the 5-E model as a checklist for assessing demonstration of science process skills.

Table 10.11 Example of Completed Checklist

Procedural Process Step	Yes	No	Rationale
Read instructions before beginning work			
Check material and supplies before activity			
Clean desk space and organize work area			
Set material and supplies neatly and orderly			
Follow step-by-step process			Student forgets to read steps 1–2 before doing steps 3–4.
Label all objects in orderly way			Student puts objects on desk but does not label them properly.
Wear safety equipment at all times			
Keep work area neat and clean			
Finish task on time			Student does not finish all steps and runs out of time.
Clean up and return materials and supplies			
Wash hands			

Table 10.12 Example of 5-E model Used as a Checklist

Inquiry Process Skill	Task	Yes	No	Comments
Engage	Asking questions, following questions, answering questions, paying attention, listening to others			
Explore	Observing, examining, using five senses, communicating			
Explain	Talking to, discussing, sharing, exchanging, interacting, etc . . .			
Elaborate	Describing, explaining, reading, using details, talking about the characteristics			Student does not describe the objects verbally with adjectives or adverbs but writes down the shapes of each object on paper.
Evaluate	Explaining, elaborating, concluding, predicting, classifying, communicating, analyzing, comparing, contrasting			

Teacher-made-rubrics may also be used to assess science process or performance tasks. Rubrics should have a minimum of three levels and a maximum of five levels. Teachers can use more levels; however, the more levels a rubric has the more complicated it is going to be. For lower grades, three levels are perfect and for higher grades, five levels should be sufficient depending on the nature of each

Table 10.13 Example of Rubric

Level	Criteria	Guidelines
Level 5	Advanced	Excellent, outstanding, quality, mastery, creative
Level 4	Proficient	Satisfactory, acceptable, creative, clear, consistent
Level 3	Intermediate	Acceptable, clear, consistent, connected
Level 2	Speech emergence	Partial, some details, inconsistent, unclear
Level 1	Basic	Unacceptable, unsatisfactory, little or no information, beginning, early production, preproduction

lesson plan. Table 10.13 shows an example of a rubric with five levels. Each level must have some criteria and guidelines to justify its ranking; otherwise, rubrics are no different from checklists.

Teachers can design rubrics with high levels of criteria for major science categories or tasks. For instance, they may want to measure student learning in specific tasks or science knowledge areas, such as knowing science processes, applying science knowledge, using science concepts and generalizations, collecting data or information, using scientific variables, doing reports and written projects, conducting experiments and investigations. These areas require detailed and specific criteria and guidelines; however, teachers rarely use rubrics with high criteria in lower grades. Normally, these criteria and guidelines are appropriate for Grades 7–12.

Teacher-made holistic scoring guides or rubrics are practical tools for judging performance tasks as well. Teachers create holistic scoring guides for specific tasks, changing the language in the rubrics for other, similar tasks. Sometimes it is necessary to avoid using the same rubric for several science processes or performance tasks. Teachers need to develop rubrics for what they want to assess, and they might be able to adapt existing rubrics they find in books; however, the newly created rubric must measure what it is purported to measure. For instance, if a food chain quiz is given to students to assess their understanding of science concepts, teachers expect students to identify the links in the chain from producer to primary consumer to secondary consumer to tertiary consumer, as shown in Figure 10.1. The task is for students to correctly draw a line or arrow connecting all boxes from the producer to the consumer or from the consumer to the producer. Teachers can create a simple holistic scoring method to score this activity as illustrated in Table 10.14.

Figure 10.1 *Sample of food chain.*

Table 10.14 Example of Holistic Scoring

0 points	1 point	2 points	3 points	4 points	5 points
No prediction, no connection, no explanation	Wrong prediction, incorrect connections, attempts to solve the chain	Two or more predictions, two or more connections, construct the chain	Correct prediction with some errors, connect most boxes, correct attempt to solve the chain	Accurate prediction, construct the chain, connect most boxes correctly	All right predications, connect all boxes correctly and orderly, construct the chain orderly and correctly

OVERALL SCIENCE ASSESSMENT

Teachers have many options for assessing science learning: *traditional, performance, authentic, alternative, rubrics, science workbooks, holistic scoring, checklists, concept maps (idea web, idea maps, thematic concepts), essay, open-ended question, focus question, open question, closed question, process, products, portfolio, progress reports, feedback, report card, self-assessment, reflective teaching,* and more. Again, there is no perfect way of assessing science knowledge in students, and teachers need to develop their own instruments to measure what they teach and how they teach science concepts to students. As Howe (2002) explained, teachers need to know how to enhance inquiry instruction through assessment, and teachers have to know the purpose of assessment because assessment and instruction are related to each other as two sides of the same coin.

Regardless of what instruments are used to assess, teachers need to make sure that students are learning science concepts. Having sound assessment instruments does not necessary means that students are learning science concepts if the inquiry instruction is of poor quality. As Howe (2002) argued, all inquiry activities in the classroom, including assessment and hands-on and minds-on activities, should be directed toward helping students achieve appropriate cognitive, affective, psychomotor, social, and academic goals.

For that reason, teachers need to make sure all students master science knowledge: facts, concepts, theories, principles, and procedures. Science content involves the following:

- Science experience charts
- Science record pages
- Science log
- Oral, verbal, and written pictorial interpretations
- Concept maps
- Anecdotal records

- Experimenting and investigating process
- Data collection, recording, and analysis
- Observation skills
- Data capture
- Scientific processes
- Charting and graphing skills
- Hands-on and minds-on activities
- Science attitudes
- Model building
- Presentation and demonstration skills
- Classroom science project
- Science fair project
- Science portfolio
- Science learning objectives and goals

For students in elementary school, teachers need to keep an up-to-date science portfolio for each student. They can select what should be included in the portfolio and what is excluded. This portfolio shows the cumulative work by which science learning took place in the classroom. Table 10.15 lists many items that could be kept in the science portfolio; however, teachers and students can work together to choose what is appropriate for the contents of the portfolio.

Overall science assessment will determine the effectiveness and quality of the teacher's teaching of science concepts to students. Teachers should consider using the assessment results to guide their planning, preparation, inquiry instruction, guided practices, selection of hands-on and minds-on activities, learning

Table 10.15 Sample Contents for Science Portfolio

Processes	Products
1. Observations	1. Journals
2. Tests	2. Projects
3. Experiments	3. Graphs
4. Investigations	4. Charts
5. Data collection	5. Drawings
6. Analysis	6. Models
7. Variables	7. Pictorial materials
8. Computer work	8. Photographs
9. Lab results	9. Pictures
10. Book reviews	10. Checklists
11. Articles	11. Presentations
12. Writing samples	12. Demonstrations
13. Classifications	13. Artifacts

objectives and science goals for all students. Most importantly, teacher self-assessment and self-reflection on instruction are valuable for maintaining quality teaching and learning of science.

INQUIRY SCIENCE PROJECTS

One of the ways to assess science performance in students is to require participation in mini-science project competitions. Mini-science projects are appropriate for elementary grades, and teachers need to adjust the difficulty level of the processes to accommodate all students. They need to provide clear guidelines for the projects but allow students to choose their topics in areas of their interests.

For higher grades, teachers need to create more complex guidelines for science projects with more criteria and require demonstration of more science knowledge and skills. Table 10.16 lists some steps for teachers to consider for

Table 10.16 Sample Guidelines for Mini-science Projects

Criterion	Guidelines for Each criterion
Project title	Select an appropriate title for the project. A title could be a question, statement, leading prompt, or catchy phrase. For instance, What detergents remove grass, ketchup, and oil stains best? Energizer batteries will outlast Duracell and other alkaline batteries.
Background information or research information about the topic or area of interest	Use different sources, such as online resources, print materials, articles, science books, newspapers, magazines, reference pages, encyclopedia, and teacher's manuals for background information.
Introduction to the project	State the purpose of the project clearly, or tell exactly what student is going to do for the project. For instance: the purpose of this project is to compare three types of detergents to determine which brand removes stains best.
Hypothesis	A hypothesis is a statement, a question, or a predication that has not been tested. A project cannot begin without a clear and concise hypothesis. The focus of the project is the hypothesis. For instance, Tide detergent will remove stains better than two other major brands.
Scientific variables	Use variables as follows: 1. Variables mean labeling or naming all objects used in the experiment. 2. Dependent variables are testing variables in the experiment. 3. Independent variables are other variables in the experiment. 4. Constancy means variables remain the same or change but still hold the same value or weight. 5. Control sample is a prototype or sample used to compare to testing sample.

(Continued)

Criterion	Guidelines for Each criterion
	6. Facts are objects that are observable and readily demonstrated.
	7. Concepts are abstractions of objects or events, accumulation of facts and attributes, or values of something.
	8. Principles are generalizations and laws related to rules or concepts that involve some sort of relationship between two or more concepts.
	9. Theories are speculations of large ideas that have been experimentally supported by concepts, facts, principles, and science processes.
	10. Scientific methods are ways the project will be conducted in an orderly or step-by-step process.
Materials	List all materials, equipment, and supplies required for this project. For instance, one hundred people over the age of 18 will be surveyed for this project.
Experimental procedures	List all steps, create clear guidelines, or organize the process for this project. For instance, step one, step two, step three, or rule one, rule two, rule three, or list all instructions in chronological order—1,2,3, or first, second, third, etc.
Flow chart	Include all processes of the experiment in order or sequence of events. For instance, trial one, trial two, trial three, or chart one, chart two, chart three, or picture one, picture two, picture three, or first, second, third, or all steps (if required).
Data collection	Explain how you will collect all data for this project. Give type of data, how it will be collected, how it will be recorded, and how each variable is named or labeled.
Graphing	Use charts, tables, bar graphs, dot graphs, cone graphs, line graphs, or artistic graphics to display data or results for this project.
Analysis of data	Discuss how you will analyze the data collected and how you will use the data in the experiment, or how you will prove, disprove, or support hypothesis of the project. The results need to be explained, elaborated on, communicated, and shared in accordance with the project's hypothesis.
Conclusion	Infer, conclude, imply, or discuss how this project measures the hypotheses, why it was supported or not supported; share reflections about this project, such as what was right, what was wrong about it, what should be done about it next time, or what needs to be included or excluded in the project; and what you learned from this project.
Recommendations for further studies	Conclude what should be done in the future to test this project again or to create a similar project for further testing; recommend what other students might do.
Bibliography or references	Include a list of references used to support this project: books, online resources, people, or personal communications.
Project display	Use a tri-fold or other board to display project in order: left side, middle, right side. For instance, the left side may have title, research, and introduction; the middle may have hypothesis, materials, procedures, and methods; the right side shows data analysis, graphs, conclusion, recommendations, and references.
Oral presentation	Present project to the class and answer any questions other students may have. Teachers decide how much time to allot for each presentation or what criteria students need to present to the class.

mini-science projects. Teachers should select all criteria that fit their students and their grade level. A mini-science project could be a simple hands-on and minds-on activity that takes a few days to complete such as planting a seed in a Styrofoam or clear plastic cup to observe germination of young plants, or making a chart to chart weather conditions or climate changes for a week.

A mini-science project must include specific processes, inquiry skills, and science knowledge. A project should require students to formulate a hypothesis for testing, use variables, conduct an experiment or investigation, collect data, and design methods of experimentation.

Promoting science projects help students learn science as inquiry because projects are hands-on and minds-on activities. Elementary schoolteachers should know how to conduct a science project before requiring their students to do them; otherwise, mini-science projects should not be part of the equation in learning science. Science projects take time, involve costs, and require diligent work to get them done. Students and teachers need to work as a team to get all projects done on time. The teacher's role is that of facilitator, guiding the process and monitoring progress to keep students moving ahead on the projects. As Figure 10.2 shows, mini-science projects can be done in different amounts of time, and teachers need to determine what timeframes work best for their grades.

As mentioned earlier, teachers need to develop scoring guides or rubrics to assess science performance tasks, and science mini-projects are hands-on and minds-on inquiry activities that need to be scored and judged carefully. Projects not only take time, effort, energy, and diligent work, but they also require application of inquiry process skills and science knowledge and skills. One cautionary note for teachers: science mini-projects have to be designed for students to do without help

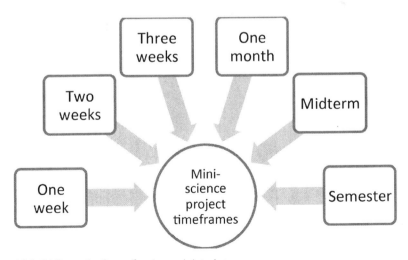

Figure 10.2 *Different timeframes for science mini-projects*

and based on students' abilities, capabilities, and comprehension levels. Teachers need to make sure parents understand that their role in these projects is to provide support only; otherwise, parents can end up doing the projects for their children. To limit unwanted parental input, teachers need to send clear guidelines to parents to warn them about academic integrity. Some children tend to depend on their parents to complete their school projects. Also, teachers need to make sure the science projects do not cost a fortune for students to do; otherwise, socioeconomically disadvantaged students will not be able to complete their projects.

Table 10.17 presents samples of scoring guides teachers can use to judge or grade science mini-projects. The grading scales or judging criteria for each individual project must take grade level into consideration. Science projects should not be limited to what students can do inside the classroom; students can go work on them outside the classroom as well.

Table 10.17 Sample Scoring Guides for Science Projects

Judging Criterion	Examples of Scoring Guides	Examples of Points System Scoring Rubrics
Title	Title is impressive, sound, logical, intriguing, amazing, or entertaining.	4: Exemplary 3: Outstanding or excellent 2: Good 1: Fair 0: Poor
Research information	Use good and adequate resources to support the project and provide sufficient background research information.	4: Exemplary 3: Outstanding or excellent 2: Good 1: Fair 0: Poor
Hypothesis	State the hypothesis clearly, concisely, and operationally.	4: Exemplary 3: Outstanding or excellent 2: Good 1: Fair 0: Poor
Scientific processes	Use inquiry process skills, scientific methods, variables, and data.	4: Exemplary 3: Outstanding or excellent 2: Good 1: Fair 0: Poor
Scientific thought	Use good problem, question, and approaches, conduct experiments and investigations, organize data collection, label and name variables, and use science processes well.	4: Exemplary 3: Outstanding or excellent 2: Good 1: Fair 0: Poor

Science knowledge and skills	Apply science knowledge and skills, such as concepts, facts, theories, principles, construction, ideas, and inquiry processes.	4: Exemplary 3: Outstanding or excellent 2: Good 1: Fair 0: Poor
Conclusion	Write solid or good conclusion, explain the outcome well, explain how results support or disprove the hypothesis, and include reflection.	4: Exemplary 3: Outstanding or excellent 2: Good 1: Fair 0: Poor
Display and presentation	Present the science board or project to the class, do good reporting, share good information, and answer all questions.	4: Exemplary 3: Outstanding or excellent 2: Good 1: Fair 0: Poor
Creativity and design	The board is creative in design; follow directions; display items orderly, visibly, and legibly on the board; and include artifacts.	4: Exemplary 3: Outstanding or excellent 2: Good 1: Fair 0: Poor
Thoroughness	The whole project is clear, convincing, consistent or partially clear, convincing, and consistent, or disorganized, with little, or no information.	4: Exemplary 3: Outstanding or excellent 2: Good 1: Fair 0: Poor
Clarity	The write-up is clear, the presentation is clear, and the display supports the contents of the project.	4: Exemplary 3: Outstanding or excellent 2: Good 1: Fair 0: Poor
Quality	The overall project is outstanding, excellent, good, fair, or poor.	4: Exemplary 3: Outstanding or excellent 2: Good 1: Fair 0: Poor

TAKE INQUIRY SCIENCE BEYOND THE CLASSROOM

Besides performing hands-on and minds-on activities in the classroom, teachers can help their students take inquiry science beyond the classroom. Normally, science beyond the classroom means field trips to gardens, museums, historical sites, zoos, farms, landmark discovery locations, or other places of interest. Teachers can do more than schedule field trips if time permits, and resources are available to help fund science projects beyond the classroom. Students can be referred to summer science camps, science and math projects, conservation corps, or community projects to learn more about how science is related to real-life situations.

Science beyond the classroom seems possible for older children, but younger children need parent involvement in their extracurricular activities in order to ensure their health and safety. So teachers need to be very careful about requiring inquiry science beyond the classroom for children in Grades K-3. If extracurricular projects are academically sound, teachers need to inform parents and obtain their approval for their children to participate. Teachers also need to make sure parents provide transportation and are responsible for any fees required.

To help teachers think about inquiry science outside the box, Table 10.18 lists some topics for science beyond the classroom. Teachers should examine these and carefully select what is best for their students. Most importantly, they must adjust to meet their students' needs instead of requiring students to meet their teaching needs, especially for inquiry science learning. Projects beyond the classroom may involve intense work, some costs, and some kind of assistance. Teachers need to factor in these concerns when planning or prescribing such activities.

Teachers can take science beyond the classroom to promote independent learning. The goal is to inspire children to learn more and know more about science.

Table 10.18 Selected Topics for Science Beyond the Classroom

Science Area	Topics
Animal studies	Ants, worms, insects, bugs, pets, snails, caterpillars, fish, birds, snakes, rabbits, hamsters
Plant studies	Roots, stems, leaves, flowers, seasons, tree rings, plant food, use of plants for real-life needs
Comparative studies	Study batteries, food oxidation, food ingredients, floating or sinking objects, static electricity, food molding
Consumer testing	Quality and quantity studies, brand names v. generic brands, soap v. soap. cereal v. cereal, wine v. wine, nutrition facts on packages
Human studies	Eye colors, hair colors, handprints, fingerprints, footprints, thumbprints, heights, waist sizes, IQ tests
Earth science	Hiking, trekking, camping, solar system, fossils, plants, animals, river, ocean, sea, ponds, basins, creeks, trees, landforms, landfill, farmland
Physical science	Objects, motions, inertia, gravity, flying, centering, positioning, balance, lifting, pushing, pulling, running, jumping, falling, throwing
Water studies	Cold, cool, warm, hot water, surface tension, water molecule, contaminated water, use of water for human consumption
Weather observations	Weather changes, warm, cold, hot, pollution, air quality, allergies, drought, wildfire, rainy, windy
Cellular phone studies	iPad, iPhone, iPod, android devices, cell phone ownership, costs

Generally speaking, U.S. children are behind in science knowledge in school because science education is implemented inconsistently across the school curricula. Remember, science is ubiquitous and teachers can help to reinforce its learning.

Last, but not least, to promote independent learning, teachers need to design inquiry science activities or independent projects that are cheap, affordable, and doable with the least expensive materials or supplies available. For instance, students can find most science supplies or materials at home or purchase them from places, such as *Dollar Tree Stores, .99 Only Stores, and The Big Lots Stores* instead of going to expensive places, like *Michaels Stores, Wal-Mart Stores, Target Stores, OfficeMax Stores, and Hancock Fabrics.* Keep in mind that some inquiry activities may not require new or additional materials or supplies at all, such as observing ants around the house, collecting different leaves and comparing them, keeping a log of weather conditions and climate changes, and learning how to bake chocolate cookies.

SUMMING UP

This chapter focused on assessment of student learning and provided teachers with many techniques for science assessment in the multicultural setting. Formal and informal assessments are used to measure student learning in science at the elementary level and traditional and performance assessments have also been used to measure students' science knowledge and inquiry process skills. There is no perfect instrument for assessing or measuring student learning because each lesson is different and each student learns science differently. Authentic and alternative assessments are as practical as any other method, and each method has advantages and disadvantages. Teacher-made-instruments are the best tools to assess student learning of inquiry science.

Teachers need to take multicultural factors and issues into consideration when assessing student learning. Assessments such as rubrics, scorings, and checklists, are good for specific areas in science; however, these tools may not benefit students who lack language skills. For inquiry science, teachers have more than one way to assess student learning. Assessment is valuable for determining the quality and effectiveness of teaching and learning in the classroom. Assessment and instruction go hand-in-hand. The bottom line is that assessment helps teachers evaluate their own performance in the learning circle. Teachers can benefit from self-assessment and self-reflection. Without professional, objective assessment tools and methodologies, teaching accountability is reduced to whatever teachers can make up to fill their days in the classroom.

CHAPTER ELEVEN

Teach Inquiry Science Creatively

Science, like life, feeds on its own decay. New facts burst old rules; then newly divined conceptions bind old and new together into a reconciling law.

—WILLIAM JAMES *THE WILL TO BELIEVE AND OTHER ESSAYS IN POPULAR PHILOSOPHY*, 1910

INTRODUCTION

In earlier chapters, much was said about inquiry science helping teachers build science foundations for the rest of their teaching careers. Science, like any other academic subject, has to be taught in ways that fit the students' needs instead of the teachers' needs. Meeting teachers' expectations is not a problem in teaching science; however, teachers need to ask themselves if they are teaching science to students as inquiry or as directed. "As directed" means that teachers control student learning; students have opportunities to learn only what their teachers expect them to know. Students have little or no chance to think things through, to process the information they receive, to conduct investigation, to try hands-on and minds-on experiments, or to construct their own knowledge and skills. They learn what they do of science through rote memory. This chapter gives teachers a tour of inquiry science and discusses ideas for teaching inquiry science concepts creatively to all students of diverse backgrounds in the multicultural setting.

NSES AND CA STANDARDS

When they teach inquiry science, teachers cannot choose what they want to teach without carefully considering the national and state standards for science instruction. Inquiry science instruction has to be standards based and has to be implemented as inquiry. Tables 11.1 and 11.2 give overviews of the national standards and California's standards. These standards are broad-based and teachers need to apply them in ways that make the content of their lessons sound and appropriate for the grade level they teach. The standards are guides that aid teachers in developing meaningful, sensible, and appropriate science lesson plans to teach students science concepts.

Science standards require teachers to teach students concepts rather than concrete science until students reach the higher grades. Teachers who teach real science, or concrete science, to elementary students can be misapplying the content standards. Teachers should get to know these guidelines and apply them in their science lesson planning; otherwise, they may approach inquiry science in ways that are inappropriate for student learning.

INQUIRY LESSON PLANNING

Science lesson plans should reflect the content standards and should have inquiry components, or criteria for inquiry activities. Teachers may have different ways of designing their inquiry lesson plans; however, lesson planning takes diligent effort to make sure the content is appropriate for inquiry-based instruction. Table 11.3 shows the difference between direct instruction and the guided inquiry approach to help teachers understand what an inquiry lesson plan should look like. There is no perfect lesson plan for every science concept, and creativity is what makes teachers the greatest artists for teaching science creatively. In other words, teachers need to find their own ways to make science fit the learning needs of their students.

Table 11.4 presents a detailed inquiry lesson plan format for teachers' consideration. This format meets most of the TPE and TPA standards requirements; it is challenging to implement a detailed lesson in a 20- or 30-minute time slot. Actually, a science activity takes much more than 20 or 30 minutes if it follows such a detailed lesson plan.

Inquiry lesson planning can be adjusted and modified to meet teaching and learning needs based on the learning objective of the lesson plan. A lesson does not have to include all the criteria or components listed in Table 11.4; however, it should contain hands-on and minds-on activities needed for students to focus on and to develop inquiry process skills and science knowledge and skills.

Table 11.1 National Science Education Standards (NSES)

Grade Level	Unifying Concepts and Processes	Science as Inquiry	Physical Science	Life Science	Earth and Space Science	Science and Technology	Science in Personal and Social Perspective	History and Nature of Science
K-4	System, order, and organization; evidence, models, and explanation; change, constancy, and measurement; evolution and equilibrium; and form and function	Ability to perform, understand, or learn scientific inquiry	Properties, objects, position, motion, light, heat, electricity, or magnetism	Characteristic of plants and animals; life cycles; and ecosystem	Properties, earth layers, objects in the sky, climate changes, and materials	Use technology, differences between natural objects and objects made by man	Health, relationships, people, society, resources, life challenges, and changes	Science as human endeavor, discovery, and invention
5-8	System, order, and organization; evidence, models, and explanation; change, constancy, and measurement; evolution and equilibrium; and form and function	Ability to perform, understand, or learn scientific inquiry	Properties, changes, matter, motion, forces, and transfer of energy	Structure, function, ecosystem, food chain/web, reproduction, heredity, behavior, people, society, adaptations, survival, and differences	Earth layers/ structure, earth history, planets, solar system, and changes	Abilities, design, understand technology, and applications	Health, resources, people, society, hazards, risks, benefits, diseases, and environments	Science as human endeavor, nature of science, and history of science

Note. Information from *A Sampler of National Science Education Standards*, by Joseph M. Peters, 2006, Upper Saddle River, NJ: Pearson Education.

Table 11.2 California Science Content Standards

Grade Level	Physical Science	Life Science	Earth Science	Investigation/Experimentation
Kindergarten	Properties of materials (clay, cloth, paper, house, car, toys, objects), observe, measure, predict, color, size, shape, weight, texture, flexibility, attraction to magnets, floating, sinking	Types of plants and animals, differences, similarities, comparing, classifying, seed-bearing, plants, birds, fish, insects, stems, leaves, roots, arms, wings, legs	Earth structures, air, wind, land, water, mountains, rivers, oceans, valleys, deserts, landforms	Observe, compare, classify, describe, communicate
First	Forms and states of matter, gases, liquids, solids, properties of substances, mixed, cooled, or heated	Plants and animals, needs, survival, adaptations, food, sharp teeth eats meat, flat teeth eats plants, shelter, nesting, physical needs	Weather patterns, wind vane, weather conditions, temperature, thermometer, observe, measure, light, rain, fog, snow, climate changes	Observe, predict, measure, describe, communicate
Second	Motions of objects, force, strength, push, pull, sound, vibration, pitch, noise, beat	Life cycles of plants and animals, germination, pollination, reproduction, growth, development, parents, offspring, characteristics	Earth is made of materials, soil, water, fossils, rocks, minerals, resources, energy	Predict, observe, measure, describe, communicate, experiment, test, record
Third	Forms of energy and matter, light, heat, water, wind, gas, fuel, food, solid, liquid, gas, evaporation, melting, substances, atoms, particles	Adaptations, behavior, survival, reproduction, growth, extinction, biomes, life forms, ecosystem	Objects in the sky, patterns, constellations, stars, planets, day, night, dark, light, seasons, lunar cycles	Predict, observe, measure, describe, communicate, experiment, test, record
Fourth	Electricity, magnetism, energy, light, motions, forces, charges, poles, compass, effects, circuits, design, motors, devices, generators, magnetic field	All organisms need energy and matter to live and grow, food chain, food web, herbivores, omnivores, carnivores, consumers, decomposers, producers, recycle of plants and animals	Properties of rocks and minerals, process of formation, igneous, sedimentary, metamorphic, rock cycles, earthquake, landslides, erosion, volcanic eruption, landforms, weathering, transportation, deposition, wind, waves	Read, predict, observe, measure, describe, communicate, infer, formulate, experiment, test, record
Fifth	Types of matter, periodic table, chemical reactions, elements, metal, nonmetal, gas, solid, liquid, chemical properties, atoms, molecules, physical properties	Plant and animal structures, respiration, transpiration, waste disposal, digestion, functions of internal organs, metabolism, chemical breakdowns	Weather cycles, patterns, conditions, seasons, evaporation, condensation, precipitation, rain, hail, snow, fog, sleet, ice, lakes, oceans, rivers, underground water, convection currents, temperature	Conduct study, read, predict, observe, measure, describe, communicate, infer, formulate, experiment, test, record

Sixth	Heat and thermal energy, climate changes, heat waves, light, radiation, flow of energy, temperature, convection currents, transfer of energy, humidity, pressure	All organisms in ecosystem, exchange energy and nutrients, sunlight, photosynthesis, produce food, food web, abiotic factors, light, water, natural energy, material resources, air, soil, rocks, minerals, petroleum, fresh water, wildlife, and forests, renewable energy, nonrenewable energy	Plate tectonics and earth's structures, geological events, earthquakes, tsunamis, shakes, motions, eruptions, layers, fossils, epicenter, faults, landforms, weather patterns, climate, shapes, topography	Conduct study, read, use technology, predict, observe, measure, describe, communicate, infer, formulate, experiment, test, record, science project
Seventh	Physical principles in living systems, light spectrum, light waves, reflection, refraction, electromagnetic light, wavelengths, lenses, eyes, magnify glass, telescope, microscope, camera, light colors, light travel	Cell biology, genetics, structure and function in living systems, cells, tissues, organs, muscles, joints, skeleton, genes, traits, heredity, recessive, dominant, mitosis, reproductive organs, sexual activity, pollens, seeds, fruit, fertilization, pregnancy, chromosomes, plant and animal cellular structures, species, natural selection, anatomy, fossil	Earth and life history, age of the earth, rock cycles, evolution of life on earth, geological processes, geological time scale, extinction, fossil, fire, flood, catastrophic events, eruptions, impacts of asteroids	Conduct study, read, use technology, predict, observe, measure, describe, communicate, infer, formulate, experiment, test, record, science project
Eighth	Motions, forces, structure of matter, density, buoyancy, forms of matter, velocity, speed, balanced, unbalanced, inertia, action, reaction, static, gravity, elastic, tension, compression, friction, atomic structure, proton, neutron, electron, properties, molecular motions, elements on periodic table, acidic, basic, neutral	Chemistry of living systems, carbon, carbohydrates, fats, proteins, DNA, principles of chemistry in living organisms	Earth in the solar system, structure and composition of the universe, milky way, stars, planets, galaxies, black hole, distance between planets, eclipse, shine, waxing, waning	Conduct study, read, use technology, predict, observe, measure, describe, communicate, infer, formulate, experiment, test, record, science project

Note. Information from *Science Content Standards for California Public Schools: Kindergarten through Grade 12*, California Department of Education, 2003, http://www.cde.ca.gov/be/st/ss/documents/ sciencestnd.pdf

Table 11.3 Basic Components of Direct Instruction and Guided Inquiry Lesson Plan Formats

Direct Instruction	Guided Inquiry
1. **Learning objectives:** Students will be able to . . . , or students will learn about . . .	1. Learning objectives: **Students will be able to . . . , or students will learn about . . .**
2. **Materials:** List all materials required for this lesson plan	2. Materials: **List all required materials for this lesson plan.**
3. **Engagement or motivation:** Ask questions, use hook-up ideas, or firsthand experiences.	3. Engagement or motivation: **Ask questions, use hook-up ideas, or firsthand experience.**
4. **Learning procedures:** Scripted presentation, guided practice, independent practice, evaluation and closure	4. Learning procedures: **Inquiry activities: observation, communication, prediction, comparing, data collection, analyze data, conclusion, evaluation and closure.**
5. **Assessment:** Traditional, performance, or project	5. Assessment: **Traditional, performance, or project**

Table 11.4 Detailed Inquiry Science Lesson Plan Format

Key components

Grade level: Select a grade level for this lesson plan

Area one: Set clear learning expectations for all:
Identify desired results, anticipate learning outcomes, and aim high to achieve them.

1. **Big idea:**
   The question provides the focus for the lesson and directs students' attention to the big idea or engager. Key questions or engagers are the foundation of inquiry-based teaching and learning.

2. **Essential questions:**
   Ask specific closed, focus, or open-ended questions to engage students.

3. **Science standards:**
   List specific standards as guides, such as science, math, language arts, social studies, ELD, SDAIE, TESOL, and SIOP.

4. **Focus students:**
   Identify ELL and SN students for focus in this lesson plan and expect instructional challenges.

5. **Knowledge and skills needed for this lesson:**
   Identify specific science knowledge and skills students may need to demonstrate in this lesson plan and explain how to meet these challenges.

6. **Related contents and resources:**
   List specific background information about this lesson, explain how it relates to standards and how the content will address the learning needs.

Area two: Determine acceptable evidence:

Specify some ideas that justify the learning outcomes in this lesson plan.

1. **Major outcomes:**
   What students will achieve or learn at the end of this lesson, or what is expected of students to be able to do in this lesson plan.

2. **Learning objectives:**
   What students will learn: the students will be able to. . . .

3. **Type of assessment:**
   Traditional approach, performance approach, or project approach. Specify how student learning will be assessed.

4. **Integrate inquiry process skills:**
   How these scientific processes will be applied in this lesson plan: Inferring, relating, communicating, organizing, comparing, contrasting, observing, predicting, concluding, analyzing, and sharing.

5. **Inquiry teaching strategy:**
   Explain what methods or strategies will be used to carry out this lesson plan, such as guided practice, KWL, graphic organizers, teacher directed, student-centered, cooperative learning, collaborative approaches, groups, and hands-on and minds-on activities for all students.

6. **Engage prior knowledge and experiences:**
   How to apply prior knowledge and learning experiences in this lesson plan, how to relate to real-life experiences, how to make relevant to other concepts, and how to make connections between construction and development.

7. **Science literacy:**
   How to promote science literacy, such as writing, reading, speaking, and listening.

8. **Connecting life experience to learning experience:**
   Discuss how hands-on and minds-on activities connect to students' real life, or ask if students have experienced conceptual change by learning inquiry science.

9. **Use reciprocal teaching:**
   Allow students to make predictions, evaluations, clarifications, inquiries, summaries, or ask questions.

10. **Apply scaffolding:**
    Allow students to learn step-by-step, provide guidance, and then withdraw support to allow students to gain independence to take control of their learning.

Area three: Planning instruction:

Use appropriate lesson plan format to carry out the instructional activities.

1. Use inquiry-based instruction or guided inquiry
2. Five-step lesson plan format
3. Three-step lesson plan format
4. Direct instruction
5. Creative approaches:
   5Ws+H, PQ5Rs, KWL, scaffolding, SIOP, ELD, SDAIE, TESOL, or TPR

(Continued)

Key components

6. Inquiry activities:
   Hands-on and minds-on activities
7. Center group activity:
   Set up centers for group activity and rotate students
8. Independent practice:
   Allow students to work on worksheets or independent inquiry activities, such as observing, classifying, comparing, or sorting.

Area four: Take it beyond the classroom: Prescribe inquiry activity for students to do for independent practice.

1. Independent mini-project or discovery:
   Ask one or two questions and allow students to conduct their own investigation or experiment to answer them.
2. Assign appropriate activities for more practice.
3. Pair student up to work on problems.
4. Allow students to ask and answer their own questions about things.
5. Make connection between home and school:
   Find something at home that you think is related to inquiry science and bring it to class for discussion tomorrow.

As mentioned in early chapters, teachers can use idea maps, idea webs, thematic approaches, concept maps, and linkages to construct integrated content across the academic disciplines.

FIVE-STEP LESSON PLANNING

In several states, especially in California, the five-step lesson plan format is quite popular because it is a format used in many teacher preparation programs and it is recognized by the state as an effective format. The five-step lesson format is similar to the three-step lesson plan format, but the two are written somewhat differently. Either format can be used in science instruction as long as the content is rich in inquiry-based activities. Table 11.5 presents both formats for quick reference.

WHAT MAKES SCIENCE FUN

As alluded to early in the other chapters, teaching science concepts through inquiry can be challenging for some teachers. For others, science is no more difficult than other academic subjects. The teacher's level of comfort with teaching

Table 11.5 Basic Components of Five-step and Three-step Lesson Plans

Five-Step Lesson Plan	Three-Step Lesson Plan
1. Anticipatory set: Engage prior knowledge, use inquiry-based approach, ask questions, or hook students up with thought provoking ideas.	1. Into: **Engagement, invitation, hook-up, and tap into learning objective; ask questions to connect prior knowledge and learning experiences.**
2. Instruction: List step-by-step process for carrying out the instructional sequences.	2. Through: **Use body of knowledge, skills, information, and relevant information to support instructional processes; teach new concepts through examples, samples, demonstrations, modeling, and scaffolding.**
3. Guided practices: Use examples, demonstrations, modeling, and samples to connect teaching and learning, engage in processes, and use scaffolding techniques.	
4. Closure/evaluation/assessment: Review, recap, check for understanding, clarify issues, reaffirm learning objectives, and assess student learning.	3. Beyond: **Bring it to closure with activity, practice learning objective, expand the concepts, connect to real-life experiences, and assess student learning.**
5. Independent practice: Prescribe worksheet for practice, engage in inquiry activities, and use hands-on and minds-on activities.	

academic subjects makes a lot difference. Teachers who feel positive, competent, and well-organized about their teaching teach better regardless of the subject matter. Teachers need to make inquiry science fun for students to learn. Figure 11.1 gives some ideas as to how teachers can make science fun. Fun does not mean students can throw things around or do whatever they want during

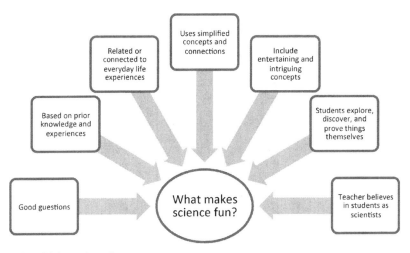

Figure 11.1 *Making science fun*

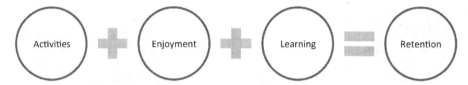

Figure 11.2 *Fun activities help retention*

science instruction. Fun means students are engaged, love the activities, are focused, and practice with constructive approaches. In other words, students learn science concepts through discovery, exploration, and understanding instead of being forced to try to absorb knowledge and skills. As Figure 11.2 illustrates, fun activities help students retain information.

THOUGHT-PROVOKING APPROACHES

One way to make learning inquiry science fun is through thought-provoking approaches. Students like to pay attention, to listen, to do with their hands, and to practice if they believe an activity will be fun or it arouses their curiosity. Curiosity goes hand-in-hand with fun. The more students are curious, the more they will try, and the more they try, the more fun they will have. Figure 11.3 illustrates how teachers can use thought-provoking approaches to engage students

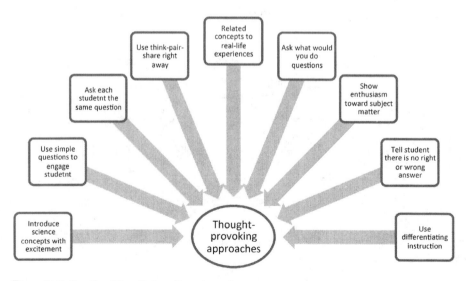

Figure 11.3 *Samples of thought-provoking approaches*

in inquiry science. Teachers have to bring themselves down to the students' level of understanding instead of expecting students to understand at their level. For instance, if teachers expect ELL, NNS, and SN students to understand everything they say or ask in the classroom, they are not accommodating all their students' needs. Not all students come from the same cultural background, and the ways they talk, communicate, and understand can be different from what is typical. Keep in mind that many students speak other languages that teachers do not speak. Teachers should rephrase questions, answers, and statements whenever necessary to accommodate all learners.

USE BRIDGE-BUILDER CONCEPTS

In order for teachers to teach science concepts effectively and reach out to all learners in the classroom, they need to incorporate specific bridge-builder concepts. There is no one-model-fits-all, and teachers need to teach science and all other academic subjects with creative practices. Bridging learning gaps helps students learn science concepts better, especially ELL, NNS, and SN students who need extra time to process new information. Teachers who do not know how to use bridge-builder concepts to connect learning and teaching leave many students to fend for themselves in the learning cycle. Table 11.6 lists key concepts for bridge

Table 11.6 Bridge-Builder Concepts

Concept Area	Applications
Guided practices	1. Use examples, samples, illustrations, demonstrations, and step-by-step processes. 2. Try out problems through scaffolding, reciprocal teaching, and coaching. 3. Model how to solve problems. 4. Guide and facilitate the process.
Modeling	1. Offer, give, or provide clear examples of learning expectation. 2. Show student work; perform illustration and demonstration.
Bridging	1. Connect and weave existing teaching schema. 2. Tap and engage students in activities. 3. Apply prior knowledge and learning experiences.
Contextualization	1. Offer and provide learning environment to explore concepts. 2. Apply concrete referents, such as visual aids, realia, pictorial materials, cards, and arts. 3. Explain and elaborate through synonyms, antonyms, metaphors, analogies, anecdotes, examples, descriptions, samples, demonstrations, illustrations, and storytelling.

(Continued)

Concept Area	Applications
Building schema	1. Use a skeletal framework to build new information, such as idea maps, concept maps, idea web, and thematic concepts.
	2. Create and provide advanced organizers for direct teaching, such as KWL, graphic organizers, charts, diagrams, mapping, Venn diagram, clustering, or grouping.
	3. Connect new information through organizers.
Questioning techniques	1. Use open-ended questions.
	2. Use referential questions.
	3. Use focus questions.
	4. Use questions with multiple answers.
	5. Allow students to question.
	6. Ask and answer questions.
Speech rate	1. Use slow speech rate.
	2. Speak slowly and clearly.
	3. Use verbal and non-verbal communications appropriate.
	4. Enunciate clearly.
	5. Reinforce key words or concepts.
	6. Use wait time whenever needed.
	7. Keep ELL, SN students, and NNS (non-native speakers) in mind while teaching.
Learning modalities	1. Allow learning process or group process.
	2. Prescribe hands-on and minds-on activities.
	3. Recognize multiple intelligences and learning styles.
	4. Use KTAV (kinetics, touching, audio, and visual) approaches.
Interactive relationship	1. Engage students in discussion, interaction, sharing, problem-solving, and learning processes.
	2. Promote identity, meaning, and civility.
	3. Allow equal opportunity for social interactions.
Meta-cognition development	1. Teach strategies, study skills, and coping skills for learner autonomy.
	2. Allow debriefing process of learning.
	3. Include plan for future use and references.
Reframing	1. Use reflective teaching to improve.
	2. Apply feedback to make changes.
	3. Explore differentiating instruction.
Checking for understanding	1. Use review to check for understanding.
	2. Engage students in independent practices, such as hands-on and minds-on activities.
	3. Use guided practices to check comprehension.
	4. Allow students to ask questions for clarification.
Monitor student learning	1. Pay attention to students.
	2. Assess progress and provide assistance.
	3. Supervise and observe student work.
	4. Collect work.
	5. Expect completion of assignments.

building in teaching science. These concepts are often parts of SDAIE, ELD, TESOL, SIOP, ESL, and other sheltered English instructional models; however, if used appropriately, they work for all students in all academic subject areas. There is misperception that these are appropriate for ELLs, NNS, and SNs only, and this is no longer true since all students benefited from them. However, without these concepts, teachers may not be able to reach to ELLs, NNS, and SNs as they are required to by state mandates.

CONSTRUCTIVIST APPROACH

In earlier chapters, the 5-E and 8-E models were discussed; the 5-E model is given in Table 11.7. To teach science concepts creatively, teachers need to use a constructivist approach to reinforce the 5-E and 8-E models. This approach recognizes the teacher's and the student's roles in the learning cycle.

Using the 8-E model, an expansion of the 5-E model, Vang (2005) illustrated teachers' roles and students' roles. They are listed in Table 11.8. These roles can be narrowed down for specific targets.

Table 11.9 illustrates how the constructivist approach is applied to teachers' and students' roles for inquiry science in the 5-E model. Teachers need to adjust

Table 11.7 The 5-E Model of Instruction

Component	Expectations	Examples
Engagement	Engage learners in inquiry-based instruction or ask questions about objects.	What do plants need to live? How many planets are in the solar system? What is the difference between insects and bugs?
Exploration	Observe, plan, or conduct simple investigation to gather data or information about objects.	Water, soil, light, space; study all the planets; compare and contrast insects and bugs.
Explanation	Use data and information to explain, use simple variables to label or sort out information, try to answer question.	What would happen to plants if there is no light, water, soil, or space? Why are planets different in size? How are insects and bugs different?
Elaboration	Learn to apply new understanding to new question, or connect learned experience to real-life experience.	Use results to explain different plants with details. Use information to tell how planets are different. Use characteristics of insects and bugs to explain differences and similarities.
Evaluation	Engage in formal and informal learning by assessing scientific knowledge, understanding, application, and abilities.	What have students learned about planets, solar system, and insects and bugs?

Table 11.8 Teachers' and Students' Roles in the Learning Cycle

Component	Teachers' Roles	Students' Roles	Focus of Both
Expectation	Set up clear learning expectation and learning objective for each lesson plan design. Expectation + objective = goal	Expect to understand the expectation and learning objective in the lesson and follow instruction.	Aim at same expectation, learning objective, and goal.
Engagement	Issue mentally challenge question to prompt inquiry. Enable students. Maintain good rapport with students at all times.	Ask, discuss, share the problem. Apply prior knowledge.	Read to tap into lesson and delivery of instruction.
Exploration	Use indirect approaches with support system and materials available. Give praise, encouragement, hints, or clues as necessary. Respond to question and provide focus.	Be an active participant, engage in activity, collect data, interpret own work and ask questions for assistance.	Facilitate, guide, model, and sort out information.
Explanation	Clarify comprehension, introduce new concepts, use appropriate teaching methodologies, and include hands-on and minds-on activities.	Learn and explain own understanding in scientific terms, apply firsthand experiences, and encode and decode new information or concepts.	Engage in discussion, clarification, questioning the answers, and investigation.
Elaboration	Provide assistance, explain procedural guidelines, guide students, and facilitate the scientific processes: observing, communicating, classifying, measuring, relating, applying, predicting, analyzing, inferring, concluding, and taking beyond.	Expand and extend firsthand experiences to gain deeper knowledge to build new concepts, and develop new questions.	Reflect and review firsthand experiences and respond to unanswered or new questions.
Experience	Encourage students to conduct experiments or investigations, inspire their science knowledge and skills to go beyond what is learned, and supervise investigative processes.	Use learned experiences to compare and contrast, apply scientific processes to explain, elaborate, and explore the results.	Connect outside experiences with inquiry activities and textbook information.
Enjoyment	Manage, monitor, supervise, assist, guide, and facilitate students throughout the scientific processes, and allow students to work individually and cooperatively. Allow flexibility, adaptation, and accommodation.	Engage in inquiry activities, use scientific processes, conduct experiment and investigation, and work in group individually or cooperatively.	Respect independent work or group work, engage in inquiry activities, provide support, guidance, direction, and follow guidelines. Minimize interruption.
Evaluation	Monitor student work, evaluate progress, prescribe test, reflect on student learning outcome, give feedback, emphasize key concepts, make adaptations, and promote academic language and science literacy.	Take test, assess own learning, apply knowledge and skills, relate learned experiences to real life, use academic language and scientific process to answer questions.	What was taught is what was tested. Use teacher-made test to evaluate student progress or learning outcome.

Note. Information from New Pedagogical Approaches for Teaching Elementary Science to Limited English Proficient Students, by C.T. Vang, 2006, *Multicultural Education, 13*(3).

Table 11.9 Teachers' and Students' Roles in Constructivist Approach

Component	Teacher's Roles	Student's Roles
Engagement	1. To mentally challenge students with an event or inquiry question. 2. Use questions that are open-ended and designed to get students started with their own investigations. 3. Ask thought-provoking question to engage students in science concepts right away.	1. To discuss, illustrate, or write about the problem. 2. Let the teacher know their prior knowledge, skills, conceptions, and beliefs. 3. Share and discuss answers to the question.
Exploration	1. Apply very indirect approach to engage students. 2. Provide materials, observe, pose questions, and assist as needed. 3. Use planned experiences that allow students to focus on particular concepts without first having been taught the concept.	1. Must be actively involved in the inquiry process. 2. Work together to test ideas by manipulating materials and data. 3. Investigate with minimal guidance from the teacher. 4. Allow students the opportunity to discover an unknown effect, fact, principle, law, or theory by themselves. 5. Allow students to clarify their own understanding of major concepts, knowledge, and skills.
Explanation	1. Clarify students' understanding and discoveries. 2. Introduce new concepts and skills for inquiry learning.	1. Propose explanations and solutions based on their understanding of the concepts and processes. 2. Allow students to construct new view of the concept or process under investigation. 3. Allow students to have conceptual change based on the new information acquired through firsthand experiences.
Elaboration	1. Assist students in applying and extending what they have just learned. 2. Pose open-ended questions for discussion and interaction about their learning experiences. 3. Clarify their understanding and comprehension whenever necessary.	1. Engage in inquiry activity to apply what they have just learned. 2. Build a better understanding of concepts or process to extend their knowledge and skills. 3. Take action on what they have learned and ask new inquiry questions.
Evaluation	1. Evaluate student progress. 2. Check for understanding and comprehension. 3. Clarify students' firsthand experiences.	1. Assess their scientific knowledge, skills, and abilities. 2. Take traditional assessment. 3. Take performance assessment. 4. Engage in inquiry activities.

the approach to best fit their needs and the needs of their students. For lower grades, some of these roles may not be appropriate; however, in the higher grades, the constructivist approach is appropriate. Moreover, states generally require that instructional adaptations be included in all lesson plan designs; therefore, teachers need to keep the ELL, NNS, and SN students in mind when planning lessons.

Furthermore, teachers must perform the following tasks throughout implementation of the constructivist approaches to make sure that all students are engaged in inquiry skills processes:

1. Facilitate and guide the process.
2. Check for understanding on a regular basis.
3. Monitor student progress and adjust as necessary to accommodate students' needs.
4. Provide continual feedback.
5. Use active participation techniques to keep students focused and engaged at all times.
6. Employ KTAV (kinetics, touch, audio, and visual) modes of learning.
7. Use strategies for diverse learners' needs: adaptations, accommodations, modifications, and interventions.
8. Prescribe individual, group, or whole-class activity.
9. Encourage use of inquiry process skills.
10. Promote science literacy through inquiry activities.

Whatever teachers do or use as they teach inquiry science, the golden rule for making teaching and learning science fun, meaningful, and purposeful is to have thoughtful planning and organization. Most importantly, teaching and learning science concepts depends entirely on the ongoing implementation of hands-on and minds-on practices; that is the focus for inquiry science.

GET READY FOR IMPLEMENTATION

Developing sequential steps for implementing inquiry science requires practice and diligent planning and organization. As mentioned in earlier chapters, teaching science concepts is not the same as teaching real science or concrete science. Many teachers are intimidated by the thought of teaching science because they believe they have to teach real science to elementary students, and that does not make any sense. Here is the key to removing the intimidation: teachers teach science concepts that relate to real science but not the real science itself until students reach the

Figure 11.4 *Components of the instructional process*

higher grades. In other words, elementary teachers apply science concepts to real science rather than using real science to teach science concepts.

The implementation of science instruction can be done in many ways; however, instruction needs to be very well organized and structured for science as for any academic subject. Figure 11.4 illustrates the components of the instructional process and their order.

Inquiry science lesson plans can be implemented orderly and chronologically in the classroom; however, implementation depends on the grade level and the age of the students. Teachers need to plan how the implementation process will work for their particular grade level or specific group of students. Table 11.10 offers some suggestions for teachers to consider in implementing inquiry science in the classroom. The steps given in the table can be adjusted to meet the needs of students. Keep in mind that all instructional processes have to be flexible to accommodate any unanticipated circumstance that might happen.

If teachers can answer the basic questions in Table 11.10, they are somewhat ready to implement inquiry science. Regardless of the nature of the inquiry science lesson plan, teachers need at the very least to keep to the allotted times, engage all students, provide hands-on and minds-on activities for all, and use the constructivist approach in their lesson planning and implementation. Remember, inquiry science should be taught as a human endeavor.

Table 11.10 Implementation Processes and Activities

Process	Examples of Activities
Physical organization	1. Is the learning environment organized and ready for inquiry science anytime during the day? 2. Is the class designed for multipurpose or multidimensional activities? 3. Is there sufficient space, equipment, materials, supplies, and resources for inquiry science?
Mental organization	1. Is the teacher mentally ready to teach science concepts based on national and state standards? 2. Is the teacher mentally organized to deliver inquiry instructions? 3. Is the teacher mentally prepared to engage all children in learning science concepts with hands-on and minds-on activities?
Time allocation	1. How much time does the teacher have for each inquiry science lesson plan? 2. What is the best way to use the time for inquiry science? 3. How to manage time during inquiry science activity or hands-on and minds-on activity?
Preparation	1. Has the teacher adequately prepared inquiry activities for individual students, small-group activity, and the whole class? 2. Has the teacher tried out or practiced these activities before giving them to the students to experiment or investigate in class? 3. Has the teacher organized materials and supplies needed for each inquiry activity?
Engagement	1. Is the teacher ready to engage students in learning science concepts? 2. What will the teacher use to engage students and for how long? 3. What roles should the teacher play during this process and what are students expected to learn from this?
Distributing of materials and supplies	1. When must the teachers distribute materials to students for inquiry activity? 2. For lower grades, does the teacher have to premake everything for the students? 3. For higher grades, how much time should the teacher allow time for getting everything ready? 4. Who should help the teacher distribute materials or supplies in class? 5. Who should help the teacher collect materials, supplies, and student work after the activity?
Exploration	1. What kind of questions should the teacher ask students? 2. How will the teacher expect students to explore the concepts and for how long? 3. What should the teacher use to guide the exploration and what are the steps the students need to take? 4. How will the teacher monitor and adjust the process? 5. What activity should the teacher for firsthand experience?
Explanation	1. What questions should the teacher use to engage students in sharing what they just learned? 2. What will the teacher expect students to share? 3. How will the teacher clarify students' understanding and misunderstandings? 4. What will the teacher do to help those who cannot explain verbally or in writing? 5. When is it time for students to process in groups to share or discuss their findings? 6. How does the teacher help students connect learning with real-life experiences?

Elaboration	1. What questions should the teacher ask students about their findings?
	2. How do students apply this learning experience to their prior learning or real-life experiences?
	3. How will the teacher engage students in discussing conceptual change?
	4. What detailed information can students share with the class?
	5. How do students explain or elaborate something that has not been taught to them?
Evaluation	1. What will the teacher do to evaluate student progress or understanding?
	2. How will the teacher assess student learning of new concepts?
	3. When is it time to clarify student understanding and misunderstandings about this new concept?
	4. How could this be related to real-life experiences or other learning experiences?
	5. What are the highlights the teacher needs to review, recap, and reemphasize?
	6. What should the teacher do about students who did not finish the work?
Feedback/ reflection	1. What kind of feedback should the teacher give to the students?
	2. What kind of feedback should the students give to the teacher?
	3. How does the teacher reflect upon the feedback and improve the next inquiry lesson?
Wrap-up	1. When is it time to call for cleanup and putting things away?
	2. When is it time to call for materials and supplies to be returned orderly?
	3. How much time does the whole class need for cleanup?
	4. When is it time for all students to wash their hands and take off their safety devices?

SUMMING UP

This chapter summarized key concepts, ideas, and approaches to help teachers better prepare to teach science concepts creatively in the classroom. It emphasized how teachers can use national and state standards for inquiry science, lesson plan formats such as the 5-E and 8-E models, and thought-provoking approaches to strengthen the instructional process and make teaching and learning science fun.

The constructivist approach was added in this chapter to reinforce the 5-E and 8-E models. Teachers' roles and students' roles are extremely important in learning inquiry science. Teachers do not want to give answers to students and students do not want to just memorize answers without doing any inquiry activities to learn something they have been taught or experienced through firsthand experiences. Moreover, bridge-builder concepts are taken from specialized lesson formats such as ELD, SDAIE, SIOP, TESOL, and other forms of sheltered English instruction and applied in inquiry science to help teachers learn how these techniques are beneficial to all learners, not only NNS, ELL, and SN students.

This chapter also briefly talked about how teachers can get ready for the implementation of inquiry science with sequential processes. Teachers need to be physically and mentally organized for any academic subject; however, teaching science demands especially thorough preparation, good organization, and thoughtful planning and structure. Without these, inquiry science is likely to be uncreative, unexciting, and irrelevant to teachers and students alike.

CHAPTER TWELVE

Practice Inquiry Science Concepts

A fact is a simple statement that everyone believes. It is innocent, unless found guilty. A hypothesis is a novel suggestion that no one wants to believe. It is guilty, until found effective.

—EDWARD TELLER

INTRODUCTION

Teachers in elementary schools teach multiple subjects and are required to master language arts, mathematics, social studies, and science whereas most teachers in Grades 7-12 teach single subjects and are required to master only one subject. Single-subject teachers have more time to practice their art and content than do multiple-subject teachers. Most teaching in single-subject areas uses repeated curricular activities, but in multiple-subject areas teachers have complex daily routines and schedules to follow and have to change academic tasks, subject matter, and content throughout the day. To master inquiry science, teachers need to find time to practice science concepts; the more they practice the better they become. This chapter describes how to practice inquiry science through hands-on and minds-on strategies. The content of this chapter provides teachers with ideas, concepts, and approaches that will improve their mastery of scientific processes, knowledge, and skills. Once teachers have mastered their art, they can design appropriate inquiry activities that enable students to discover new experiences with joy and explore the wonder of science with curiosity.

SCIENCE AS A HUMAN ENDEAVOR

Science means different things to different teachers. Science concepts do not determine what science is; however, the understanding of science concepts helps students learn the content of science itself.

Science is about the surroundings and the natural world that can be explored through firsthand experiences, or science is simply the process of asking and answering questions about the surroundings and the natural world. As mentioned in earlier chapters, there is no single definition for science. Scientists could not agree on one definition, so dictionaries and teachers have multiple definitions. However, science is broad and needs to be taught with an open mind through inquiry-based approaches that allow students to explore what science really is. Remember, science is ubiquitous; it is found everywhere. But without proper teaching and learning, science is hard to find.

For this reason, teachers have to realize the challenges and responsibilities they have in teaching the intricacies of science in the multicultural classroom. Every child learns differently, and every science lesson requires inclusive teaching. Teachers are responsible for teaching science concepts in ways that enable their students to learn the content and discover what science is about and what it is not. Practicing science concepts will improve the students' mastery of those concepts only if the practice is thoughtfully planned and well organized. Science is about the development of knowledge and skills through the construction of inquiry process skills; it is a human endeavor that connects everything in life to the known and unknown in the natural world.

INQUIRY PROCESS SKILLS

There are many ways to teach and practice science concepts, but the proper way to engage students in learning inquiry science is through the inquiry process skills of observing, communicating, predicting, comparing, contrasting, classifying, measuring, inferring, analyzing, concluding, and investigating, as shown in Figure 12.1 and Table 12.1. Teaching science is a process, and learning science is also a process, as the 5-E model illustrated in Table 12.2 indicates. Teachers need to require students to practice inquiry skills to learn scientific processes. Regardless of cultural

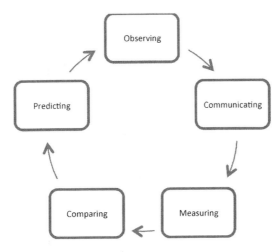

Figure 12.1 *The inquiry process*

backgrounds, nearly all children have had science experiences; however, without knowing the proper process to learn science concepts academically, knowing science could be meaningless because there is little or no connection between experiences and learning. Acquiring inquiry skills allows students to engage themselves in scientific processes to make learning science concepts meaningful, making a connection between learning and their real-life experiences as required by national and state science standards.

Table 12.1 Examples of Inquiry Skills in Science

Words Associated with Inquiry	Examples of Inquiry Skills
Observe	Use, apply, or allow five senses to examine, feel, determine, or learn about an object or event
Classify	Sort, put, collect, organize, separate, or place things that are the same, different, or similar in a group, or organize things that share properties together in a group
Measure	Use or apply numbers or rulers to find, label, name, or identify the size, length, distance, time, volume, area, mass, weight, height, or temperature of an object or an event
Infer	Decide, form, conclude, interpret, or finalize an idea from facts, concepts, principles, theories, results, or observation
Communicate	Discuss, interact, exchange, talk, share, elaborate, or explain the information, data, or results
Interpret	Explain, tell, discuss, share, elaborate, or exchange information, data, or results of investigation or experiment

(Continued)

Words Associated with Inquiry	Examples of Inquiry Skills
Hypothesize	Form, make, ask, or write a statement or question that can be tested to answer a question
Experiment	Use variables to perform a test to support, confirm, or disprove a hypothesis or a question of interest
Use variables	Use, identify, or label things to be changed, controlled, manipulated, or monitored in an experiment
Predict	Guess, estimate, state, or tell the possible results, number, or outcome of an event, investigation, or experimentation
Make a model	Design, craft, make, produce, or create something to represent or replicate an object or event of experiment
Use numbers	Name, label, identify, order, count, add, subtract, multiply, or divide to explain data or results of an experiment
Record data	Note, write, log, keep, arrange, store, collect, or organize information, data, or results in science investigation or experiment
Analyze data	Decide, infer, observe, measure, communicate, apply, or use the information, data, or results collected or gathered to answer questions or to solve problems or hypotheses

Table 12.2 Processes of 5-E Model

Component	Expectations	Examples
Engagement	Engage learners in inquiry-based instruction or asking questions about objects	What do plants need to live? How many planets are in the solar system? What is the difference between insects and bugs?
Exploration	Observe, plan, or conduct simple investigation to gather data or information about objects	Water, soil, light, space; study all the planets; compare and contrast insects and bugs
Explanation	Use data and information to explain, use simple variables to label or sort out information, try to answer question	What would happen to plants if there is no light, water, soil, or space? Why are planets different in size? How are insects and bugs different?
Elaboration	Learn to apply new understanding to new question, or connect learned experience to real-life experience	Use results to explain different plants with details. Use information to tell how planets are different. Use characteristics of insects and bugs to explain differences and similarities
Evaluation	Engage in formal and informal learning by assessing scientific knowledge, understanding, application, and abilities	What students have learned about planets, solar system, and insects and bugs.

USE MIND-FOCUSED STRATEGIES

Practice is a tool for the mastery of science concepts; however, inquiry practices need to include mind-focused strategies that inspire students to learn. Table 12.3 gives some examples of mind-focused strategies that teachers can use as part of their hands-on and minds-on activities. Keep in mind that NNS, ELL, and SN students require more than mind-focused strategies. They need instructional adaptations, accommodations, modifications, and interventions; without these helps, inquiry practices such as hands-on and minds-on activities may not benefit them at all.

Table 12.3 Samples of Mind-Focused Strategies

Strategies	Examples of Activities
Thought-provoking questions	Use focus, closed, or open-ended questions to introduce inquiry science concepts.
Use prior knowledge	Engage students' prior knowledge, learning experiences, and life experiences right away.
Student interests	Know and recognize student interests and use inquiry activities to inspire their interests.
Student curiosity	Use questions, prompts, props, perks, and ideas to make students curious about inquiry science.
Make science fun to learn	Make teaching and learning science concepts messy, sloppy, slimy, dirty, and tasty.
Use intriguing ideas	Apply intriguing ideas, concepts, questions, or thoughts to engage students in critical thinking, such as: what would happen if I do. . . .
Use entertaining ideas	Bring entertaining ideas to class such as drawing your partner's face without looking at your paper, or use funny questions about science, like how big is an ostrich egg?
Make science enjoyable	Allow students to have fun while doing inquiry science activities, prescribe hands-on activity to work on in groups, and allow them to take things home to show parents and others.
Believe that everyone can learn	Realize that every child in class can learn science and everyone is a scientist.
Realia	Use books, pictures, arts, crafts, samples, examples, real objects, artifacts, and drawings to enhance learning.
Visual aids	Use pictures, posters, drawings, art, artifacts, cards, books, and video clips to enhance learning.
Books	Big books with pictures, small books with big prints, books related to topic of activity, and story books.
Pictorial materials/ pictures	Use realia, visual aids, books, posters, crafts, art, examples, samples, objects, drawings, and pictures to enhance learning.

(Continued)

Strategies	Examples of Activities
Samples or examples	Bring objects, plants, insect pictures, animal pictures, or show video clips.
Cooperative learning	Assign students to work in groups or pairs; allow socialization, group process, and interactions; sharing; communicating; collaborating; and team work.
Group process	Use group for hands-on and minds-on activities; facilitate group process; guide group work; provide assistance; allow students to share how they learn science.
Video clips	Select appropriate video clips to enhance instruction and activities; use 5- to 10-minute videos.
Animated resources	Online resources include animated video clips; 1- to 5-minute videos.
Hands-on and minds-on activities	Use appropriate, cheap, effective, and easy hands-on and minds-on activities to engage students in science.
Use challenging ideas	Ask challenging questions and allow students to work in groups or pairs to solve the problems, like proving that anything can walk on water.
Center approaches	Use centers or stations for activities, rotate students if necessary, or work in small groups to finish a task.
Student-centered approaches	Inquiry science is based on student-centered approaches; use questions, prompts, props, and perks to inspire students; base activities on students' abilities, knowledge, and skills.

Mind-focused activities should be used to prep students or to tap them in to inquiry instruction or activities. Before beginning hands-on and minds-on activities, teachers need to make sure students are focused on learning science; otherwise, teachers may have to repeat directions or processes. Keeping students focused means teachers spend less time directing and redirecting attention when students are supposed to be doing hands-on and minds-on activities.

CONCEPTS TO CONCRETE

Teaching science concepts is not the same as teaching real science. Elementary students need to be taught from concepts to concrete, not from concrete to concepts. The elementary grades can be divided into three major groups, as illustrated in Figure 12.2. The progression from teaching concepts to teaching concrete science in Grades K-12 is depicted in Figure 12.3. If teachers follow this model, the content of their teaching will be consistent with national and state science standards. In the science standards, science concepts are taught in the early grades and concrete science in the later grades. Without this progression, science education would be a mixed bag with a piecemeal curriculum, and that will not benefit students.

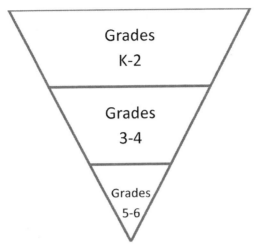

Figure 12.2 *Major groups of elementary grades*

CONTENTS OF LESSON PLAN DESIGNS

Regardless of the format of a lesson, all children must be included in learning science concepts. NNS, ELL, and SN students are often left out of the learning process because they need special instructional assistance from their teachers as required by TPE and TPA mandates. In some cases, teachers mistreat these students by not considering them or recognizing their needs as important. Ryan and Cooper (2001) and Good and Brophy (2000) described some of the ways teachers

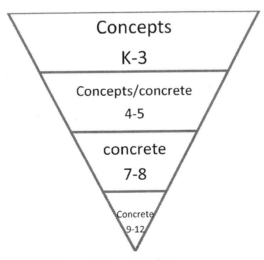

Figure 12.3 *Progression in teaching concepts to concrete science*

fail to meet the needs of low achievers; some are given in Table 12.4. Table 12.5 lists examples of instructional adaptations teachers need to consider for these students. Otherwise, they become seat warmers, silent learners, and ghostlike students in the classroom. Hands-on and minds-on activities must be designed for all, and the constructivist approaches should be implemented with care in order to include all learners in the learning cycle during inquiry science activities.

At the very least, teachers need to show respect for all learners regardless of their cultural backgrounds, language skills, special needs, and academic abilities. Remember, children are enrolled in school to be taught, to learn, and to socialize, not to be humiliated, insulted, or put down by teachers. As mentioned in earlier chapters, teachers should learn to become multicultural educators who can create and maintain a positive learning environment for all learners in the multicultural setting. The construct of a lesson plan has to be inclusive; otherwise, some students are ignored for nonacademic reasons and non-inclusive instructional practices are detrimental to the quality of education all students deserve. Teachers who fail to consider multicultural issues and factors in their daily teaching do a

Table 12.4 Ways Teachers Sometimes Treat Low Achievers

Type of Treatment	Possible Causes
Give little time for lows to ask a question	Assume lows don't understand the question, don't know the answer; or don't want to waste time.
Allow no clue, no hint, or no opportunity for lows	Expect lows to understand the question and know the correct answer right away.
Reward inappropriate behaviors or incorrect answers	Expect lows to have middle-class values or focus on the behaviors more than the needs.
Criticize lows for failure	Blame lows for not knowing or not understanding.
Praise them for success less frequently	Fail to promote lows, lack cross-cultural education, or hold prejudicial biases.
Give less response and less public feedback	Hold stereotype, bias, prejudice, or rejection.
Pay less attention or interact less with lows	Avoid lows for many reasons, focus on other students, or ignore lows' needs.
Call on lows less	Expect the right answers, presume incompetent, or hold cultural grudges.
Seat them farther away	Focus on loud, noisy, rowdy, or assertive students and avoid quiet and polite students.
Demand less from them	Assume lows don't have skills, have problems speaking English, or won't know the answers.
Give lows more private than public interactions	Put pressure on lows to learn, expect lows to adapt, or make sure assignments are done.
Closely monitor lows in class	Focus on lows' weaknesses, expect lows to learn at the same rate, or have no time for lows.

Give lows more structured activities	Expect lows to learn specific skills, give lows different activities, or use strict rules.
Give lows no benefit of the doubt in borderline cases	Grade down instead of grading up, make errors too serious, expect to be like other learners.
Give lows less friendly interactions, fewer smiles, and less support	Present negative attitudes toward lows, shut them off, or give no attention at all.
Give lows shorter and less informative feedback	Fail to encourage lows; give good, not good, or okay remarks; or send "see me" notes.
Make less eye contact with lows and respond less attentively	Avoid lows, consider lows to be "ghost like" students, or expect nothing from them.
Use less effective lessons and less time-consuming instructional methods for lows	Give content compatible, not content obligatory, or watered-down instruction.
Give less accepted and lower use of their ideas and input	Assume lows to be followers, not leaders, or expect lows to be listeners, not actors.
Use impoverished and improvised curricula with lows	Use whatever they can think of, give lows easy assignments, expect lows to do just enough, give lip services for lows, provide lows with cosmetic education, or offer lows nonacademic instruction.

Table 12.5 Examples of Lesson Plan Adaptations

Accommodations	Modifications	Adaptations	Interventions
Use list of vocabulary words, preview, review, engage prior knowledge, think-pair-share, pair-up, group, cooperative learning, ELD lesson, SDAIE lesson, scaffolding	Definitions, word bank, read out loud, choral reading, repetition, recitation, review, pair up, graphic organizers, graph sheet, grid, group activity, cooperative learning, video clips	Use realia, pictures, placards, word cards; model sentence; use sentence frame, cloze, cognitive learning, KWL, graphic organizer, primary language support, bilingual materials, practicing, exercise, drills, make-a-word dictionary	Use individualized instruction, one-on-one conference, pull-out, center instruction, small-group activity, special lesson plans, formal and informal assessment
Use scaffolding, reciprocal teaching, open court reading, bridging, connecting, contextualization, schema building, thematic approaches, text representation	Use BIA, TA, translator, interpreter, bilingual materials, RTI or SIOP approaches, ELD/SDAIE approaches, TESOL, ESL, SEI approaches, slow pacing, clear enunciation, slow speech, wait time, parts to whole or whole to parts, TPR	Use hands-on and minds-on activities, practicing, drills, exercises, review, study guide, modeling, guided practices, examples, samples, demonstration, grade- and age-appropriate materials, illustrations, processing information, check for understanding, white boards	Use 180 program, reading clinician, pullout, ability grouping, ELD rotation, cluster grouping, paraprofessional assistance, RTI, SIOP

disservice to the students who need their help the most. Learning life, earth, and physical science can be as challenging as the learning of any other academic subject. For this reason, teachers need to prepare all learners for trying, practicing, and doing inquiry science activities.

SCIENCE MATERIALS AND SUPPLIES

As mentioned in early chapters, teachers need to organize all science materials and supplies before they begin a lesson to have them ready for practicing inquiry activities. Each lesson may require different kinds of materials and supplies, so teachers need to know where to find their science resources. Inquiry science cannot be taught effectively without having proper materials and supplies handy so students can practice. For lower grades, teachers have to pre-make all materials or supplies for hands-on and minds-on activities in order to save time; in the higher grades, teachers can expect students to make models themselves. For inquiry activities, teachers need to allow a few minutes in the activity schedule for distributing materials or supplies to students. Ideally, a well organized plan and thoughtful structure will save time and minimize disruptions and awkward transitions. Figures 12.3 and 12.4 list some of the materials and supplies that teachers may need to have. These materials and supplies need to be stored in a safe place for future use. Also, teachers need to recycle or reuse materials whenever possible

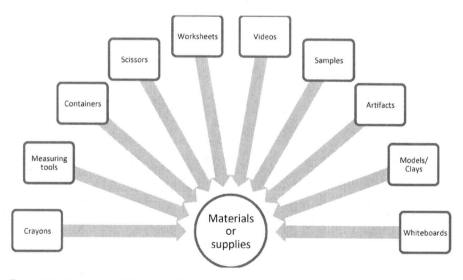

Figure 12.4 *Science materials and supplies*

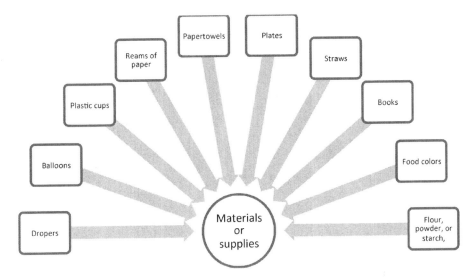

Figure 12.5 *Additional science materials and supplies*

in order to save money. Inquiry science activities do not have to be expensive, and teachers can adapt or simulate hands-on and minds-on activities as long as the learning objective is clear.

LIFE SCIENCE CONCEPTS

In accordance with the NSES and California Science Standards for K-12 grades, as listed in Tables 12.6 and 12.7, teachers have to use inquiry-based approaches to engage students in learning science concepts, and inquiry process skills are required for all science areas.

In order to practice life science concepts with students, teachers must apply the K-6 life science conceptual frames given in Table 12.8. Teachers can develop a series of inquiry activities for hands-on and minds-on activities based on these conceptual frames and use them to guide their teaching and learning objectives. Life science is centered on plants and animals and their environments.

The national and state science standards require that all students develop an understanding of the characteristics of organisms, the structures and functions in living systems, life cycles of organisms, and organisms and their environments. Teacher need to make connections between these learning expectations and the conceptual frames.

Table 12.6 National Science Education Standards (NSES)

Grade Level	Unifying Concepts and Processes	Science as Inquiry	Physical Science	Life Science	Earth and Space Science	Science and Technology	Science in Personal and Social Perspective	History and Nature of Science
K–4	System, order, and organization; evidence, models, and explanation; change, constancy, and measurement; evolution and equilibrium; and form and function	Ability to perform, understand, or learn scientific inquiry	Properties, objects, position, motion, light, heat, electricity, or magnetism	Characteristic of plants and animals; life cycles; and ecosystem	Properties, earth layers, objects in the sky, climate changes, and materials	Use technology, differences between natural objects and objects made by man	Health, relationships, people, society, resources, life challenges, and changes	Science as human endeavor, discovery, and invention
5–8	System, order, and organization; evidence, models, and explanation; change, constancy, and measurement; evolution and equilibrium; and form and function	Ability to perform, understand, or learn scientific inquiry	Properties, changes, matter, motion, forces, and transfer of energy	Structure, function, ecosystem, food chain/web, reproduction, heredity, behavior, people, society, adaptations, survival, and differences	Earth layers/structure, earth history, planets, solar system, and changes	Abilities, design, understand technology, and applications	Health, resources, people, society, hazards, risks, benefits, diseases, and environments	Science as human endeavor, nature of science, and history of science

Note. Information from *A Sampler of National Science Education Standards*, by Joseph M. Peters, 2006, Upper Saddle River, NJ: Pearson Education.

Table 12.7 California Science Content Standards

Grade Level	Physical Science	Life Science	Earth Science	Investigation/ Experimentation
Kindergarten	Properties of materials (clay, cloth, paper, house, car, toys, objects), observe, measure, predict, color, size, shape, weight, texture, flexibility, attraction to magnets, floating, sinking	Types of plants and animals, differences, similarities, comparing, classifying, seed-bearing, plants, birds, fish, insects, stems, leaves, roots, arms, wings, legs	Earth structures, air, wind, land, water, mountains, rivers, oceans, valleys, deserts, landforms	Observe, compare, classify, describe, communicate
First	Forms and states of matter, gases, liquids, solids, properties of substances, mixed, cooled, or heated	Plants and animals, needs, survival, adaptations, food, sharp teeth eats meat, flat teeth eats plants, shelter, nesting, physical needs	Weather patterns, wind vane, weather conditions, temperature, thermometer, observe, measure, light, rain, fog, snow, climate changes	Observe, predict, measure, describe, communicate
Second	Motions of objects, force, strength, push, pull, sound, vibration, pitch, noise, beat	Life cycles of plants and animals, germination, pollination, reproduction, growth, development, parents, offspring, characteristics	Earth is made of materials, soil, water, fossils, rocks, minerals, resources, energy	Predict, observe, measure, describe, communicate, experiment, test, record
Third	Forms of energy and matter, light, heat, water, wind, gas, fuel, food, solid, liquid, gas, evaporation, melting, substances, atoms, particles	Adaptations, behavior, survival, reproduction, growth, extinction, biomes, life forms, ecosystem	Objects in the sky, patterns, constellations, stars, planets, day, night, dark, light, seasons, lunar cycles	Predict, observe, measure, describe, communicate, experiment, test, record
Fourth	Electricity, magnetism, energy, light, motions, forces, charges, poles, compass, effects, circuits, design, motors, devices, generators, magnetic field	All organisms need energy and matter to live and grow, food chain, food web, herbivores, omnivores, carnivores, consumers, decomposers, producers, recycle of plants and animals	Properties of rocks and minerals, process of formation, igneous, sedimentary, metamorphic, rock cycles, earthquake, landslides, erosion, volcanic eruption, landforms, weathering, transportation, deposition, wind, waves	Read, predict, observe, measure, describe, communicate, infer, formulate, experiment, test, record
Fifth	Types of matter, periodic table, chemical reactions, elements, metal, nonmetal, gas, solid, liquid, chemical properties, atoms, molecules, physical properties	Plant and animal structures, respiration, transpiration, waste disposal, digestion, functions of	Weather cycles, patterns, conditions, seasons, evaporation, condensation, precipitation, rain,	Conduct study, read, predict, observe, measure, describe,

(Continued)

Grade Level	Physical Science	Life Science	Earth Science	Investigation/Experimentation
		internal organs, metabolism, chemical breakdowns	hail, snow, fog, sleet, ice, lakes, oceans, rivers, underground water, convection currents, temperature	communicate, infer, formulate, experiment, test, record
Sixth	Heat and thermal energy, climate changes, heat waves, light, radiation, flow of energy, temperature, convection currents, transfer of energy, humidity, pressure	All organisms in ecosystem, exchange energy and nutrients, sunlight, photosynthesis, produce food, food web, abiotic factors, light, water, natural energy, material resources, air, soil, rocks, minerals, petroleum, fresh water, wildlife, and forests, renewable energy, nonrenewable energy	Plate tectonics and earth's structures, geological events, earthquakes, tsunamis, shakes, motions, eruptions, layers, fossils, epicenter, faults, landforms, weather patterns, climate, shapes, topography	Conduct study, read, use technology, predict, observe, measure, describe, communicate, infer, formulate, experiment, test, record, science project
Seventh	Physical principles in living systems, light spectrum, light waves, reflection, refraction, electromagnetic light, wavelengths, lenses, eyes, magnify glass, telescope, microscope, camera, light colors, light travel	Cell biology, genetics, structure and function in living systems, cells, tissues, organs, muscles, joints, skeleton, genes, traits, heredity, recessive, dominant, mitosis, reproductive organs, sexual activity, pollens, seeds, fruit, fertilization, pregnancy, chromosomes, plant and animal cellular structures, species, natural selection, anatomy, fossil	Earth and life history, age of the earth, rock cycles, evolution of life on earth, geological processes, geological time scale, extinction, fossil, fire, flood, catastrophic events, eruptions, impacts of asteroids	Conduct study, read, use technology, predict, observe, measure, describe, communicate, infer, formulate, experiment, test, record, science project
Eighth	Motions, forces, structure of matter, density, buoyancy, forms of matter, velocity, speed, balanced, unbalanced, inertia, action, reaction, static, gravity, elastic, tension, compression, friction, atomic structure, proton, neutron, electron, properties, molecular motions, elements on periodic table, acidic, basic, neutral	Chemistry of living systems, carbon, carbohydrates, fats, proteins, DNA, principles of chemistry in living organisms	Earth in the solar system, structure and composition of the universe, milky way, stars, planets, galaxies, black hole, distance between planets, eclipse, shine, waxing, waning	Conduct study, read, use technology, predict, observe, measure, describe, communicate, infer, formulate, experiment, test, record, science project

Note. Information from *Science Content Standards for California Public Schools: Kindergarten through Grade 12,* California Department of Education, 2003, http://www.cde.ca.gov/be/st/ss/documents/ sciencestnd.pdf

Table 12.8 Life Science Conceptual Frames for Inquiry Activities

K Grade	First Grade	Second Grade	Third Grade	Fourth Grade	Fifth Grade	Sixth Grade
Plants:	*Plants:*	*Plants:*	*Plants and animals:*	*Plants and animals:*	*Plants and animals:*	*Plants and animals:*
1. Parts of plants	1. Plants are living things	1. What plants need to survive	1. Looking at plants and animals	1. Kingdom of life for plants and animals	1. Plant and animal kingdom	1. Classifying plants and animals
2. What food plants need	2. Parts of plants	2. How plants make new plants	2. Needs of plants and animals	2. Plant and animal cells	2. Plant and animal cells	2. Systems in plants and animals
3. How plants grow and change	3. Different plants	3. How plants are alike and different	3. Classifying plants and animals	3. Classifying plants and animals	3. Classifying plants and animals	3. Plant and animal cells
4. Examining plant parts, like leaves, flowers, fruits, and stems.	4. How plants grow and change	4. Plant habitats: forests, hot place, cold place, or deserts	4. Plant parts and animal parts	4. Reproduction of plants and animals	4. Systems in plants and animals	4. Plant and animal microorganisms
5. People use plants for what	5. Plants live in different places	5. Plant kingdom	5. How plants and animals grow and change	5. Plant kingdom and animal kingdom	5. Plant and animal reproduction	5. Cell theory
Animals:	6. Examining flowers, fruits, seeds, leaves, stems, and roots of plants	*Animals:*	6. Plant life cycles	6. With and without backbone animals	6. Plant and animal life cycles	6. Genetics
1. Animals are everywhere	*Animals:*	1. Animal groups	7. Animal life cycles	7. Life systems in plants and animals	7. Traits and heredity	7. Traits and heredity
2. What food animals need	1. Learn about different animals	2. How animals grow and change	8. Parents and children	8. Plant and animal life cycles	8. Relationship in ecosystems	8. Animal and human genetics
3. Bugs and insects	2. Where animal live	3. Animal habitats, land, water	9. Plants and animals relationship in ecosystem	9. Ecosystems and biomes	9. Food chains, food webs, adaptations, and energy flow	9. Ecosystems
4. Reptiles and their differences	3. How animals grow and change	4. What foods animals need	10. Food chains, food webs, and different ecosystems	10. Animal adaptations	10. Survival in ecosystems	10. Food chains, food webs, and changes in ecosystems
5. Water animals and land animals	4. Different habitats: land, water, and desert	5. Food chains or food webs	11. Plant and animal adaptations	11. Changes in ecosystems	11. Biomes and ecosystems	11. Comparing ecosystems and changes in ecosystems
6. People and animals	5. Plants and animals live together		12. Plants and animals living environment	12. Plant habitats	12. Changes in land and water ecosystems	12. Plant and animal adaptations
7. How animals grow and change			13. Changes affect plants and animals	13. Animal habitats	13. Life cycles in biomes and ecosystems	
				14. Relationship of living things		
				15. Survival in ecosystems		

These life science conceptual frames are standards-based and are ready for implementation with minor modifications to meet the learning objectives the teachers set in the classroom. For instance, teachers can easily engage kindergarten students in learning plants by asking: *What plants can you see out there in the school yard? Can anyone tell me about them? What parts of plants do you know? Or what do the plants you see have in common?* Teachers can do the same for animals: *What kinds of animals do you see on a farm? What kinds of animals do you see in the local zoo? What kinds of animals do farmers raise? What kinds of animals do people use for racing? What kinds of animals do people use for food? Or what kinds of animals are good for pets?* These are examples of inquiry questions for students to investigate, think, and reason about. Most importantly, these questions connect to real-life experiences or prior knowledge and skills. Remember, teachers have to bring science concepts to the students' level of understanding and comprehension.

EARTH SCIENCE CONCEPTS

Teachers can apply similar approaches to teaching earth science concepts to students; they can use the earth science conceptual frames listed in Table 12.9. These conceptual frames are based on national and state standards and are guidelines that provide teachers with clear ways to engage students right away in inquiry process skills through hands-on and minds-on activities. A series of inquiry activities can be created easily from the conceptual frames. Keep in mind that it is not what the teachers want to do in science that matters, but rather, it is what and how the teachers get the students to do in science that is more important. Earth science is based on concepts involving the earth, weather, and the sky.

PHYSICAL SCIENCE CONCEPTS

According to national and state inquiry science standards, all students should develop the ability to ask questions about objects, organisms, and events in the environment; to plan and conduct inquiry investigations; to use appropriate tools, applications, and techniques to gather and interpret data; to apply evidence and science knowledge and skills to develop explanations; and to communicate with others about inquiry investigations, data, and explanations. These are learning goals for all science concept areas. In order for students to reach these goals, teachers need to understand the physical science conceptual frames in order to prescribe meaningful hands-on and minds-on activities for inquiry practices. Table 12.10 presents physical science conceptual frames for teachers to consult in planning a

Table 12.9 Earth Science Conceptual Frames for Inquiry Activities

K Grade	First Grade	Second Grade	Third Grade	Fourth Grade	Fifth Grade	Sixth Grade
Earth: 1. Land and water 2. Soil 3. Rocks 4. Landforms 5. Water 6. Recycle and reuse of resources 7. Concepts of earth *Weather and sky:* 1. Exploring weather conditions 2. Examining clouds and climate changes 3. Seasons: fall, winter, spring, and summer 4. Day and night 5. Sunlight, shadows, heat energy, and power	*Earth, weather, and sky:* 1. Examining the earth's surface 2. Earth's shapes 3. Rocks, soil, and minerals 4. Land and water 5. Change of landforms 6. Earth resources 7. Use and protect earth's resources 8. Weather and seasons 9. Weather cycles 10. Climate changes 11. The sky 12. How earth moves 13. Earth and other planets	*Earth, weather, and sky:* 1. Land and water 2. Changes on earth 3. Earth's natural resources 4. Rocks, minerals, soil, and fossils 5. Weather conditions and climate 6. Weather cycles 7. Earth and space 8. Day and night 9. How seasons change 10. Solar systems 11. Earth, sun, moon, and stars	*Earth, weather, and sky:* 1. Earth changes 2. Earth's features and shapes 3. Weathering and erosion 4. Earth's resources 5. Rocks, minerals, soil, fossils, fuels, air, and water resources 6. Weather conditions and climate changes 7. Water cycles 8. Weather seasons 9. Planets, sun, moons, stars, and the sky 10. Relationships of planets and earth 11. Land and water 12. Sudden changes: weather conditions, seasons, drought, melting, and flooding	*Earth, weather, and sky;* 1. Earth's shapes and features 2. Earth layers 3. How earth moves 4. Weathering and erosion 5. Weather conditions and climate changes 6. Use and protect earth's resources 7. Rocks, minerals, soil, land, and water 8. Landfill, pollution, conservation, and recycle 9. Air and weather 10. Water cycles 11. Examining weather and climate changes 12. The solar system 13. All planets 14. Constellations	*Earth, weather, and sky:* 1. Earth's features 2. landforms 3. Continents 4. Plate tectonics 5. Earthquakes 6. Volcanoes and eruptions 7. Earth resources 8. Rocks, minerals, soil, land, water, fossils, energy, and fuel 9. Weather patterns, conditions, and seasons 10. Climate changes 11. Atmosphere 12. Clouds, precipitation, sunlight, rain, hail, thunderstorms, hurricane, flooding, and earthquakes 13. The universe, space, planets, solar system, and their relationships	*Earth, weather, and sky:* 1. Changes on earth 2. Earth's shapes and features 3. How earth moves 4. Continents and plate tectonics 5. Landforms and water 6. Geological changes 7. Earth resources 8. Rocks, minerals, soil, land, and water 9. Air and climate changes 10. Use and protect resources 11. Weather and climate 12. Atmosphere, precipitation, clouds, sunlight, day, night, and planets 13. Astronomy 14. The solar system, planets, and their relationships 15. The galaxies, space, and beyond

Table 12.10 Physical Science Conceptual Frames for Inquiry Activities

K Grade	First Grade	Second Grade	Third Grade	Fourth Grade	Fifth Grade	Sixth Grade
Matter:	*Matter, motion, and energy:*	*Matter, motion, and energy:*	*Matter, motion, and energy:*	*Matter, motion, and energy:*	*Matter, motion, and energy:*	*Matter, motion, and energy:*
1. Exploring matter	1. Matter is everywhere	1. Examining matter	1. Observing matter	1. Properties of matter	1. Observing matter,	1. Classifying matter
2. Wood, metal, soil, objects, and water	2. Describe matter	2. Describing matter	2. Properties of matter	2. Describing matter	2. Describing matter	2. Physical properties of matter
3. Investigating matter concepts	3. Solids, liquids, and gases	3. Solids, liquids, and gases	3. Measuring matter	3. Observing matter	3. Measuring matter	3. Elements and compounds
	4. Changes in matter	4. Changes in matter	4. Solids, liquids, and gases	4. Measuring matter	4. Comparing matter	4. Periodic table
Motion:	5. Mixture of matter	5. States of matter	5. States of matter	5. Classifying matter	5. Properties of matter	5. States of matter
1. Moving objects	6. Heat and matter	6. Mixture of matter	6. Physical changes	6. Changes in matter and states of matter	6. Elements of matter	6. Solids, liquids, and gases
2. Wheels	7. Position and matter	7. How things move	7. Chemical changes	7. Solids, liquids, and gases	7. Periodic table	7. Mixture of matter
3. How things move around	8. Pushes and pulls	8. Position and motion	8. Forces and motion	8. Mixture of matter	8. Metals, nonmetals, and metalloids	8. Chemistry
4. Ups and downs	9. How machines move	9. Forces and friction	9. Position and motion	9. Compounds of matter	9. Atoms, protons, electrons, and neutrons	9. Chemical changes
5. Sounds	10. Energy, sounds, and light	10. How machines move	10. Work energy	10. Forces and motion	10. Physical and chemical changes in matter	10. Chemical properties
6. Exploring magnets	11. Energy and heat	11. Exploring magnets	11. How machines move or work	11. Change motion, speed, and velocity	11. States of matter	11. Atoms and energy
	12. Electricity and power	12. Using energy, heat, sounds, light, electricity, and power	12. Forms of energy, heat, light, sounds, electricity, power, and fuels	12. Work energy and use energy	12. Mixture of matter	12. Exploring forces
				13. How machines move or work	13. Solids, liquids, and gases	13. Forces and motion
				14. Energy sources	14. Acids, bases, salts, and alkaline	14. Changes in motion
				15. Heat, light, sounds, electricity, circuits, generators, branches, and power	15. Compounds of matter	15. Work energy and use energy
				16. Magnetism and electricity	16. Using forces, motion, force and motion	16. How machines move and work
					17. Work energy and use energy	17. Exploring energy
					18. How machines work and move	18. Waves and sounds
					19. Sources of energy, heat, light, wind, air, sounds, electricity, and magnetism	19. Properties of light
						20. How lights work and their colors
						21. Heat, electricity, power, and magnetism

series of physical science activities; learning objectives should be based on these conceptual frames. Moreover, teachers can connect these frames with science standards to guide instruction. In physical science, students in Grades K-6 should be able to develop an understanding of the properties of objects and materials and changes in the properties of matter. Physical science is based heavily on matter and motion.

PHYSICAL EDUCATION CONCEPTS

Despite the Healthy Hunger-Free-Kids Act of 2010 and the Women, Infants, and Children (WIC) Reauthorization Act of 2004, in today's inquiry science, physical education concepts are often kept completely out of the kinesiological equation. Most schools and teachers do not offer students meaningful physical education and activities but expect students to come to school healthy and physically fit. The nation's media report over and over again that many school-age children are obese and the incidence of childhood obesity is rising every year. The fast food industry is often blamed for childhood obesity. In fact, these laws require public schools to establish local school wellness policy to address the physical fitness and wellness of all students.

In recent years, some states have reconsidered the importance of including physical education activities in the normal school academic curriculum. However, such thinking has not been consistent or strong enough to require public school systems to implement a physical education requirement for elementary school students. Many teachers do not teach physical education or design lesson plans about the importance of routine physical exercise and sports. If schools do not have physical education programs, the only children enrolled in extracurricular activities such as baseball, soccer, basketball, football, and recreational pursuits are those whose parents can afford the cost. Students in low socioeconomic circumstances are generally minimally engaged in physical education activities during school hours. Perhaps, the school system is relying on parents to teach their children physical education at home; however, this is a poor choice because the school system is academically responsible for teaching physical education.

Following are some activities teachers can use to help students learn about physical activity. All children know how to perform physical activities; what they need is the opportunity to engage in them. Keep in mind that some children are not able to participate in these physical education activities because of their special needs, limitations, and disabilities. Therefore, teachers need to find other meaningful ways to engage them in appropriate physical education activities.

Physical Activity: Ball Skills with Music

Grade level:	K-3
Music:	Sweet Georgia Brown
Balls:	6-inch rubber balls
All students:	Each student has to have a ball

Physical objectives:

1. Physical exercise
2. Total physical response
3. Have fun
4. All participate
5. Learn ball skills
6. Improve locomotor and psychomotor skills
7. Uses total physical response: sitting, catching, bouncing, kneeling, bending, moving, coordinating, controlling, balancing, visual skills, physical abilities, etc.
8. Correlation with neurogenesis

Game rules:

Level one:

1. Set a number of bounces for practice (10 right hand and 8 left hand, or 5 right hand and 5 left hand).
2. Bounce the ball with right hand first and count the number of bounces.
3. Bounce the ball with left hand and count the number of bounces.

Level two:

1. Set a number of bounces for practice
2. Bounce the ball with alternate hands (right and left, or left and right)
3. Count the number of bounces.

Level three:

1. Bounce the ball with both hands simultaneously.
2. Catch the ball on its return.
3. Repeat the process over and over again.

Physical Activity: Elimination Tag Game

Grade level:	K-6
Equipment:	None
Materials:	None
Space:	Large open area, gym, or field

Physical objectives:

1. Physical exercise for all
2. Total physical response

3. Have fun
4. All participate

Game rules:
1. Line up students at one end of the gym or other space.
2. Designate one or two students as "it" and place them in the middle of the gym.
3. The "it" students are allowed to tag other students.
4. Once tagged, the student must sit down at the location where tagged.
5. Down students can tag others running by to be revived and reenter the game.
6. The process continues and all students are physically engaged in activity.

Physical Activity: Stuck in the Mud Game
Grade level: K-6
Space: Open area, gym, field, basketball court, or classroom area

Physical objectives:
1. Physical exercise
2. Have fun
3. All participate

Game rules:
1. Select a student to be "it" to start the game.
2. If tagged, the student is down and must freeze on the spot.
3. The downed student must stand up and stretch the legs apart to leave a space between the legs.
4. Once another student crawls through the space between the legs, the downed student is revived and reenters the game.
5. The game is over when the last student is tagged and all are stuck in the mud together.

Physical activity: Crab Soccer Game
Grade level: K-6
Equipment: None
Materials: A few dodge balls
Space: Open area, gym, basketball court, or field

Physical objectives:
1. Play soccer game
2. To outscore the opposing team
3. Physical exercise
4. Total physical response

5. Have fun
6. All participate

Game rules:
1. Divide students into teams (small, medium, or large teams).
2. Explain the crab-like position.
3. Students must be in a seated position with their hands behind them.
4. Legs and feet are out in front.
5. Make sure their bottoms do not touch the ground or floor.
6. No hands to be used during game to catch the ball.
7. Leave position to retrieve the ball only if out of bounds.
8. Only the goalie can use hands to block ball traveling above the head.
9. Touching the ball with hand is called "handball" like in soccer.
10. For any "handball," the other team gets a free kick from the spot it occurred.

How to play the game:
1. Set a score (2, 3, 4, or 5).
2. Two balls are placed at the center of the playing field to start a "face off" for the game.
3. Allow only three players to start the "face off."
4. To gain advantage, a coin is tossed.
5. Once balls are in play, there is nonstop play until there is an infraction.
6. First team to score the designated score wins the game.

Physical Activity: The Six Corners Game

Grade level:	K-6
Equipment:	None
Materials:	One foam die
Music:	Any appropriate music

Physical objectives:
1. Physical exercise
2. Total physical response
3. Use locomotors skills
4. Have fun
5. All participate

Game rules:
1. Number each of the four corners and two sides of the room 1 through 6.
2. Everyone must travel in the same direction and in the same way.
3. Choose locomotors skills for this game: skipping, galloping, walking, dashing, etc.

4. When music starts, students must follow the given directions and travel in the same way as told.
5. When music stops, everyone has five seconds to get to a numbered corner or side of the room.
6. While waiting at a corner, the teacher rolls the foam die.
7. All students in the corner with the same number as on the die come to the middle of the room and do 5 or 10 sit-ups
8. The game continues when they finish the sit-ups.
9. This process repeats until the game is over.

Physical Activity: The Chimp Race Game

Grade level:	K-6
Equipment:	None
Materials:	None
Space:	Open area, gym, field, or classroom

Physical objectives:
1. Physical exercise
2. Total physical response
3. Have fun playing game
4. All participate

How to play the game:
1. Divide students into two or three groups of equal numbers.
2. Line students up in each group.
3. Model how to play the game.
4. The first student of both teams bends over with feet apart and grabs his or her ankles.
5. On "go," the students race down the course and back without letting go of their ankles.
6. Each team member races in a relay.
7. The first team done wins the game.

Physical Activity: The Turtle Chase Game

Grade level:	K-6
Equipment:	None
Materials:	None
Space:	Open area, gym, field, or classroom

Physical objectives:
1. Physical exercise
2. Total physical response

3. Have fun
4. All participate

How to play the game:
1. Select a student to be the "it" to start the game.
2. All students are free players.
3. "It" chases free players.
4. All players are unsafe unless they become safe by lying down on their backs with feet and hands up in the air like a turtle.
5. The game is over when all players are safe.

Physical Activity: The Sole-to-Sole Game

Grade level:	K-6
Equipment:	None
Materials:	None
Space:	Open area, gym, field, or classroom

Physical objectives:
1. Physical exercise
2. Total physical response
3. Have fun
4. All participate

How to play the game:
1. Select a student to be "it" to start the game.
2. All students are free players.
3. "It" chases free players.
4. All players are unsafe unless they sit down on their bottoms with the soles of their feet or shoes touching another player's.
5. The game is over when all players are safe.

Physical Activity: The Everlasting Dodge Ball Game

Grade level:	K-6
Equipment:	None
Materials:	A few very soft dodge balls
Space:	Open area, gym, field, or classroom

Physical objectives:
1. Physical exercise
2. Total physical response
3. Have fun
4. All participate

How to play the game:

1. Select a student to be "it" to start the game.
2. Go over rules for the game.
3. Hit players below the shoulders only.
4. If someone catches the thrown ball, the thrower is out of the game.
5. If a ball hits someone below the shoulder, that player is out of the game.
6. But when the catcher or striker is out, the downed students automatically reenter the game.
7. This process repeats until the time is gone.

FOOD AND NUTRITION CONCEPTS

Remember, many states are now requiring students in 5th, 7th, and 9th grades to take the physical fitness test (PFT); however, physical education and food and nutrition facts are not being offered consistently in primary grades to prepare students for such requirements.

The food pyramid is posted in many classrooms; however, the teaching of inquiry science concepts on food and nutrition facts is completely absent in today's school science education curriculum. Similarly, schools and teachers expect students to know about food and the nutrition facts in order to eat healthy food and stay healthy, but the fact of the matter is that many parents lack this knowledge themselves and nutrition facts are not part of familial life. Children usually eat whatever parents give them at home. Learning about food and nutrition concepts is an integral part of inquiry science that teachers need to allow and encourage in the classroom. If teachers neglect education on nutrition facts, dietary supplements, and food calories, they should consider the impact on children's life when they do not learn what they are supposed to know about nutrition facts in the classroom.

How will students of diverse backgrounds and parents who have little or no education understand the kind of information shown in Tables 12.11 and 12.12, which is part of everyday life, if they are not taught how to apply this information to their daily lives? Food and nutrition concepts should be introduced to children as early as they are able to grasp the concepts of healthy diets and food allergies. Teachers are warned about certain foods that could cause severe allergic reactions, such as peanuts, chocolate, milk, and cheese, but they have not taken the time to design meaningful inquiry activities to engage students in learning more about nutrition facts and the benefits of different foods. For instance, children should be taught that Vitamin C helps protect the body, heals cuts and wounds, and assists the immune system in fighting infections and sickness. Children can get vitamin C from fruits and vegetables; however, many elementary children do not eat a healthy amount of fruits and vegetables.

Table 12.11 Example of Nutrition Facts

Serving Size: ½ cup of strawberries, sliced (83g)
Calories 27
Calories from Fat 0 g

	% Daily Value
Total Fat 0g	0%
Saturated Fat 0g	0%
Trans Fat 0g	0%
Cholesterol 0mg	0%
Sodium 1mg	0%
Total Carbohydrate 6g	2%
Dietary Fiber 2g	7%
Sugar 4g	
Protein 1g	

Vitamin A 0%, Vitamin C 81%, Calcium 1%, Iron 2%

Table 12.12 Example of Fruit Recipe

Asian Banana Split Recipe

Makes 1 serving
Prep time: 5 minutes

Directions:
1. Cut banana in half lengthwise
2. Spoon yogurt into a bowl
3. Place banana halves on both sides of yogurt
4. Top yogurt with granola and berries, then serve

Ingredients:
1 small peeled banana
½ cup of low-fat vanilla yogurt
1 tablespoon of low-fat granola
½ cup of sliced strawberries

Nutrition information per serving:
Calories 259, Carbohydrate 55g, Dietary Fiber 5g, Protein 8g, Total Fat 2g, Saturated Fat 1g, Trans Fat 0g, Cholesterol 6mg, Sodium 98mg

PRACTICE SCIENCE LITERACY

Howe (2002) stressed the importance of mastering the four areas of science knowledge, as shown in Table 12.13, in boosting science literacy in children. Despite the fact that national and state science standards do not require the practice of science literacy while learning science concepts, teachers need to promote science literacy in children as early as possible; otherwise, science words and meanings will

Table 12.13 Four Types of Science Knowledge

Type of Knowledge	Examples
Arbitrary	Names, symbols, conventions, rules, places, procedures, authentic ideas, labels, originality
Physical	Light, heavy, rough, smooth, coarse, shiny, round, oval, shapes, bright, dull, sink, float, description
Logical	Analysis, conclusion, concept, interpretation, inference, application, implication, shapes, size, mass, volume
Social interactive	Interaction with others, interpersonal relationships, cooperation, team work, think pair share, group work, communication, sharing, discussion

not become part of their daily vocabulary and will slip away from them. To help students learn scientific language, teachers should use integrated content to teach science words and terminology and require students to practice them in academic forms, such as writing, spelling, defining, and speaking. Teachers may ask students to look up a new word in the dictionary to find out what it means, or teachers may use a word bank to list all new vocabulary words and ask students to define them and write sentences for each of them. For long words, teachers may ask students to break them down using prefixes, roots, and suffixes, or separate different parts of the word by syllables.

Academic language in science is a powerful tool and children need to master it in order to learn science concepts. The more words they know the better they will perform in science assessments. The following are science goals that depend on science literacy:

1. Knowing or having the skills for inquiry; developing an understanding of and ability to engage in scientific inquiry.
2. Knowing or having scientific knowledge; developing a base of factual, conceptual, and theoretical knowledge and skills of the surroundings and the natural world.
3. Knowing and having scientific attitudes and habits of mind; recognizing and applying scientific attitudes and habits of mind to learn science.
4. Knowing and having knowledge and skills in science and technology; developing understanding of the connections between science and technology, recognizing how science and technology affect people, life, and society as a whole.
5. Knowing and having knowledge and skills to use facts, concepts, principles, theories, and laws of science to apply to real life experiences or events.

Furthermore, science literacy will help students understand that science is dynamic and continually changing as it revolves around life and the natural world.

For that reason, teachers should do their very best to promote science literacy in children, encouraging the learning processes that boost science knowledge and understanding of scientific concepts and processes through the meaningful practice of hands-on and minds-on inquiry activities. As mentioned in earlier chapter, Bybee (1997) defined six types of science literacy:

1. *Illiteracy in science* means that students have the inability to understand a question or locate the question in a given disciplinary domain.
2. *Nominal literacy in science* means that students understand the disciplinary basis of a question or topic but display misunderstanding in response.
3. *Functional literacy in science* means that students have the knowledge of scientific vocabulary with a specific context, such as using a new word in a sentence, identifying a new word on a test, recognizing the definition of a new word, or connecting concepts to the meaning of a new word.
4. *Conceptual literacy in science* means that students understand the way that disciplinary concepts relate to the whole discipline, like knowing the parts to whole approach, and have the knowledge of both the parts and the whole of a discipline.
5. *Procedural literacy in science* means that students understand the process of inquiry and the knowledge and skills required to complete this process successfully, like following written instructions or directions step-by-step, and are able to link concepts to the scientific methods and procedural processes of inquiry used to develop new knowledge and skills with in a specific discipline.
6. *Multidimensional literacy* means that students understand science as a cultural enterprise, as interconnected with society, and are able to incorporate the history and nature of science into practical use.

Perhaps these six definitions will help teachers as they guide their students to progressively higher levels of science literacy as they teach science concepts.

SUMMING UP

This chapter highlighted the practical applications of teaching and learning science concepts and presented the conceptual frames for life, earth, and physical sciences. Effective teaching of science concepts depends heavily on allocating time for students to practice their understanding of science concepts. Multiple-subject teachers may not have time to practice science as they should; however, without the mastery of basic science skills and knowledge, they may find that teaching science is more challenging than teaching other academic subjects.

Therefore, it is imperative for teachers to give time for practicing science with hands-on and minds-on activities.

Whatever lesson plan formats teachers choose to use, the content and strategies must be appropriate for all learners in the multicultural setting. Low achievers are often ignored by teachers and sometimes treated unfairly during instruction. Without instructional adaptations as required by state mandates, NNS, ELL, and SN students are frequently left out of real instruction and relegated to the position of silent learners or seat warmers in the classroom. Teachers need to make sure that inquiry activities are accessible for everyone regardless of language skills, cultural background, science knowledge and skills, and academic ability.

Teaching science concepts is not the same as teaching real science. Teachers need to move from concepts to concrete science, not from concrete science to science concepts. Developing meaningful inquiry activities using the conceptual frames presented in this chapter will boost student learning. Teachers should find practical ways to promote science literacy in children to inspire their desire to acquire science knowledge and skills for life-long learning.

References

American Association for the Advancement of Science. (1993). *Benchmarks for Science Literacy*. New York: Oxford University Press. Online version retrieved from http://www.project2061.org/publications/bsl/online

Banks, J. A. (2008). *An introduction to multicultural education*. Boston: Pearson Education.

Biological Science Curriculum Study. (1989). New designs for elementary school science and health: A cooperative project of Biological Science Curriculum Study (BSCS) and International Business Machine (IBM). Dubuque, IA: Kendall/Hunt.

Bybee, R. (1997). *Achieving scientific literacy: From purposes to practices*. Portsmouth, NH: Heinemann.

California Department of Education. (2003). *Science content standards for California public schools: Kindergarten through Grade 12*. Retrieved from http://www.cde.ca.gov/be/st/ss/documents/sciencestnd.pdf

California Department of Education. (2011). *California English Language Development test (CELDT): Explaining and using 2010–2011 summary results*.

Center for Science, Mathematics, and Engineering Education. (1996). *National science education standards*. Washington, DC: National Academies Press. Retrieved from http://books.nap.edu/html/nses/html/overview.html#content

Charles, C. M., & Senter, G. W. (2002). *Elementary classroom management* (3rd ed.). Boston: Allyn and Bacon.

Cummins, J. (1981). The role of primary language development in promoting educational success for language minority students. In California State Department of Education, *Schooling and language minority students: A theoretical framework* (pp. 3–49). Sacramento: Office of Bilingual Education, California State Department of Education.

Echevarria, J., & Vogt, M. (2011). *Response to intervention (RTI) and English learners: Making it happen*. Boston, MA: Pearson Education.

Flannery, Mary Ellen. (2006, January 1). Language can't be a barrier (425 first languages). *NEA Today*.

Gardner, H. (1983). *Frames of mind: The theory of multiple intelligences*. New York: Basic Books.

Gardner, H. (1993). *Multiple Intelligences: The Theory in Practice*. New York: Basic Books.

Gollnick, D. M., & Chinn, P. C. (2009). *Multicultural education in a pluralistic society* (8th ed.). Upper Saddle River, NJ: Pearson Education.

Good, T. L., & Brophy, J. E. (2000). *Looking in classrooms* (8th ed.). New York: Addison–Wesley Education Publishers.

Heacox, D. (1991). *Up from under-achievement: How teachers, students, and parents can work together to promote student success*. Minneapolis, MN: Free Spirit.

Howe, A. (2002). *Engaging children in science* (3rd ed.). Upper Saddle River, NJ: Merrill Prentice Hall.

International Society for Technology in Education. (1999). National education technology standards for students: Connecting curriculum and technology. Eugene, OR: Author.

Jacobson, W., & Kondo, A. (1968). *SCIS elementary science sourcebook*. Berkelely, CA: Science Curriculum Improvement Study.

Karplus, R., & Their, H. (1974). *SCIS teacher's handbook*. Berkeley, CA: Science Curriculum Improvement Study.

Kohlberg, L. (1969). Stage and sequence: The cognitive development approach to socialization. In D.A. Goslin (ed.), *Handbook of socialization theory and research*. Chicago: Rand McNally.

Kottmeyer, W., Claus, A., & Dockery, R. (1973). *Student notebook*. San Francisco, CA: McGraw-Hill Book Company.

Lessow-Hurley, J. (2000). *The foundations of dual language instruction* (3rd ed.). New York: Addison Wesley Longman.

Manning, L. M, & Baruth, L. G. (2009). *Multicultural education of children and adolescents* (5th ed.). New York: Pearson Education.

Manning, L. M., & Bucher, K. T. (2007). *Classroom management: Models, applications, and cases* (2nd ed.). Princeton, NC: Merrill.

Maslow, A. (1954). *Motivation and personality*. New York: Harper and Row.

McNamara, B. E. (2007). *Learning disabilities: Bridging the gap between research and classroom practice*. Upper Saddle River, NJ: Pearson Education.

Mercer, C. D., & Pullen, P. C. (2005). *Students with learning disabilities* (6th ed.). Upper Saddle River, NJ: Merrill/Prentice Hall.

National Research Council. (1996). *National science education standards*. Washington, DC: National Academy Press.

National Research Council. (2000). *Inquiry and the national science education standards: A guide for teaching and learning*. Washington, DC: National Academies Press.

National Council of Teachers of Mathematics. (1989). *Curriculum and evaluation standards for school mathematics*. Weston, VA: Author.

Peters, J. M. (2006). *A sampler of national science education standards*. Upper Saddle River, NJ: Pearson Education.

Piaget, J. (1965). *The child's conception of the world*. London: Routledge and Kegan Paul.

Ryan, K., & Cooper, J. M. (2001). *Those who can, teach* (9th ed.). New York: Houghton Mifflin.

Science. (2001). *Webster's college dictionary*. New York: Random House.

Science. (2004). *Longman Dictionary of American English*. Upper Saddle River, NJ: Pearson Education.

Science. (2005). *Scholastic Pocket Dictionary*. New York: Scholastic Inc.

Sunal, D. W., & Sunal, C. S. (2003). *Science in the elementary and middle school*. Upper Saddle River, NJ: Merrill Prentice Hall.

Training Center for Indochinese Paraprofessionals, Boston University School of Social Work. (1982). *A mutual challenge: Training and learning with the Indochinese in social work*. Boston: Boston University School of Social Work.

U.S. Department of Education. (1999). *To assess the free appropriate education of all children with disabilities: Twenty-first annual report to Congress on the implementation of the Individuals with Disabilities Education Act (IDEA)*. Washington, DC: Author.

Vang, C. T. (2006). New pedagogical approaches for teaching elementary science to limited English proficient students. *Multicultural Education, 13*(3).

Vang, C. T. (2010). *An educational psychology of methods in multicultural education*. New York: Peter Lang Publishing.

Index

Educational PSYCHOLOGY

Critical Pedagogical Perspectives

Greg S. Goodman, *General Editor*

Educational Psychology: Critical Pedagogical Perspectives is a series of relevant and dynamic works by scholars and practitioners of critical pedagogy, critical constructivism, and educational psychology. Reflecting a multitude of social, political, and intellectual developments prompted by the mentor Paulo Freire, books in the series enliven the educator's process with theory and practice that promote personal agency, social justice, and academic achievement. Often countering the dominant discourse with provocative and yet practical alternatives, *Educational Psychology: Critical Pedagogical Perspectives* speaks to educators on the forefront of social change and those who champion social justice.

For further information about the series and submitting manuscripts, please contact:

Dr. Greg S. Goodman
Department of Education
Clarion University
Clarion, Pennsylvania
ggoodman@clarion.edu

To order other books in this series, please contact our Customer Service Department at:

(800) 770-LANG (within the U.S.)
(212) 647-7706 (outside the U.S.)
(212) 647-7707 FAX

Or browse online by series at:

www.peterlang.com